WIDE-OPEN WORLD

WIDE-OPEN
WORLD

*How Volunteering Around
the Globe Changed One
Family's Lives Forever*

John Marshall

Ballantine Books
New York

Published in the United States by Ballantine Books, an imprint of Random House, a division of Random House LLC, a Penguin Random House Company, New York.

BALLANTINE and the HOUSE colophon are registered trademarks of Random House LLC.

All photos by the author and his family.

ISBN 978-0-345-54964-8
eBook ISBN 978-0-345-54965-5

Printed in the United States of America
on acid-free paper

www.ballantinebooks.com

2 4 6 8 9 7 5 3 1

First Edition

Book design by Donna Sinisgalli

For Traca, Logan, and Jackson

CONTENTS

PART FOUR: VOLUNTHAI

PART FIVE: THE GOOD SHEPHERD
AGRICULTURAL MISSION

We travel, in essence, to become young
fools again—to slow time down and get
taken in, and fall in love once more.

—PICO IYER

PROLOGUE

FROM INSIDE THE HUMAN KITCHEN, I WATCHED THE SPIDER MONKEYS begin to arrive. *They don't look so tough*—or so I told myself as they climbed onto the bars that separated me from them. They were docile, for one thing, hanging out like bored visitors at a human zoo, not baring their teeth or trying to get in. One, two, then three monkeys; they all just scratched their red belly hair with their long black fingers, searched for the right grip with their wandering prehensile tails, looked at us—at me—with their black unfathomable eyes, and waited. Soaking wet and full grown, spider monkeys weigh around fifteen pounds, but they have ten times more muscle mass per body weight than your average human, which makes them incredibly strong. A spider monkey, hanging only by her tail, can pick up a sixty-pound bag of ice and swing it playfully around like a loaf of bread. One monkey at the sanctuary even broke into a bathroom, ripped a ninety-pound toilet off its bolts, and threw it out the door! Plus they have sharp teeth and lightning-quick reflexes, and they can be unpredictable and territorial and jealous. Especially with guys like me.

Several months before we left home, before we bought our tickets to Costa Rica, I received an email warning. Carol, one of the sanctuary founders, was writing with some advice about volunteering. Along with suggestions on what to bring and descriptions of what we would be doing, she slipped in a couple of lines that caught me by surprise. She wrote, and I quote:

> Sweetie is growing out of her propensity to attack white males, but Winkie seems to be the culprit now. John: there are a few special guidelines that you will have to follow until they realize you are not a threat to The Troop.

Now, several words jumped out at me right away, the first being "attack," the second being "white," and the third being "male," two of which describe me pretty well. My wife, Traca (pronounced TRAY-sa), laughed the warning off, as white women on the non-attack list are prone to do, but I was a little freaked out. It didn't help that I received this email right after seeing the interview Oprah Winfrey did with Charla Nash (the woman who had her face chewed off by a chimpanzee in 2009); and though I knew spider monkeys are much smaller than chimps (especially the two-hundred-pound male chimp that got Charla), I suspected they were still capable of peeling me like a big white male banana should the desire arise.

As I watched the monkeys at the window, wondering which one was Sweetie and which one was Winkie (or whether it mattered), I noticed two scarlet macaws fly from above the Human Kitchen, screeching like show-offs, as if their spectacular red and blue plumage wasn't attention-grabbing enough. They soared across the grounds, through the dense jungle growth, landing together in a palm tree that curved out across the Golfo Dulce. Beside me, Traca looked awestruck, as if witnessing a miracle, and our two kids—Logan, our seventeen-year-old son, and Jackson, our fourteen-year-old daughter—were as focused as I've ever seen them. If they were still harboring any reservations about this trip, they weren't letting on. They looked enchanted, alive, overloaded by the sheer density of wildlife, the potential for danger, and the pure novelty that surrounded us all.

Our home for the next month would be the Osa Wildlife Sanctuary, a little orphanage/rehab center for all kinds of abandoned or injured rainforest animals. Creatures like kinkajous, peccaries, coatis, tayras . . . though I was focused strictly on the spider monkeys. While all the other sanctuary residents were being cared for in cages, the spider monkeys were the only animals allowed to roam free. Which meant one very critical thing for me and my family: For the next thirty days, *we* would be living in cages. Whenever we stepped outside, we'd just be part of the monkey troop.

"Well, let's see how this goes," Carol barked in her usual forceful voice. She reached for the security latch on the kitchen door, then turned to me. "Just don't show any fear or it's all over," she warned, clearly not paying attention.

Short of holding an I AM AFRAID sign, I'm not sure how I could have exhibited any more fear signals than I was exhibiting at that moment. I was sweating liquid fear. My legs were weak. My heart was racing like a rabbit's heart in Coyote Canyon. I knew this sensation. When I was a kid, I had an irrational fear of dogs; not just big scary dogs but all dogs. Even friendly golden retrievers could get my blood pumping in a panic, and as Carol opened the door, I had that same reaction: pure, instinctual fear.

"You okay, Dad?" Logan asked me, a white male himself but, according to Carol, too young to be perceived as a threat by the monkeys.

"I guess so," I said. "If they go to eat me, save yourself." I hoped he knew I was joking.

"They're not going to attack you," Jackson said, rolling her eyes as if she was annoyed. But I could tell she was a little worried, too.

Then, right before we stepped outside, I caught Traca's eye. She flashed a big excited smile and I knew exactly what it meant. This was her dream. She'd wanted to take a trip like this ever since we first met, and now here we were, at the threshold of our first big adventure.

Click. The latch opened and out we went.

Leaving the safety of the Human Kitchen, I felt unprotected, but I wasn't—not really. Surrounding me like bodyguards, moving as a single unit, was my family: my wife of nearly twenty years, my son, and my daughter. I knew that we wouldn't always be together, that life and change would pull us inevitably apart. But as Sweetie (or was it Winkie?) casually dropped from the cage bars and made her way toward us, toward me, there was no future. There was only this moment, the whole world narrowing to a single small, hairy shape. No matter what happened next, one thought stood out in my mind like a red macaw against a blue tropical sky:

We're doing it.

After years of talking about it, we're actually doing it.

Part One

BEFORE
THE TRIP

A journey is like marriage.
The certain way to be wrong is
to think you control it.
—JOHN STEINBECK

1

OUT OF THE BLUE

Taking a trip around the world was at the very top of Traca's bucket list long before I met her and it became a recurring topic of conversation in our marriage over the years. We dreamed about it from time to time, mapped out routes, imagined the adventure. For my part, I was mostly playing along with this fantasy, not really thinking we'd ever go, but Traca never let it die. Even when there was no practical way a big trip made any sense at all, when we were busy with young children or in debt up to our eyeballs, she loved to toss the idea of world travel onto the floor like a magic carpet and see if it took us anywhere. It's just part of her makeup. Foreign cultures and unknown languages and passport stamps and airport terminals fire her imagination like nothing else. It's not so much wanderlust. It's more like *fernweh,* another German word, which means "an ache for the distance." That's Traca. She *aches* to go and explore . . . she *yearns* to experience the world . . . as if she is pulled by a gravity I simply do not feel.

It's not that I'm against travel. I love it. I guess I'm just more practical than she is. While Traca would happily spend the last of our meager savings on a spectacular two-week trek in Peru, I tend to analyze a specific trip and calculate whether the cost of plane tickets, hotels, and restaurants and the sheer hassles involved would make a good investment for a family on a budget.

We did manage to spend a wonderful, impractical year in a Portuguese fishing village back in 2000 when our kids were seven and five—but a complete circle of our enormous planet? That was different. The timing just wasn't right, or it was too expensive, or I wanted to focus on my career, or it would be better when the kids were older, or we'd do it later. In fact, I probably could have stalled like that forever (because it's never really the *right* time to take a trip around the world), until one day, as if the universe were advocating in Traca's behalf, three words popped into my head, and even I couldn't resist the idea any longer.

I wasn't thinking of anything particular at the time the three words occurred to me. I wasn't really thinking at all. I was just sitting on an airplane, looking out the window, marveling at the Windex-blue water of the Caribbean. I had a ginger ale in front of me and a tan on my face, and I was feeling better, more centered, than I'd felt in a very long time. Maybe ever.

This *bliss*—for lack of a better word—was the result of a weeklong yoga retreat Traca and I had just completed, and it came as a total surprise to me. When she proposed the idea, I had zero interest in a yoga vacation, even a tropical one. Traca was the yoga instructor and daily practitioner in the family. Time spent in a rigid ashram environment might seem like heaven on earth to her, but to me it sounded like a descent into backbend hell, and an expensive one at that.

Still, I had been pretty stressed out. Professionally, my work as creative director at a few local TV stations in Maine felt uninspired, and my eyes were almost constantly red from too much computer time. I felt listless, unmotivated, going through the motions of life— which was a fairly accurate description of my marriage at the time, too. After sixteen years of raising children, Traca and I were more like chaperones than lovers, treading water in the deep end of the parenting pool, just passing the time. We got along well enough. We were committed to our kids. There was no cheating or plate throwing, but there wasn't a lot of passion, either. While I buried myself in work and focused on my career, Traca got deep into yoga and meditation and shamanism and Reiki therapy. We were drifting and we both knew it, but there were so many other things preoccupying us. I always assumed we'd reconnect when the kids went off on their own; it would just mean three more years of treading water, which I knew would pass quickly.

As for the yoga vacation, I didn't expect it to fix any or all of these problems, but since it was the only thing Traca wanted for her birthday that year, I signed us both up. I packed my swimsuit and my stretchy pants, resolved to leave my cynicism and my judgment at home, and flew to Paradise Island in the Bahamas for a little downward-facing dog and, hopefully, some time on the beach.

My first impression of the ashram, other than the palm trees and the warm sun, was "These people do *not* look very friendly." I said this out loud to Traca, which I could tell instantly annoyed her, but it was true. Everywhere I went on the ashram property, residents and instructors followed me with their eyes as if I were a shoplifter. When I passed people on the lush, overgrown paths, said hello, and tried to be friendly, many of them looked right through me or looked away. It didn't make any sense. Where were the enlightened smiling faces and the "Thanks for spending so much money with us" hospitality? Feeling judged and defensive, I decided to forget about everyone else and just focus on myself. For better or worse, I committed wholeheartedly to the regimented ashram routine.

So I woke up while it was still dark, walked silently down the beach with the other guests, sat in meditation as the sun came up, then did my best to chant the *hour-long* Sanskrit song that began and ended every ashram day. For most of this epic chant, I had no idea what I was saying—but I did recognize the famous Hare Krishna lines that devotees used to sing in airports back in the seventies. I remember spotting a group of these chanters while on a family vacation as a kid. It was as if my two brothers and I had found a nest of rare, hilarious birds, and we couldn't help laughing at them as they banged on their tambourines, twirled in their robes, and whipped their thin, solitary braids around on their otherwise bald heads.

Hare Krishna, Hare Krishna, Krishna Krishna, Hare Hare . . .

The first time I said these words at the ashram, I was sitting in a group of chanters, all of them swaying and vibing on the rhythmic chant energy. Sandwiched between Father Granola and Sister Moonstar Rainbow Brite, I looked up to try to catch Traca's eye. She was sitting across from me, head down, with her own sway and vibe going on. Then, as if she knew I needed her, she lifted her head and looked right at me. For a beat, we just looked. Then she smiled and shrugged, which for some reason sent me into a fit of laughter. If my brothers could have seen me at that moment, I knew they'd be laughing, too.

After morning chant, two hours of yoga awaited. I did my best, but sadly, I was like the Tin Man, with welded hips and steel bars for legs. (And not much heart, either, now that I think of it.) Most classes, I was a million miles from the perfect pose the rubber-limbed yogis would demonstrate, but I was there. I was trying.

"Now hold your foot to your breast like a baby," a rail-thin instructor said one afternoon, sitting cross-legged on the floor in front of me. To demonstrate, he lifted one foot effortlessly to his chest, rocking back and forth. "And feed your baby gently," he said, now breast-feeding his own foot. "And kiss your baby," he said, drawing his foot to his puckering mouth.

As I sat on my mat, having trouble just keeping my back straight without support, I managed to lift my foot a full eight inches off the ground. But it was not going any higher, not without tearing a few ligaments.

Naturally, the instructor was just getting started. "And finally, rest your baby behind your head like this and lift your other baby to your chest." I watched him sitting there with one ankle tucked behind his neck, the other suckling at his bosom, and I thought: *I would need to fall off a building to end up in a pose like that.*

"What'd you think?" Traca asked me at the end of the class. She was smiling, firing on all cylinders, clearly in her element.

"I think my babies are going to go hungry," I said.

But I didn't give up. Day by day, I ate the mega-healthy meals (just brunch and dinner), attended every yoga class (four hours per day), received a small ovation when I did my first unassisted headstand, chanted with all the sincerity I could muster, even tapped a tambourine during one evening program.

Then a funny thing happened. In just seven days, all the people at the ashram went from unfriendly to friendly. "The people here are so nice," I said to Traca with a laugh, knowing that the change had happened within me. For the first time in years, I felt light and joyful, my mind was still and clear, and I saw Traca—really *saw* her—not simply as a mother and a homemaker but as the beautiful woman I had fallen in love with so many years ago. The coldness that had permeated our marriage for too long was breaking up. We held hands. We kissed. It was an epiphany, really. As though I'd been sitting in the dark for years and suddenly someone had pulled open the shades.

"You are feeling better?" a swami asked me as I was leaving.

I said that I was. Much better.

"I can tell," she said with a big smile. "Your eyes are *shining.*"

With this peaceful easy feeling, I boarded a plane headed back to Portland, Maine, with a stop in Atlanta. Traca took the aisle, I took the window. Below, the bright blue water matched the clarity I was feeling when the three words appeared in my mind like a non sequitur from God. Though I wasn't looking for them at the time or fishing for them in any way, they felt urgent—if not a sign, then at least an inspired nudge. Three simple words:

Year of Service.

It's a strange feeling, getting an answer to a question you did not know you were asking, but I knew exactly what the words meant, and—in spite of my newfound calm—they both thrilled me and freaked me out. I also had the superstitious notion, right away, that if I spoke these words out loud, they would take on a life of their own, that Traca would chomp down on them like a pit bull and never let them go. Even I couldn't resist the idea they suggested, and I began planning in my head almost immediately.

Up until that point, my biggest resistance to the idea of a trip around the world had always been the cost. I read a book once called *One Year Off* by David Elliot Cohen in which the author packed up his wife and three small children (and an au pair!) and hit sixteen countries over the course of thirteen months. While I loved the author's "leave it all behind" attitude and his close encounters with hippos and holy men, my biggest impression was: *This must have cost a bloody fortune!* In one eleven-day period, the Cohens went on a five-day safari at Chobe National Park in Botswana, a three-day safari at the Hwange National Park in Zimbabwe, and a white-water rafting trip below Victoria Falls. As if that wasn't enough, they then flew to South Africa for *another* three-day safari at a place called Makalali in Kruger National Park! I won't even begin to speculate on how much this week and a half must have set the family back; even with the best possible bargain hunting, I'm sure it was a lot. And while I have no problem with the Cohens spending whatever they wanted to spend on their adventure, I just knew that this kind of lavish traveling was not going to be our story.

But a *Year of Service* . . .

I'd read about the idea in a magazine. "Voluntourism," it's called; vacations with a purpose. All over the world, people are combining travel with service and creating much more meaningful experiences. In exchange for some work and usually a placement fee, volunteers get food and a bed to sleep in. If we planned it carefully, I reasoned, it probably wouldn't cost very much at all. We'd need airfare, but after that we'd just need to find organizations that needed volunteers. We wouldn't just be sightseeing. We'd be helping. Instead of impersonal hotels and budget restaurants, we'd be in communities where we were needed, making connections to local people, eating with them, living with them. Some people report having their lives forever altered by a single *week* of overseas service. So what could a whole year do?

The more I thought about it, the more excited I got. What an amazing gift to give our kids! Like most every other teenager in America, our daughter, Jackson, was totally addicted to Facebook and her cell phone. What if we could unplug her for a full year? Wouldn't that be worth almost any price? And our sixteen-year-old son, Logan, would be gone from home soon. What if we could show him the world together before he headed off into it alone? How would the trajectory of his young life be changed after such a trip? How would all our lives be changed?

I looked at Traca and she smiled. I looked back out the window. In my mouth the three words rolled around like marbles.

Year of Service . . . Year of Service . . .

In Atlanta, I was biting my tongue, not speaking, afraid the words would tumble out if I so much as yawned. I carried them down the moving sidewalks, past the magazine racks, up to our gate. Did I even want this? A whole year of service? I was excited, but I was scared. What was I scared of? Nothing had actually happened yet. The words weren't a burning bush or anything. I had a career. I had kids in high school to think about, college coming up. I wasn't some flaky Hare Krishna.

Year of Service . . . Year of Service . . .

And then . . . we were talking about it. We were eating some lunch, waiting for our connecting flight, and I just started saying it all. I opened my mouth and the marbles rolled all over the table.

2

THE BEST PART

As expected, Traca embraced the idea with all the passion of a child accepting a trip to Santa's Village, and we talked about it all the way home. By the time we touched down in Portland, Maine, and drove to our hometown of Gorham, we had it pretty much figured out. Largest order of business: Fix up our home and get it ready to sell. That's how we'd pay for the trip—that's how committed we were to the idea. After that, all the other details seemed petty. We'd pick countries and causes that intrigued us, contact them, buy plane tickets to the places that invited us to visit. Then we'd leave jobs and bills and schools when the time came and, if everything fell together just right, we'd be on the road by the first of September. It was the beginning of May. We had four months to make it happen.

The real wild cards in all of this were the kids. Would they be into it? Would they dig their heels in and clutch their friends? Logan would be a high school junior in the fall. Jackson would be a freshman.

Logan would be easy. He wasn't really all that entwined in high school life. His friends were not his organs. His teams were not his blood. He was a good kid—an honor student, a top-ranked cross-country runner, an artist; a solitary figure in many ways, but not a loner. He was popular at school, generally happy. And he was easy to have around the house. He liked his sister, he loved his mother, and while many of his friends were sickened by the sight, sound, and all-around existence of their fathers, he still liked his.

If I *had* to pinpoint one area where Logan needed some work, I'd probably say confidence. He was a little shy at times, reluctant to speak up, not a big risk taker; but then, he'd always been that way.

When he was less than two years old, I once found him at the top of our stairs. He was just standing there like a ledge jumper, while I stood at the bottom. A single misstep and he would cartwheel and tumble like a rag doll into my arms. "Easy, buddy," I said softly, not wanting to startle him. My legs were coiled springs, ready to leap. My eyes scanned his small vulnerable body, his curly blond hair, his pudgy little shape, while my mind calculated angles, distances, options. I put my hands up, palms facing him as if holding the air between us, pushing it and him back from the edge with my mind. Other boys his age might have walked unaware and happy off the edge of a cliff, running for the open air again if you were lucky enough to pull them back from the plunge the first time. But not Logan. At the top of the stairs, with his eyes locked on mine, I could see his less-than-two-year-old brain thinking it through. Then he lowered himself carefully to the ground, shaking his head. "No, no, no," he said as he crawled slowly backward to safety.

People have called him an old soul and I know what they mean. He came into this world centered in a way that many adults are not, he is thoughtful to the same degree that many of his peers are reckless, and under all the Axe body spray and the smelly socks, there is a sweetness and a wisdom to Logan that are undeniable.

When he was seven, before we left on our yearlong trip to Portugal, I wanted him to be excited about the adventure. He was in the first grade and I thought he might resist the idea of leaving his buddies or his school. Jackson was only five at the time, and she was up for anything, but I thought Logan might need a little convincing. So I laid it on thick, name-dropping all the cool things there were to see and do on the planet, whether they were on our itinerary or not.

"How'd you like to see a volcano?" I asked. "Or a Komodo dragon? Or an iceberg? Wouldn't that be fun?"

Logan nodded at all these suggestions and then said the most surprising thing. I'll never forget it. "But that's not the best part," he said, completely serious.

"It isn't?" I replied, ready to toss the Eiffel Tower or the Great Pyramid of Giza at him if necessary.

"No," he said. "The best part is, I'll get to spend a year with you."

Ten years later, as Logan approached adulthood and prepared to begin the part of his life that took place away from home, away from me, I knew exactly how he felt back then. If I could spend one more full year with him, without distractions, without routines, I knew I would never regret it. Because with only two years of high school left, no matter how we spent it, our time together was incredibly short. He was not the pudgy, curly-haired little kid at the top of the stairs anymore. He was nearly six feet tall, thin like the long-distance runner that he was, poised and ready to launch. And this time, no matter how much I wanted to hold him still with my upraised hands and my force of will, he *was* going to jump, tumbling and cartwheeling past me, out the door and into his own life.

Time flies when you're raising kids. You hear it all the time, particularly when your kids are little and you're talking to parents whose kids have already left home. "It goes so fast," they say. "Don't miss it. Enjoy every second you have with them." And I did. I was there. I worked nights when Logan was little so I could be around during the day. I soaked it up, no regrets. Even so, selfishly, greedily, I wanted this trip and all the time together that it represented. I wanted to wander in jungles and trek up mountains and play games by headlamps and talk because there was nothing else to do and because we were the only people who spoke English for miles around and because we were living in the same room. Beyond all that, I wanted the world to inspire Logan's generous heart and embolden his cautious nature. I wanted to give him one last great experience with his family before he jumped out into the big puddle of life by himself and made his own splash.

But that wasn't the best part.

More than anything else, I just wanted to hang out with him for a while longer, and I was thrilled—though not really surprised—when he accepted the trip idea for the adventure that it was and hopped right on board.

3

DOWN THE ELECTRONIC
RABBIT HOLE

Then there was Jackson.

When I told her I was going to write a little bit about her for this story, she confronted me at my desk with this piece of character advice:

"If you make me out to be some self-centered little bitch," she said, "I will tear out those pages and burn them. Are we clear?"

In the interest of avoiding a fiery edit, I'll start with this: The moment I first learned I had a daughter was the happiest moment of my life so far.

Not that having a son wasn't a thrill and a celebration, but Logan's birth was more stressful than Jack's. Traca and I didn't know what to expect when our first child was born. Everything was new. Plus, Logan's delivery was a long, painful process that scared us as much as it excited us. Jackson's birth was just . . . different.

Secretly, I wanted a girl that day. Of course, I said all the politically correct things parents are obligated to say to superstitiously avoid birth defects or to appear unselfish. Things like "Another boy would be perfect," and "So long as it's healthy," but honestly, deep down, I wanted a girl.

As Traca went into labor, we didn't know the sex of the child, but we didn't have to wait long to find out. Unlike Logan's slow, exhausting delivery, Jackson's arrival was like the birth of a comet: fast, blazing, intense, producing a concentrated pain within Traca the likes of which I can only—thank the Lord—imagine. Through the fire, I kept saying "her" and "she" as in "Here she comes," and, "We almost have her," but I didn't know, not for sure. It wasn't until Traca finally pushed Jackson's little body into the world and our midwife held her up like baby

Simba, her wrinkled pink bum facing us. Then Traca and I watched, suspended, breathless, as Jackson made her first grand entrance . . . a slow, dramatic turn . . . until there was no mistaking the anatomy. A girl! A beautiful baby girl. My heart exploded like fireworks.

Then fourteen years passed.

One day, after Traca and I returned from the Bahamas, I stood in the doorway of Jackson's room, watching her. The place was a disaster. The floor was covered with dirty clothes as if a laundry bomb had gone off. She was sitting up in bed, laptop on her lap, cell phone in her hand, headphones in her ears, ignoring me. I knew she knew I was there but she didn't look up. So I just waited, wondering: *When did she get so long?* She was five foot six, beautiful in ways you didn't have to be her father to recognize. She had long brown hair like her mom's, naturally wavy but pin-straight at the moment, hanging like a silky curtain around her pretty face. Most of her girlfriends were straightening their hair for school, so Jack ironed hers every morning as well. It wasn't my choice. I loved her full tangle of hair. But on teen fashion issues, my opinion didn't matter. Her friends mattered, belonging mattered, and if straight hair was the highest price she had to pay, I was all for it. Still, I worried about her sometimes.

I've always had a good connection with Jackson, right from the start. When she was very small, maybe two years old, I once woke up in the middle of the night and couldn't fall back to sleep. The house was still and quiet, and as I lay there in the dark, I started thinking about my daughter. Her room was separated from mine by a wall, and as I pictured her sleeping in her crib, I found myself silently repeating her name like a mantra:

Jackson . . . Jackson . . . Jackson . . .

"Daddy?" she answered, calling out as if she'd read my mind.

I took this as proof of our special bond, but she clearly wasn't tuned into me so acutely as I stood in her doorway. I know it's normal, that the little girl she used to be was long gone, but the sentimental truth was: I missed her. I missed being with her, talking with her, giving her horsey rides up the stairs every night . . .

"Horsey?" she used to say, patting my hair, my flowing mane. "Carry me, please."

So I'd flop down on the ground, prance a bit, snort and buck, until she said, "Good horsey. Easy, boy." Then she'd climb onto my back and hold my neck tight as I galloped up the stairs, always rearing midway, soothed only by a kiss on the cheek. We did this every night for years until one night she just climbed the stairs on her own. I watched her from the couch, feeling like an abandoned toy, snorting my horse sound to get her attention.

"Not tonight, Horsey," she said tiredly. Just like that, it was over.

Of course I had known it wouldn't last forever; even while it was happening, I knew to savor it. She used to call me from her bed after I'd already tucked her in. "Daddy? I want a drink of water," she'd say. So I'd bring some water and hold it for her little mouth and tuck her in again. Then, when I was back downstairs for all of thirty seconds, she'd say, "Daddy? Can you read me a story?" So I'd go back up and grab a book, snuggle beside her, and read it with as much dramatic flair as I could muster. When it was over, I'd kiss her head and go downstairs and wait. "Daddy? I'm scared," or, "Daddy? I dropped my teddy," or "Daddy? Can you read me another story?"

One night as I prepared to bound up the stairs for something like the fifth time, Traca stopped me. "She's just playing you," she said. "She doesn't need any of this. She needs to go to sleep. She'll keep calling you if you keep going up."

"I know," I said. "But she won't be calling me forever."

Jackson . . . Jackson . . . Jackson . . .

I stood at her door thinking her name, but I got nothing. She just clicked her stupid computer keys and answered her annoying cell phone and listened to her inane hip-hop music about shaking your booty down to the ground or doing it all night long. It was a sad tableau, really.

Traca and I resisted getting Jackson a cell phone for as long as non-Amish parents can be expected to hold out, long after all her friends were flaunting their second cute-as-candy flip phones, but eventually she wore us down. Once armed, Jack took to texting like a prodigy, racking up over eight thousand texts in her first month. With only 420 waking hours in the average month (assuming fourteen hours a day for thirty days), that means Jackson received or sent nearly twenty messages every hour of the day, or one every three minutes. This number becomes even more impressive when you subtract the six hours per day that phones are not allowed in school, leaving a near-constant texting marathon for Jackson's fingers to run. Add to this all her favorite shows, favorite songs, favorite stars, favorite causes, favorite everything—all offering their incessant Twitter–Facebook feeds like tiny doses of crack to the strung-out teen info-junkies of the world . . . it's amazing Jack had time to eat, much less do homework.

Now, I know what all you better parents are saying. *Shut it off, you whiner! Pull the plug if you don't want it.* And we did . . . once. When we thought Jackson's usage was getting *way* out of hand, we cut the cord and took away her computer and phone indefinitely, which—as any parent who's ever taken this hard-line stance with a teen daughter can attest—is the opposite of LOL. We tried to reason with her, explain our good intentions . . . but Jack wasn't listening. When she realized we were serious, she stood up, threw her phone against the wall, said she hated us for the first (and only) time in her life, and stormed out of the room.

Then an unexpected thing happened. The next day, she started talking. Maybe out of boredom, but who cares? She hung around after dinner. She played a board (bored) game with me. In a few days, she seemed relaxed and focused, engaged and full of humor. It was a beautiful transformation that lasted for a full *six months*—until the day we reluctantly returned her electronics to her, and she began to withdraw once again.

More than for anyone else in the family, I wanted the trip for Jack. I wanted her to leave the phone and the computer and the hair straightener at home. I wanted her to unplug from her social networks, to have a chance to get to know herself beyond her user name and password, to look up from cyberspace and see the great big world all around her, to reach beyond herself to someone, anyone, who clearly needed more than she did. I wanted her to imagine, to dream, to relax, and to see how good that feels. The fact that she would miss a year of high school senior boys—I was okay with that. The fact that we might one day find ourselves somewhere in the world walking arm in arm like the old friends we used to be . . . I was okay with that, too.

When we told Jackson about our plans, she resisted the idea, as I had known she would. "Freshman year is kind of a big deal," she said, as if reminding me of a great and obvious truth. But before long, she started to soften, using phrases like "*If* we go," and "I'm not saying I'm in, but," which basically meant she was in and we were going.

With just a few months left before we hit the road, I stood in her doorway, watching her, thinking her name, wanting her to turn my way as she had done on the day she was born. Though I couldn't carry her up the stairs anymore without real effort, I wasn't ready to let her go just yet. I was her horsey, her storyteller, her biggest fan.

Come on, Jackson.

At last she looked up. "What?" she said, annoyed.

"Hi," I said.

"Creeper. Get out of my room," she said flatly before disappearing down the electronic rabbit hole once more.

4

BIG LOGISTICAL DUCKS

With the kids either on board or moving slowly toward the dock, it was time to launch into full-scale "set sail" mode. There was a lot to do. Planning a full year on the road and finding volunteer organizations to welcome a family of four with underage children, then linking all our stops with plane tickets, while somehow keeping it all under our ridiculously low budget, was challenging enough. Add to this: Paint the house, organize the basement, reshingle the roof, remodel the bathroom, find a real estate agent *and a buyer* while working full-time, and do it all in a few months . . . I was exhausted just looking at the list.

It didn't help that the euphoria, the *bliss* that Traca and I brought back with us from the Bahamas, was quickly fading along with our tans, and soon our relationship felt as if it was right back to its pre-yoga-retreat state: a little distant, a little cold, a little less happy than two people planning a world trip should probably be. It's not that we were fighting or even angry. We just didn't seem to be on the same page. In fact, as the days ticked by and I began to stress over the many details of our complex yearlong journey, Traca seemed utterly uninterested in planning even the smallest part of it.

To be fair, Traca's never been much of a planner, particularly when it comes to travel. She's more of an adventurer, an "avid" explorer, you might say, as in "diva" spelled backward. Give her an all-inclusive stay in a fancy resort with guided tours of sterile tourist traps and you will absolutely *ruin* her vacation. Traca wants the real thing, the local people, the local food. She wants to take overcrowded buses without air-conditioning. Even better: She wants to walk until her feet are sore and get completely lost at some point in the day. Through it all, no matter what happens, she believes, in a deeply spiritual way, that the universe will guide her to the people, places, and experiences she needs the most at just the right time.

It can be an exciting way to spend a weeklong vacation, and it has certainly added a degree of spontaneity to my life—but for a full year of travel? Internationally? With kids in tow? Drifting like four corks in the jet stream? Call me a boring stick-in-the-mud, but I wanted a little more structure than that.

At the very least, I wanted twelve stops to pin the trip on. Twelve known destinations with dates attached and people waiting. Tickets would be cheaper that way, I reasoned, and the kids would know what was coming up next if any particular stop proved to be an intolerable mistake. I wasn't looking to wring all serendipity out of the adventure. I just wanted my big logistical ducks in a row.

But Traca wasn't interested in big logistical ducks. She didn't try to stop my research or scheduling, but she didn't pitch in, either. It may sound crazy to all the careful planners of the world, but I honestly believe a part of her just wanted to go—to pick a place, go there, and stay until another opportunity showed up or the travel gods pointed us in a new direction. At first, I saw this lack of involvement as unsupportive, even reckless. Then one night, on the eve of our wedding anniversary, I flipped through an old photo album and realized: Traca wasn't the problem. As I looked at the pictures of our younger, happier faces . . . our first summer together, our wedding day, our newborn babies . . . I could see we had simply grown apart. We had stopped listening. We had stopped talking. Worst of all, I had completely forgotten how much I used to love her spontaneous, planless approach to life.

I met Traca on the beach in Kennebunk, Maine, the summer after I graduated from college. It was 1987. We were both twenty-one. I'd just come off a long, brittle relationship with my high school sweetheart and I had vowed not to get involved with anyone, no way, no how, before heading out to Los Angeles to write movies in the fall.

So I was walking down the beach with a friend who happened to know Traca and we stopped at her blanket. Traca was very tan, wearing a bikini, still wet from the ocean, and she flashed her big smile at me when we were introduced. It probably didn't look like much to the other beachgoers; we spoke for just a minute or two, hardly more than a quick hello. I'm sure I appeared calm on the outside, but inside I felt like one of those Tex Avery cartoon wolves, with my eyes shooting out of their sockets and my tongue crashing to the sand on a river of drool.

The next day, back on the beach, I spotted Traca lying on her blanket maybe fifty yards away. A girl sitting next to me was saying something, but I wasn't listening. I was watching Traca . . . watching her sit up . . . watching her stretch and stand and turn in my direction . . . watching her start to walk. It was ridiculous, but I imagined that she was actually walking to *me*. I even put it into a sentence: *I wish you would walk over here and sit down right next to me.* I said these words in my head like an incantation, then watched as she grew larger and larger, moving across the shimmering sand like a mirage. The girl beside me was still talking, but she seemed to recede into oblivion the nearer Traca got. Until at last, to my utter amazement, this stranger, this vision, this red-hot beach goddess was standing, then *sitting*, right in front of me.

That's when we started talking.

For the next few days, that's all we did. We met on the beach, sat side by side, and talked about everything we cared about: movies and music, books and politics, fears, hopes, religion, philosophy, travel, and on and on. We listened and talked, talked and listened, like the waves that rolled in and out effortlessly all day.

Traca was unlike anyone I'd ever spent time with. In spite of our very similar conservative New England upbringings, she was attracted to anything alternative. She'd just gotten back from a semester in London, where she'd shaved her head on a whim along with the other punks. She talked passionately about music I had never heard of; she bought records based strictly on album art, which seemed like the height of recklessness to me. She was a vegetarian, a flaming liberal. She gushed about poetry and the environment, social justice and world peace. Though she could barely draw, she was thinking about studying art—which she ultimately did. In years to come, our walls would be covered with huge free-form Jackson Pollock / Found Object paintings that emerged onto canvas the way lava emerges from a volcano. Technique never slowed her down. Planning or sketching was a waste of time. She'd start with some paint, add a hundred layers if necessary, then press cigarette butts and rubber gloves and used sanding disks and whatever else she had lying around into the congealing goo.

But it all started on the beach. In those first few days, we talked as if time was running out, pouring our stories onto the sand, mixing our childhoods, family histories, and adventures, so focused on the connection, so spellbound and rooted, we each got sunburned on just one side of our bodies.

After a full-on summer romance, we moved to Los Angeles together, where I wrote a string of imaginative screenplays that no one offered to produce while Traca created a growing gallery of abstract paintings that no one offered to buy. It didn't matter. We were dreamers back then, young artists gripped by a shared sense of destiny, with nothing but huge success ahead of us, just around the next corner. "This is the week," we used to say. And we meant it, every week, for years. We worked when we needed to, took long blocks of time off whenever possible, and spent every minute together. It sounds silly now, but we used to lie in bed or on the beach or in the grass somewhere private and we'd press ourselves together, entwining like two snakes, arms and legs wrapped tight, faces touching, feet touching. In this way, we'd breathe into each other and we'd say: *We are physically closer at this moment than any two people on the entire planet.*

We got married three years after we met, and Logan arrived two years after that. Another two and Jackson joined us. By then, we'd traded L.A. for a small house in Maine and the chance to raise a family. Without question, Traca and I both loved being parents, but I'm not sure either of us was really prepared for the change children brought into our lives. Traca never saw her free-spirited self as a homemaker, yet suddenly there she was cooking, cleaning, shopping for organic baby food . . . which left me with the role of breadwinner, a task I struggled to fulfill and one that fit me about as well as one of Jackson's diapers. Though we had our beautiful kids to wrap our love around and though life was mostly good, we often felt . . . what? Tired?

Broke? Stressed? All of the above? Over time, we laughed a little less and argued a little more. We certainly were not the two closest people on the planet any longer.

We did get one painful wake-up call. In 1999, with the death of Traca's beloved father, Larry, and the murder of my best friend, Shayne—tragedies that took place within two weeks of each other—we were suddenly, vividly, shaken back to life. In the aftermath of so much loss, Traca and I clutched each other, we kissed as if the world were ending, we vowed to savor every moment we had left, and we made an impulsive decision to move to Portugal for a year. It was a totally arbitrary destination; we had zero connections and virtually zero plans, but we went and it was beautiful. We ended up in a tiny fishing village on the pristine Algarve coast. Logan and Jackson were so young, seven and five, they began to speak Portuguese in no time, as if absorbing the language out of the salty sea air. And while they attended the local public school, Traca and I rediscovered each other, squandering days eating figs and ripe clementines, almonds and olives. It was a magical time. Over the course of that carefree year, our wounds healed, our spirits lifted, and we promised never to forget as we returned to Maine, ready to play house again.

Then nine more years went by in a blink.

We did forget, of course; routines can be hypnotic. In time, I began to climb my own corporate ladder once again while Traca dived ever deeper into her spiritual practice, widening the gap between us. It happened gradually, the way glaciers move—until one day we found ourselves in our mid-forties, with two teenage children and a nineteen-year-old marriage, disagreeing about whether to carefully plan a world trip or to let it unfold like a Sunday drive.

We just have to get out the door, I thought.

The world and travel would heal us again. I knew it. It could take us back to the two kids we once were on the beach. The happy ones. The dreamers. The ones with the half-sunburned faces. All we had to do was clear our schedules, pack our bags, and climb on that first plane.

5

LIFTOFF

OBVIOUSLY, WE TOOK THE TRIP, BUT FOR THE RECORD, WE DIDN'T MAKE our September departure. In spite of my best efforts and overwhelming motivation, I just couldn't get it all together in time. And with the collapse of the housing market, our house didn't sell, which meant we didn't have the money to take the trip anyway. On the day Logan and Jackson started the new school year, I took down the world map we had hanging on our kitchen wall, rolled it up, and stored it in the basement. Somehow that made it official—our *Year of Service* was not going to happen.

That really hit me hard. I'm not sure if I was depressed in a clinical sense, but that's the word that comes to mind. As the days began to pass, I had less and less energy. I couldn't concentrate at work or connect at home. I felt miles away from Traca, as if our ship had sunk and we were floating in opposite directions.

Four months later, on the morning of December 21, my forty-fourth birthday, I stood before my bathroom mirror feeling old for the first time in my life. I barely recognized myself. My hair was thinning, going gray. My skin was pale, with a growing collection of age spots speckling my face. I had the beginnings of a spare tire around my waist and a dull pain in my back that I could not explain. Worst of all, I had no light in my eyes, no spark. It was as though I was looking at a scary wax version of myself. It certainly wasn't anyone I wanted to be.

Contrary to my sad reflection, I've always thought of myself as a happy person, full of energy, quick to smile, optimistic, maybe even a little overconfident at times. Hell, as a younger man I was downright cocky.

I remember being twenty-two, when I moved out to Los Angeles to write movies. It didn't matter that I'd never read an actual screen-play or that I knew only a single person in the business, a friend named Tim Metcalfe, who was one of four writers credited on *Revenge of the Nerds*. In spite of the long odds and my complete lack of training, I had no doubt that Hollywood fame and fortune would be mine. All I had to do was write something.

Five weeks after arriving in L.A., when my dot matrix printer fin-ished slowly tapping out my first readable draft, I was ecstatic. Of course that manuscript was garbage, but all I saw back then was tri-umph. It was after midnight and I felt like shouting with joy from the top of the Hollywood sign. Amped on adrenaline, I made an impulsive decision. I drove to an all-night copy center, printed a few duplicates, then raced into the Hollywood Hills to find my one contact, Tim, and get my success started.

As I drove up the twisting slope of Mulholland Drive, the Los Angeles Basin lit up with a million lights behind me, I honestly felt I was on a collision course with destiny. I was even a little nervous, fearing that success was happening too fast, certain that the story I'd just written was my ticket to the big time.

It was nearly two in the morning when I pulled in to Tim's drive-way. Without hesitation, I grabbed my script, marched up to his house, and rapped on the door. "Tim?" I said. "You up?" I knocked louder, pounding with my fist like a policeman at a crack house. *"Tim! Tim, it's John! I finished my script!"*

Maybe Tim was out or asleep. Maybe he was inside, looking through the security peephole, watching me the whole time. If he was in there, I'm not surprised he didn't answer the door, because the lon-ger I knocked and the louder I called, the more sincerely frustrated I became. It never once occurred to me that this might be a bad time or that my expectations might be a little high. All I felt—for reasons I cannot now fathom—was cheated out of something that was sup-posed to have happened. Reluctantly, I left my script on Tim's door-step and glided back toward the shimmering lights of Los Angeles, cursing my bad luck that success would have to wait until morning.

For all his youthful hubris and naïve sense of urgency, I've always loved that boy pounding on the door. I was filled with enthusiasm back then. I had a conviction—a joyous deep knowing—that nothing was impossible.

Where did that go?

Half a lifetime later, as I looked at myself in the bathroom mirror, I knew I needed to make a change: start running, eat better, write something. "This is the week," I told myself, but I could tell that the old man looking back at me didn't really believe it anymore.

"Come on, Dad!" Logan shouted from the kitchen. "We're ready!"

I went downstairs for my birthday breakfast and found a few presents waiting for me. "Happy birthday," Jackson said. She sounded hungover and looked half asleep, dragged out of bed for the celebration. Traca had food on the table and a place prepared for me to sit. It was a familiar scene.

After the usual scones and fruit smoothies, we got around to the gifts. With a big smile on her face, Traca handed me her card. "Hope you like it," she said.

The card was homemade, as usual, this time with a single heart drawn on the front fold. Inside, I fully expected to find the same loving thoughts that Traca wrote every year, but when I opened it, what I found instead was nothing short of a magic carpet. Another burning bush. An answered prayer, of sorts. Four words this time:

LET'S TAKE THE TRIP!

It made no sense; that ship had already sailed. But somehow . . . seeing the possibility written down . . . seeing Traca's hopeful smile . . . I recommitted then and there. Without worrying about the money or how it would actually happen, I grabbed on to the idea like a life raft and never let go.

For those who like numbers and logistics, I've included a detailed account at the back of the book describing how we pulled this resurrected trip together in less than two months. Budgets, packing, shots, insurance, schools, jobs . . . it's all there.

We officially launched on February 20, 2010, leaving snow-covered New England below and behind us after leasing our home to some dubious renters: a shifty single mom named Joyce and her two teenage kids. To say I did not trust this woman would be a gross understatement, but we were out of time and she was offering money.

Once we handed over our keys and said goodbye to all our worldly possessions, the world awaited. Our plan was to spend at least thirty days with each volunteer organization, long enough to get the lay of the land and hopefully have a little impact. Since Logan wanted to be back in time for his senior year, we now had only six months to travel, but that still seemed long enough. And though I had only our first and third stops officially arranged, a fact that was more than fine with Traca, I was just happy to be flying away with my family.

Beyond that, the whole thing was up in the air. Would Logan discover the confidence I was hoping for him? Would Jackson unplug gracefully? Would Traca and I find each other? Would I find myself? Or would we all just freak out and kill each other in some one-room hut, crazy with the heat and frothing from a terminal case of family closeness?

I posed that last question to Jackson as we flew toward Costa Rica, and she didn't hesitate.

"If I had to bet right now," she said, "I'd put my money on kill."

Part Two

THE OSA WILDLIFE SANCTUARY

The scientific name for an animal that doesn't either run from or fight its enemies is lunch.
—MICHAEL FRIEDMAN

6

IS NOT OKAY

WHICH BRINGS US BACK TO THE HUMAN KITCHEN AND THE SPIDER monkeys and the threat of imminent attack—also known as the Osa Wildlife Sanctuary. Quite honestly, I chose the sanctuary as our first stop because I thought it would be easy. Feed a few baby animals, sweep a couple cages, all on the tropical coast of a secluded rainforest preserve. This was my attempt to wade into the shallow end of the world service pool. But, as we discovered, nothing on the Osa is particularly easy.

To begin with, you really have to want to visit the Osa Peninsula. Statistically, most visitors on a short Costa Rican vacation head north of San José, taking in the Arenal Volcano and enjoying the popular zipline canopy tours just a few hours beyond the capital. But the Osa is for the bold. It's in the southwestern corner of the country and it's mostly unbroken rain forest. It's been described as the most biodiverse place on the planet and it has never been described as easy to get to. You can either fly from San José or you can drive, depending on which side of the time/money seesaw you happen to find yourself on. As a general rule for our trip, whenever two modes of transportation were offered, we almost always chose the cheaper one, which meant we bypassed the fifty-minute Nature Air flight at $114 per person and opted for the nine-hour Autotransportes Blanco bus ride for just $8 a head!

It started at 9:00 A.M. on a Sunday. We'd arrived in San José the night before and spent a forgettable night at the Isla Verde, a cheap city hotel. The next day, we arranged for a special oversized taxi van to take us and our mountain of luggage to the bus station. At the request of the Wildlife Sanctuary, we were traveling with four large and lockable plastic trunks. (Apparently, these were necessary to keep the monkeys from pilfering our possessions with their long prehensile tails—even with tight bars on our cabin windows.) We also had an extra-large Igloo cooler that would serve as our refrigerator during our stay. Add to this our backpacks, carry-on bags, and Traca's yoga mat, and we made for quite a formidable invading army.

When the van arrived, we loaded up, sped across town, and began a journey that Jackson would describe later that night as "the worst day of my life!" And this was only day one.

First off, the bus station was packed. I mean *really* packed. People were lined up, hundreds of them, like rabid concert fans waiting for the box office to open. Traca, being our fearless foreign language expert, launched into the crowd to see about tickets, leaving me all but paralyzed in a sea of Spanish speakers. I've never been good with foreign languages. Some travelers, like Traca, genuinely seem to enjoy the communication challenge a new language presents. They use hand gestures and big smiles and a few meager vocabulary words to make themselves understood. Other tourists barely seem to notice they're in a new country at all, continuing to use English, speaking louder and slower whenever they need to get their point across. If only I could be so oblivious. In my case, I do two things when faced with a language I have no working knowledge of: I completely shut my mind off, and I begin to sweat from head to toe. Not the best or most useful ways to express yourself.

So I was standing there, blank and dripping, when a painfully thin Costa Rican man appeared, grabbed two of our trunks, nodded, and started carrying them away. Before I could protest, a young official-looking man with a gold tooth and a white uniform said, "Is okay, is okay," and patted me on the back. When the Thin Man returned, nodding and grabbing, I watched him carry two more of our packs into the mass of people. Then he came back and hauled the rest of our luggage away piece by piece. In a few minutes, our taxi van was empty and our taxi van driver drove off . . . exactly as Traca returned with the news.

"We're at the wrong bus terminal," she said.

The right bus, she discovered, was roughly thirty minutes away, on the other side of San José, and it left in exactly thirty minutes. With our specially arranged, oversized van long gone, we scrambled for our things, found them stacked neatly near the front of the line, tipped the Thin Man for not robbing us blind, piled into two separate cabs, and raced back across the city. With just minutes to spare, we got our tickets, braved the nastiest bathroom this side of a Panamanian prison, hopped on board a road-weary tour bus, and set off on a ride that would soon inspire Jackson to vow, "You will have to put a gun to my head to ever get me back on that thing."

The first six hours were actually pretty incredible. Though we were moving slowly, we were passing through breathtakingly beautiful countryside along switchback jungle mountain roads. Actually, "slowly" isn't really the right word to describe the way we were traveling. We were *inching* our way over one-lane bridges and *creeping* up rutted dirt hills. Jackson had to pee so badly at one point, she actually burst into tears—but with mountains on one side and sheer cliffs on the other, we couldn't get the driver to stop. Logan pretty much chilled, listened to music, tried unsuccessfully to teach me some Spanish. But when the sun set and an intense downpour began, all conversation stopped. As passengers closed their windows to keep dry, the temperature inside the bus began to rise. Soon, humidity surrounded us like a suffocating life-form and the air smelled like body odor mixed with diesel fuel. For the final three hours, our bus bounced from one rain-filled pothole to the next, leaving us numb and staggering for the exit when the driver finally opened the doors.

By the time we arrived in Puerto Jiménez (the largest town on the Osa), it was late and still pouring. Luckily, we found a taxi truck driver, lugged our wet mountain of stuff into the back of his covered truck bed, then squeezed our soaked selves into the cab for the four-hundred-yard drive to our hotel. Naturally, it was closed for the night. Dripping, exhausted, hungry, dumped on the sidewalk, and standing under a leaky canopy in a random Latin American alley—this was not the way I had pictured our adventure getting started.

"We shouldn't even *be* here!" Jackson snapped, and she was not comforted in the least when a friendly drunk offered her a cigarette and a swig off his bottle.

In the end, some locals rescued us, carrying our trunks through the rain and dropping them around the block at what appeared to be the only hotel that was still open: the Cabinas Bosque Mar. It wasn't the cleanest hotel we've ever stayed in, but we were grateful for the shelter. Still, the bizarre shower contraption we found in the bathroom deserves special mention. Technically, it was an on-demand hot water system that heats the water in the shower head with electricity. No tank, no waste—but no safety precautions, either. Stepping into the dirty shower stall after a day of sweaty bus travel, we were met with live exposed wires; it looked like a homemade torture device. I later learned that the locals call it a "suicide shower," and when I heard that, I was glad we all just went to bed filthy.

That night I had a dream.

Traca and I were traveling down a swollen turbulent river, standing—for some reason—on top of a large metal shipping container. As violent brown waves coursed around us, I used a long pole to help guide us through the frenzy. Though it was never mentioned in the dream, somehow I knew everything we owned was in the box beneath our feet.

At one point, the water became so dangerous, I steered us to shore and moved to a small shack to wait for the storm to ease. But as I stood inside the dimly lit shelter and looked out through a window, I saw Traca heading off downriver without me. She was clutching the steering pole, standing on top of the container, riding it into the choppy brown rapids. The waves tossed the long metal box like a toy boat, but there was nothing I could do. Before I could react, Traca slipped into the churning maelstrom and disappeared from sight.

A short time later, in just a blink of dream time, Traca was standing back beside me in the shack, soaking wet, with a small smile on her lips.

"Did you sink it all?" I asked.

"Yes" was all she said.

7

MAAAWN-KAY RULES

IN SPITE OF THE ONE-STAR ACCOMMODATIONS AND SCARY DREAMS, no one was robbed, electrocuted, or carried away to Bedbugland during the night, and soon the Costa Rican sun poked above the tree line and began drying the puddles in the dirt roads outside. It was time to meet the woman who would be our hostess for the first thirty days of our journey.

As promised, we were met promptly at 8:00 A.M. by Carol Crews, the female half of the husband–wife team that founded and ran the Osa Wildlife Sanctuary. Carol was sixty-two and had lived on the Osa for fifteen years. She used to be a lumber trader in another life and an army brat before that. She wore her hair short, talked loudly and forcefully, and speed-walked through the streets of Puerto Jiménez, shouting *"¡Buenos días!"* to everyone as if she were the mayor. Even I had to occasionally trot just to keep up with her. Though she was educated as a business major, we all came to know Carol as a top-notch biologist who ran the wildlife sanctuary like an animated and kindly drill sergeant. Most important, in the monkey troop, she was the alpha—the leader—so, for protection, she was the one I needed on my side.

After gathering a few supplies, we headed for the dock, piled aboard a rented boat, and motored out across the Golfo Dulce, the Sweet Gulf. Over the whine of our small boat's engine, Carol screamed the following instructions at us:

"Okay, maaawn-kay rule number one!" she shouted. (As her own term of endearment, she always pronounced the word "monkey" *maaawn-kay,* accenting both syllables the way a pirate might.) *"Never hold a maaawn-kay! Let them hold you! In the wild, nothing holds a maaawn-kay unless it's going to eat it!"*

It was like receiving a briefing before going to war. Carol had our undivided attention.

"Maaawn-kay rule number two!" she continued. *"If a maaawn-kay wants something of yours, give it to her! If she wants to climb on you, let her! Got it?"*

Got it. Be a good sharer. Be a jungle gym.

"Maaawn-kay rule number three: Do not touch or reach for a person holding a maaawn-kay! Maaawn-kays get jealous and will bite the person they are sitting on."

This had recently happened with a young couple, Carol told us later. The guy had a monkey in his arms, his girlfriend stepped over to greet them both, and the monkey bit the poor guy on the chest as if hungry for some heart. I made Traca vow she would not be overly affectionate with me in public, and with matching sarcasm, she said she'd do her best.

"Maaawn-kay rule number four: If a maaawn-kay gets into your room or another maaawn-kay-free zone, blow a whistle or call for help! Do not attempt to pull them or stop them in any way!"

No problem, I thought. No pulling or stopping. If Carol was the alpha, then I would be the omega male: docile, compliant, about as threatening as a Costa Rican dishrag.

As we approached the shore, we saw towering palms curved gracefully along a black sand beach, mountain cliffs rising dense and verdant in all directions, and not a man-made structure in sight. When we stepped onto land, our eyes were wide with wonder. "Welcome to Jurassic Park," Logan said.

The property was incredible. It went deep into the jungle with a hundred yards or more of beach frontage. On the far right were the tour grounds, where visitors came each day to view a menagerie of animals that could never be released. On the far left, where we were headed, were the living quarters for the Crewses and for volunteers. There were no cars at the sanctuary, no roads in or out. No electricity if the generator was off. No hot water at any time. Drinking water came from a flowing stream. Showers were outside in the jungle. Windows had no glass, only bars to keep the *maaawn-kays* out—which was a choice the Crewses had made early on.

If you decide to take in orphaned or injured baby monkeys, you have to make a call right from the start: to cage or not to cage. If you choose the cage (and most everybody does), your job will be infinitely easier, but you will never be able to release your monkeys into the wild. Monkeys need a free-swinging, social, foraging, boundless world to grow up in, and cages are the very antithesis of monkey life. Knowing this, Carol and Earl made a bold choice, opting to raise their little brood without restraints. It was a lot of work, like raising abnormally fast and strong (and hairy) human infants. But the Crewses are committed to returning animals to the wild whenever possible, and so the first human/spider monkey troop was born.

On the day we arrived, the Crewses had three cage-free orphan spider monkeys in their care: Poppy, a large, sexually mature female who was listless and depressed after miscarrying her first baby; Sweetie, a scrawny volatile adolescent female who was on steroids for an unidentified skin condition; and Winkie, a playful younger female with a healthy thick coat and a mischievous nature.

As we walked up from the beach, Carol told us the monkeys were with Earl on the other side of the property, curious about the latest tour visitors. "So you all get a free pass," she said as she led us past an anteater cage . . . past something howling in the trees . . . and into a structure she called the Human Kitchen. When we were all safely inside, she latched the gate behind her, locking us in.

Like all buildings for humans at the sanctuary, the kitchen was really a cage, with heavy mesh bars on the large window openings. It functioned as dining area, mess hall, and general command center for sanctuary operations. It was also the place about which the spider monkeys were the most territorial, and before long, all three of these amazing primates showed up, climbed up on the bars, and looked in.

At first glance I thought they were boys. They each had a curious pink appendage, not unlike a penis, that science poetically calls a pendulous clitoris. This limp little pinkie of flesh proved to be the source of much monkey attention as they pulled it and rubbed it throughout the day—and it reminded Carol of an additional *maaawn-kay* rule that Logan and I needed to know. "Never shower naked outdoors with a *maaawn-kay* around," she warned. Apparently, they would be infinitely curious about any man's "pendulous clitoris" and beyond eager to inspect it thoroughly.

"Okay. Time to meet the *maaawn-kays!*" Carol called as she opened the Human Kitchen door. And out we went.

As I've mentioned, I was scared to death. Even with my family around me like a human shield. Even though I weighed more than ten times as much as my potential attackers. We headed back toward the ocean, a place the monkeys were not crazy about. With 1 percent body weight in fat, spider monkeys sink like hairy stones and avoid the water at all costs; I was instructed to dive in fast if things went south. But I never got close to the Gulf. Within the first five steps, it was Sweetie—the most possessive of the troop—who jumped off the kitchen bars, landed lightly on her hind legs, parted Logan and Jackson with a wave of her four-fingered hands, and climbed, without teeth or force or any effort at all, up my body and onto my head. Her feet were on my shoulders. Her hands were resting on my forehead.

As you might guess, sitting on someone's head is a form of dominance. It basically says: *Look what I can do. I'm bigger than you. My tail is wrapped around your throat and my pendulous clitoris is pressed to the back of your neck. How do you like that, Tough Guy?*

I certainly got the message.

"Now find a place to sit," Carol instructed. "Let's see what happens."

So I sat. A few moments later, Sweetie climbed down to my lap and extended her leg to me. Above her ankle, she had a disgusting raw patch of oozing skin, and she pulled my hands toward the wound. *Rub it,* she seemed to say. So I did . . . around it, anyway. We sat this way for a while, me the subservient little leg rubber, Sweetie the all-powerful fifteen-pound Queen of the Jungle. As far as first dates go, I thought it went pretty well.

When this meet and greet ended without injury, we all set out across the gorgeous property to see where the tours were given, and Sweetie hitched a ride with me. I walked up jungle trails, down steep slopes, over plank bridges, all of it with a monkey on my head. Spider monkeys have a body temperature that runs 104 degrees, so I was drenched with sweat by the time I got to the tour grounds. But I got there. We both did.

If you'll excuse the prison terminology, I believe Sweetie made me her bitch that day. I wanted to think that we were becoming friends, but either way, so far, so good.

Or, as Carol enthusiastically declared back in the Human Kitchen at the end of that first day: *"No blood so far. We're off to a great start!"*

8

DADDY? CAN YOU TUCK MY SCORPION IN?

LIFE IN THE JUNGLE WAS A STRING OF NEW EXPERIENCES. AROUND every corner, from hour to hour, we saw, did, felt, said, heard, tasted, and smelled things that none of us had ever dreamed of before. And it started as soon as our eyes opened in the morning.

Each day at 5:00 A.M., the howler monkeys started howling. These monkeys were wild, living somewhere in the dense canopy that surrounded us, and their early morning calls were hard to miss. For their size, howler monkeys are capable of making the loudest land animal noise on the planet, and when an entire troop begins its deep-voiced howl, it builds and rolls, sweeping through the darkness like an advancing devil army. Very similar, in fact, to the typical *T. rex* roar used in most dinosaur movies, only deeper and more layered; Satan's choir in full voice or, to us: our alarm clock.

Before leaving our cabin at 6:00 A.M. for work, we tied up our mosquito nets, checked our shoes for scorpions, and locked our possessions in our plastic trunks. Like the Human Kitchen, our cabin was a "maaawn-kay-free zone" as Carol described it, meaning it had heavy-duty bars on the large glassless window openings, keeping Sweetie and Company out but allowing in everything else that could squeeze through a three-by-three-inch square—which included lizards, spiders, bugs, and any snake smaller than my forearm. We were tucked up on a hill overlooking the crashing waves of the Gulf, nestled into the intense overgrowth and surrounded at all times by a cacophony of clicks, chirps, rustles, squawks, and buzzes. Wild toucans rubbed their yellow beaks on the branches outside our windows. Scarlet macaws shrieked like car alarms every time they passed by. Accommodations were cramped and rustic, but we had everything we needed: a queen-sized bed, two single beds, a working toilet, and a small wooden dresser that we never used after we discovered it was riddled with termites.

Throughout the day, each of us had jobs to do, and all jobs were performed at a very leisurely pace. Jackson's main responsibility was taking care of the new kinkajou. A kinkajou is a long-limbed mammal with a long tail and a *really* long tongue. They're not endangered, but they are hunted for the pet trade. (Apparently, Paris Hilton had one as a pet and it bit her on the face. Score one for the kinkajous!) Still, you won't often see these creatures in the wild. They're arboreal and nocturnal, meaning they live in trees and hunt at night, mostly for fruit. When fully grown, they can open a raw coconut with their kinka-claws—but Jackson's little guy was just a baby and looked more like a helpless, brown, furry alien than anything capable of physical violence. She named him Kaylor (after her two best friends, Kali and Taylor), and she doted on him all day long. She bathed him, cleaned his cage, and fed him a mix of Pedialyte, mashed-up bananas, and milk four times a day. Carol inspected Kaylor one afternoon and was proud to report that, in his new mama's care, he was positively thriving.

Logan had new parental responsibilities as well. In addition to maintenance duties, he was also the attentive father to seven baby parakeets. These birds looked nothing like the resplendent adults they would grow up to be. Their feathers were tiny, their bones were thin as paper, and they peeped pathetically whenever they were hungry, which was most of the time. Like his sister, Logan was handy with the feeding tool—in his case, an eyedropper—that filled and shut these little buggers up. The trick was to fill their crops—a little flesh balloon at the front of their chests—until they were about to pop, then, without making them puke it up, carefully set them back in their towel-lined colander nest so they could digest before the next feeding. The biggest risks for the baby birds were dehydration and something called "crop sour," in which undigested food turns toxic and hardens. So every two hours, Logan checked for white specks in their para-poop (indicating the presence of urates that signaled proper hydration) and checked their crops for lumps. It was a lot of work, and it made us all wonder how Mama and Papa Parakeet managed to raise such a brood in the wild without a refrigerator of food at the ready.

Traca had her helping hands in just about everything, often work-ing in the Animal Kitchen over on the tour grounds, chopping veggies and fruit, cleaning dishes, and chatting happily in Spanish with the merry band of Costa Rican women who made up the kitchen staff. With Carol at the helm, there was a lot of mothering energy at the sanctuary, and Traca fit right in like a natural part of the ecosystem. As expected, she loved her new jungle life without complaint, even tolerating the mosquitoes that made her a must stop on their nightly feeding tours. One morning, in a very quick look, I counted seventy-five bites between her right knee and her right ankle. One leg, one side, seventy-five bites and counting!

For my part, I was assigned to the grounds crew along with a group of Costa Rican men. Together we raked paths, cleaned cages, and fed the animals that made up the sanctuary tour. This collection consisted of forty or so inmates, from rare birds to fierce capuchin monkeys to endangered jungle cats, all too injured, tame, or deranged ever to be released into the wild. My favorites were the sloths: slow-motion dudes who usually live far removed from humans, high in the trees, upside down, and chilled out like the stoners of the rain forest. Hunters don't often shoot sloths because sloth meat tastes terrible and because, even when they're dead, sloths don't usually let go of their branches. They eat a mix of low-energy, mildly toxic leaves, which gives them their slow speed and nasty flavor. But Logan wondered if their diet could be improved.

"We should feed them healthy food for a while," he proposed one day. "Maybe they'll start running around."

They certainly could use the exercise. Sloths typically remain so still that algae grow on their skin, allowing countless bugs to live in their coarse fur. I did an oral report in eighth grade on sloths, even carved one in woodworking class that year. Now, every time I entered the sloth cage to feed them, every time they looked up at me with their brown rotten-grape eyes and slowly chomped onto a leaf with their sparse sharp teeth, it was a wonderfully intimate connection for me, like having lunch with one of my junior high school heroes after so many years.

In spite of the Osa's remote location, a steady stream of tourists visited the sanctuary each day, ferried by local captains who offered snorkeling and snacks in addition to the two-hour animal tours led by Carol's husband, Earl. When needed, we acted as chaperones on these tours, keeping visitors from wandering off, escorting those in need to the bathroom, and sharing our knowledge of the rain forest, which at the beginning wasn't much.

Once the tours were finished for the day and the animals had been fed and watered for the second time, the day was ours to enjoy: swimming, playing with the monkeys, reading, exploring—but you never really knew what was going to happen. One evening after dinner, when a huge unseasonable thunderstorm blew in off the water, the kids grabbed their suits and took off for the beach. The rain was torrential, warm and loud, and the kids were jumping off a fallen palm tree stump that acted as a diving board, screaming up at the sky before launching themselves into the Gulf. As they played, Winkie, the three-year-old spider monkey, was laughing along with them from a palm frond overhead, hanging by her tail and spinning like a top. It was a spontaneous, intense, unplugged scene that Traca and I watched from the safety of the Human Kitchen, surrounded by deafening rain, holding hands.

Far from the routines of work and school and suburban life, our first few days on the Osa were a series of sentences that none of us had ever uttered before. Sentences like "I need a long-sleeved shirt, I'm going to feed the anteater," and "Watch your toes, Dad, there's a crab under the table," and "Can you come up to the cabin? I think there's a scorpion in my bed."

I took charge of that last one, but I wasn't crazy about it. This was nothing like the "Can you read me another story?" moments I missed from when the kids were little. Fact is, scorpions give me the creeps. Basically, they're tiny pieces of armor filled with black goo, with more weapons per square inch than most creepy-crawlies you're likely to find in your bed. As if their pinchers aren't bad enough, their curved and barbed tails are filled with venom that—though none of the fourteen scorpion species found in Costa Rica will kill you—feels like a hot poker being jabbed in your skin. That was a sensation I was seriously hoping to avoid.

Because we had no electricity in our cabin, I had to hunt by headlamp, illuminating a single spot in front of me in an otherwise pitch-black space. To make the fight less fair, I was armed only with a plastic jar and a notebook to be used as a lid. Traca was against all killing and suggested, from her humanitarian heart, that scorpions had the right to live, too—though I thought even the president of PETA wouldn't have argued in the scorpion's behalf had he or she been in my position at that moment.

Beside Logan's bed, there was a cross-bracing board that bowed out away from the wall a bit, and sure enough, tucked back in the gloom, a six-inch scorpion was waiting to strike. With the kids watching breathless behind me, in the ninety-degree heat, dripping sweat like a coal miner, I eased my notebook below the board, causing the scorpion to scramble reluctantly into the light. With my adversary now exposed, its tail twitching, its claws yearning to strike, I overpowered my natural desire to notebook-slap it back to hell and managed to secure it under my jar, capturing it for closer inspection.

After a quick peek and a major case of the heebie-jeebies, Logan and Jackson insisted I take it out of the room *right then* and not wait until morning. So I carried it down our jungle path to the Human Kitchen, with wild kinkajou eyes probably watching my every move, up where the wild sloths were fast asleep or at least faking sleep. I was probably the only human out for miles around, and at one point between the cabin and the kitchen, I stopped to listen. It was actually a little scary. The nighttime rain forest was alive with sound: things out hunting, things being hunted, with layers of frogs and insects creating a single drone . . . and a warm wind giving the jungle trees a rustling voice . . . and the Gulf's gentle waves snoring in the background. There were jaguars out there somewhere and deadly snakes in the blackness, but I didn't move. I just stood there in the middle of it all, so amazed to be so far from home that I almost forgot I was holding a live scorpion in a jar.

9

IN THE JUNGLE,
THE BITEY JUNGLE

FOR ALL OF YOU READY TO PACK YOUR BAGS AND BOOK YOUR OSA WILD-life Sanctuary volunteer adventure, I offer this bit of caution to the men: Most large white guys who visit for any length of time will get bitten. That's just the way it goes, fellas. Women are totally fine. Kids: no problem. But guys are pretty much scars waiting to happen. So why would a grown man knowingly put himself in such a perilous position? Because—and this is coming from someone with his own battle scars to talk about—it is a rare, rare privilege to live with monkeys.

Sweetie, Winkie, and Poppy are not exhibits. They are free. They go where they want, eat what they want, do pretty much what they want—unless Carol or Earl decides otherwise. They can't go into the cabins or the clinic or the Human or Animal Kitchens, but other than that, they have the run of the place. For the most part, this is a harmonious arrangement.

But I got careless. After my initial relief that Sweetie accepted me and didn't eat me, I stopped being afraid. I carried her whenever I had the chance, offering her a ride if she was nearby. As we walked together, she started holding tight to my chest instead of riding on my shoulders, a much less dominant posture for her. In time, she allowed me to break a few *maaawn-kay* rules, setting her down when *I* wanted to or gently pushing her away when I needed some space. One afternoon, I even managed to retrieve her from the jungle when no one else could, which filled me with a dangerous sense of pride and lulled me into a false sense of security. It got to the point where I was actually seeking her out—because, honestly, it was fascinating to be with her. When we were together, she'd look into my eyes and touch my face with her black fingers as if trying to figure me out. Or she'd hold my hand like an old friend, gripping my palm with her tail as we both watched storm clouds move in across the water. She was affectionate, curious, clearly intelligent, offering an intimate connection with the wild that few humans will ever experience. And I must confess to a certain completely unwarranted ego boost as well: Where most men needed to cower, I—the Great Monkey Whisperer—could walk up to the Human Kitchen with Sweetie in my arms, swing her to the ground, and enter her most territorial space without batting (or losing) an eye. At least such was the baloney I was feeding myself before the attack.

Here's how most monkey bites happen. In the jungle, biting is a routine part of daily life. When some troop member steps or swings out of line—*bam!* You bite 'em to say: Know your place, kid! Or, when someone takes your mango or rubs your pendulous clitoris the wrong way—*bam!* You bite 'em to show 'em who's boss. Luckily, monkey skin is very elastic and covered with hair. Plus, the bitee can react with equal speed and strength to minimize any damage. In the wild, most monkey-on-monkey violence doesn't amount to much, but humans—with our nearly bald, tight, completely vulnerable skin and our slow, frail defenses—do not, I'm sad to report, fare so well.

It was around dusk, a tricky time in Monkey Land (or so they told me as I was bleeding into the sink); like young human children, the monkeys are tired, less patient, less predictable in the early evening. Having spent most of my afternoon with Jackson working as crowd control on the daily tours, I hadn't seen Sweetie very much that day and I was hoping to spend some time with her before nightfall. I also *really* had to go to the bathroom. For men, this was an action that could be taken anywhere on the sanctuary grounds, so my plan was: quick pee break, long Sweetie break. The only trouble was, Sweetie found me right away. She climbed up on my chest, we hugged, said hello. For a few seconds, I was actually thinking of bringing Sweetie with me while I relieved myself, but Carol, who somehow read my mind, knew this was a terrible idea.

"Do *not* go in front of her!" she warned from the Human Kitchen. "She'll be *very* curious about what you're holding!"

Coming to my rescue, Carol lured Sweetie away with some Gummi Bears, her treat of choice, leaving me free to accomplish the first item on my checklist. When that bit of business was complete, I came back up from the beach and found Sweetie sitting on the ground in a happy Gummi trance. She did not look up when I called her name. Then Winkie came around the corner with Poppy not far behind. This was not good. One on one they were fine, but they did get jealous. With all three right in front of me, my survival instincts—long dormant as they were—told me to get away. The door to the Human Kitchen was maybe twenty-five feet to my right, six big steps. It was latched and would take a few seconds to open. If I walked fast . . .

After just two steps, Winkie caught me. Always playful, she ran between my legs, looked up my shorts, and then put her teeth on my ankle. It was not to hurt me. She did this in play like a dog with a soft mouth, but Sweetie did not like it *at all.* In a flash, she ran at me and—before I could react—slammed an eyetooth into the flesh above my left ankle, then made a smaller bite on my right leg and a third gash on my lower left calf. The whole thing lasted maybe ten seconds and left me shaking, afraid to move, and surprised when Sweetie and Winkie simply sat on the ground like good dogs and looked at my bleeding leg. I looked down, too.

I had never seen my own blood pouring out of my body. Sweetie's first bite had punctured one of the large veins in my lower leg, and I was gushing like a horror movie extra. Carol shouted for me to come inside, and I did. I walked past the monkeys to the locked door, which Carol opened for me, then across the kitchen floor, leaving bloody footprints on the terra-cotta tiles, and hopped up on the sink for the cleanup.

Often when Sweetie bites, she will continue to try to get at her victim, shaking the bars of the kitchen, stroking her tail up and down, clearly not finished with the altercation. But as Carol washed out my wounds, Sweetie just hung on the bars beside me, watching, curious, even chirping the spider monkey happy sound like an abuser with amnesia.

Other than me, Jackson had the hardest time with this incident. She was feeding her baby kinkajou at the kitchen table as I bled my way to the sink, and when she saw me, she turned chalk white, drawing my entire triage team to her side. "My lips and fingertips were tingling," she told me later. "I thought I was going to faint." She even described the attack in a letter to a friend, saying: "This is possibly the most dramatic, scary, petrifying, dangerous, full of tears day of my life!" On the plus side, Traca was in full mothering mode for the rest of the day, alternating between me and the kids, doing a thorough scorpion search before bed, protecting her own troop from further damage. I've got to say, I liked the attention.

I spent the next few days in solitary, leg up, monkey-free. Carol advised against stitches or even Band-Aids (which didn't stick in the humidity anyway), insisting that open air was the best tonic in the tropics. She also said not to worry about rabies or tetanus or other random monkey mouth diseases, assuring us that there was nothing we could catch from them, though they were apparently highly susceptible to our illnesses.

Sweetie came to visit me in my cabin the day after the bite. She sat on the free side of the bars, showing me *her* sore leg, gently pulling my hands toward her injury. *Rub here,* she said. So I did.

No one knew why her leg was such a mess. Several vets had checked her out and they had no idea. I just hoped to God it wasn't contagious. The hair had fallen out around a lesion about the size of a mango seed, and it appeared to be getting worse: bleeding, tender, chewed raw. I could even see a shiny tendon inside the exposed meat, and it made my worst bite look like a bad paper cut by comparison. At one point, I held up my own injured leg, careful to keep it at a safe distance from Sweetie's inquisitive grip. "See what you did?" I asked her. She chirped and pulled my fingers back for more rubbing.

This may sound insane, but . . . I really missed her. My plan was to heal up a bit more, then go outside and apologize for whatever unspecified *maaawn-kay* rule I had broken. I'd get some Gummis, carry her on my head, even hum "The Bitch Is Back" if it would help. Until then, I was on my side of the cage and she was on hers, wounds elevated, both in need of some healing.

10

LIFE AND DEATH

OUR TIME IN THE JUNGLE MOVED REALLY SLOWLY, AND I KNOW WHY: It's because everything we did there took absolute, 100 percent, full and total attention.

At home, whenever we wanted to go outside, it was never much of a production. We didn't have to think or plan in any way. Back in Gorham, we could just grab the doorknob, open the door, and step into the world like unconscious drones.

But in the jungle, every time we wanted to enter or exit a door, we needed to be on guard. The monkeys *loved* to get into the kitchen or the bedrooms. If they were around, even if it seemed as if they weren't paying attention, they were looking for a crack to slip through. So we'd pause at every doorway, scan the perimeter, ready the latch. Then, quick as we could, we'd slip out, close the door, and secure the latch behind us. If the monkeys got into any of the monkey-free zones, they would wreak holy havoc on whatever they could find—dinner plates, food supplies, laptops—so we needed to exit and enter with speed and military precision.

The same was true for nearly every other aspect of daily living. Want to take a walk down the path? Keep your eyes sharp for pinchy lines of leaf-cutter ants and the serpentine buttress roots from the surrounding trees. Ready to rake out the macaw cage? Stay clear of their beaks. Macaws can exert more snapping power than a pit bull. Forget your book up at the cabin? Be on the lookout for poisonous vipers—as Jackson learned firsthand one night.

We heard her before we saw her. *"I just stepped on a giant snake!"* she screamed, high-stepping back to the Human Kitchen. Without hesitating, Earl grabbed a machete, ran outside, chopped the snake's head off, then brought it back and placed it coiling and looping (and headless) on a kitchen cutting board. The snake in question was the *terciopelo,* or fer-de-lance, "the most feared and dangerous of the Central American snakes"—at least according to Les Beletsky, author of the *Travellers' Wildlife* series on Costa Rica that Carol let me borrow. How dangerous is the fer-de-lance? One story I heard from a grounds crew member concerned a local farmer who was bitten while working in his field. With no medical attention available, he went home and had his wife take care of his wound as best she could. The next day, the farmer died. The day after that, the wife died! As the story goes, she got enough venom in her system through a cut on one of her hands to reunite her with her husband and give the snake another victim.

Was this actually possible? To find out, I asked Earl, Carol's husband and our resident animal expert. If anyone would know, he would.

Earl was in his late fifties, wore a mustache, and had sandy-blond hair tossed to the side like the aging surfer that he was. He had worked in construction for many years, then as a commodities broker, before landing in the Osa like a coconut washed up on the beach. He could build most anything and cook most anything, and he had an encyclopedic collection of animal, bird, plant, insect, and general facts tucked beneath his sun-bleached hair. During the info-packed tours he led, I never saw him stumped by a visitor's question.

"What kind of tree is this?" a woman might ask, pointing to one specific tree in a jungle of trees.

"Oh, that's a saragundi," Earl would say. "You can tell by the leaves. They close up at night and are a popular medicine for arthritis." And off he'd go. When it fruits, who eats the fruit, peculiar adaptations, and so on. He wasn't pompous, just knowledgeable. He was easy to talk to, easygoing, and as cool as Carol was fiery.

As for the two-for-one snakebite? "It's a rural legend," Earl explained. "The fer-de-lance poison turns into a separate protein when it interacts with human blood and begins to digest your muscles from the inside out. When this happens, the wife would never come in contact with it." He went on to explain the science behind the snakebite venom, but I really wasn't listening at that point. I just kept picturing my daughter nearly stepping on one of these deadly muscle liquefiers on the path leading up to our cabin. We certainly weren't in Gorham anymore.

Back home, virtually nothing threatened to pinch, bite, or sting us in any serious way. Nothing died in front of us from week to week. But on the Osa, we were forced to face all kinds of large and small threats, actual life-and-death dramas, throughout each day.

Another example: Logan's bed continued to be a hub for scorpion activity in the rain forest. After our first "Save the Scorpions" rescue mission, he found a new one a few nights later lurking behind the same board just to the right of his pillow. Clearly, a message needed to be sent. Working again by headlamps, and away from the gentle glow of Traca's compassion this time, Logan flushed it from below with his journal and I skewered it from above with my pocketknife, pinning it to the wall just through the spot where—if it had a heart—its heart would be. As I suspected, there was nothing to kill in this creature, because it simply would not die. No matter how much I twisted the knife or dripped sweat onto Logan's bed, the scorpion continued to strike the knife handle with its barbed tail, eventually working itself free, cutting itself nearly in half, and falling into the darkness under the bed. When that happened, Logan, Jackson, and I screamed at the same time, an earsplitting sound I'm sure the howler monkeys envied, all of us jumping frantically onto a bed or a trunk, protecting our suddenly vulnerable bare feet from the pissed-off, rampaging, nearly-split-in-two arthropod somewhere in the blackness below us. When the girlish shrieking stopped (and trust me, this took a while), I gathered my courage, pulled the bed aside, and splatted what was left of the scorpion with my sandal. In my memory, this event plays out in super slow motion, though it probably took all of three minutes to unfold.

The parakeets were also having their own wild ride on the life-and-death roller coaster. When Logan neglected to fill out his daily feeding log one too many times, Earl reassigned him to the maintenance crew with me, and Traca took over as surrogate mom for the birds. But a few days later, she woke up to find her little nestlings peck-peck-pecking on heaven's door. We'd started with seven, but lost a few of the weaker ones early on. Now another was dead, and the rest had a bad case of the dreaded crop sour. Carol tried to extract the rotting, hardened gunk from their gizzards with a tube and a syringe, but it didn't look good. In her professional opinion, and she had raised generations of these fragile green guys, none of them would make it. But Traca was determined. She sat and massaged their crops, no doubt pouring all the love and Reiki energy she could into their little blanket-covered colander of dimming life. While we all did our sanctuary thing, she did not leave them, not for one banana-picking minute, until Carol inspected them late in the day.

"Well, what do you know?" she said with a fellow nurturer's respect. "I think they just might have turned the corner."

When this prognosis was announced, Traca turned and looked at me with more relief and pride on her face than I'd seen since the day Jackson was born.

As for Sweetie: three days after she bit me, I walked out of our cabin to see what would happen. My plan was to head straight for the water and dive in if I needed to, but I never made it.

"John! She's coming!" Traca called.

I turned to find a monkey tearing across the lawn, heading right for me. Earl later said that Sweetie had been high in a tree when she saw me out in the open. Like a frantic fireman, she zipped down a vine and hit the ground running, up on her hind legs, arms raised and swaying back and forth for balance. I could have run. I'm much faster than she is, especially when adrenaline is coursing through me, as it was right then—but I didn't want to escape. I wanted to rejoin the troop, and Sweetie was the gatekeeper. I watched her close the gap between us, her sights set only on me. As contact was imminent, all I could do was take a deep breath, extend my hand, and pray she didn't bite it off.

Thankfully, it was nothing so dramatic. Sweetie climbed up, perched on my shoulders, and hitched a ride to a nearby chair, where we sat down. Reunited and it felt so terrifying, but good.

After that, as with all things in the jungle, I was ever vigilant. Though Sweetie was nothing but sweet to me, I was still on guard. Where was Winkie? What would my escape route be? It wasn't constant fear, just a heightened sense of awareness, an animal sense of my surroundings.

We all felt it. We were four animals released back into the wild, waking up day by day to the beauty and the danger, the life and death, all around us all the time.

11

SEIBO

IF THIS MONKEY STORY WERE A MOVIE, THE VILLAIN WOULD NOT BE Sweetie; it would be Seibo. In Mayan mythology, Seibo is the Supreme God, the creator and destroyer of the world. For the purposes of our story, however, Seibo will be a huge mantled howler monkey.

Howler monkeys are the most common monkeys in Costa Rica. They eat leaves, have black fur, and make that deep fearsome howl I mentioned. (Earl said it can be heard up to two miles away.) Under ordinary circumstances, howler monkeys would have no reason to bother us at the sanctuary, but Seibo was no ordinary monkey. Carol said, "He's the biggest howler you will ever see." Physically, he was an enormous male with huge teeth and a massive bright pink scrotum. But as with all the best movie villains, there was a lot more going on beneath his frightening exterior than simply a loud voice, big balls, and a bad case of acacia-leaf breath.

When he was just two days old, after his mother was shot by poachers, little Seibo was sold by the side of the road to a missionary couple who brought him to the sanctuary. Carol and Earl did their best to raise him as part of their fledgling troop, but the spider monkeys were not as welcoming. As a leaf eater, Seibo was slower-moving than his new fruit-eating sisters, and Sweetie and Poppy were often cruel to him. They would hold him by his tail twenty feet in the air and drop him to the ground. They would shake him violently. Sweetie even once swung from his ponderous testicles, back and forth, as a wicked sisterly prank.

Seibo endured this treatment until he was fully mature, then joined the first passing troop of wild howlers and left to live in the jungle. But he didn't go far.

Releasing an animal back into the wild can be tricky. With no separation between the jungle and the sanctuary grounds, animals have been known to return, looking for food or just out of habit. Even so, no former resident ever came back with as much vengeance as Seibo.

We awoke one day to the sound of fierce shouting. *"Haaaa! Ahhhhh!"* It was Carol's alpha cry; clearly something was wrong. The jungle was not awake yet, it was before 5:00 A.M.—but Traca and I were up, sitting in bed, on alert.

"Earrrrl! Earrrrl!" Carol screamed.

"I'm coming!" Earl responded, not far from our cabin.

Then Seibo roared. To hear howler monkeys in the distance is creepy and loud enough, but to have one on your property, raging right outside your door, is a sound so terrifying that it still echoes in my mind. Logan and Jackson looked powerless and small under their mosquito nets in front of Traca and me, all of us surrounded by roaring and shouting and freaked-out spider monkey barking.

I asked Carol later if she ever got scared, and she shrugged. "No, not really," she said, "but this morning with Seibo . . . I was a *little* worried."

Carol had more than enough reason for alarm. She had a large male spider monkey named Guapo in her arms whom Seibo was trying to attack. Guapo was rescued near the Panamanian border wearing a leather collar connected to a heavy chain. He was a guard monkey for a junkyard down there, and he was good at his job: fierce, feral, a little crazy from captivity. After being delivered to the sanctuary, Guapo remained on a long leash, allowing him to be as free as possible and stay out of a cage. Sadly, he simply could not function without his collar and restraint, the only security he had ever known. He now spent his days climbing up and down a giant strangler fig like a monkey yo-yo, patrolling his slice of the rain forest, protecting his territory.

But on the morning Seibo showed up, Guapo was literally at the end of his rope. He jumped into Carol's arms, then snarled and gnashed his teeth as she backed into a corner. With nowhere else to go, they could only watch as Seibo moved closer, huge teeth flashing in the predawn light, roaring like a *T. rex* in surround sound with Carol shouting *"Haaaaa! Ahhhhh! Earrrrl!"*

Just another day in paradise.

Before Earl could arrive with backup, Seibo retreated into the jungle, and things quieted down around the sanctuary. After that we actually had a few days where nothing unexpected happened. When Logan and I raked the long jungle trail that connects the Human Kitchen side of things with the tour grounds, the task was time-consuming but relatively uneventful. Carol told us to be careful, that *terciopelos* liked to hide in the fallen leaves that littered the path, but as we inched our way along, feeling more like minesweepers than maintenance men, we did not rake up a single snake.

The same thing happened when we went upriver to release two adult opossums. True to their "no creature left behind" philosophy, Carol and Earl had raised these smelly, black-eyed beasts from demanding, hairless pouch dwellers into the vicious, sharp-toothed mega-rats they grew to be. "Wildlife is wildlife," Carol often proclaimed, and for that, the opossums should be thankful. We released them in a beautiful area that a ten-foot crocodile was known to frequent, but while the bald-tailed varmints slipped peacefully off into the jungle, the massive croc did not show up to welcome either them or us. Another hypothetical bullet dodged.

So jungle life rolled on. We assisted with tours, cleaned cages with the staff, prepped animal food for feedings, and spent lots of time with the monkeys. Traca started doing yoga with them each morning, acting as instructor and jungle gym for the curious primates, while Logan chased them all around the grounds in an ongoing but futile game of tag.

"I want to climb trees like Winkie," he said one day, genuinely impressed. I believe he would have traded his thumbs for half the speed and agility the monkeys so effortlessly exhibited.

Jackson made up a new game of her own, grabbing a hairy arm and a tail, then spinning in a tight circle until either she or her monkey playmate was too dizzy to continue. (To get the full Jackson experience, shout *"Flyyyyy-ing maaawn-kay!"* at the top of your lungs as you do this.)

As for my own rainforest romance . . . Sweetie and I were an item again; wherever I went, she was usually not far behind. I didn't seek her out anymore, never encouraged her to come snuggle—but when I had no choice, when she decided I was her taxi or perch or wound massager du jour, I was happy to go along for the ride. In spite of the danger, I still liked her and felt lucky that she liked me, even if it was in a *Fatal Attraction* sort of way.

I knew it could all change in the blink of a monkey's eye, but it finally felt as if the troop had found its balance. Carol was at the top, from the sheer force of her personality, followed by Earl. (Even though he was a white male, Earl helped raise the orphan girls and they treated him with a patriarch's respect.) After that, the pecking order looked like this: All the monkeys from oldest to youngest, then Traca, Jackson, Logan, and last and certainly least . . . me. Honestly, I was just grateful to be included on the list at all.

The monkey story we were living was barely half over, and as with any good movie, we had absolutely no idea how it was going to end. When Seibo came back a few days after his first attack and slashed the hand of Felicia (another spider monkey on a long leash), there was more screaming, crying, and drama out there in the distance, more alpha shouts, more *T. rex* roars. And in our little cabin, wrapped in mosquito nets and predawn light, Traca, Logan, Jackson, and I just sat there, eyes wide like rapt moviegoers, looking up at the brightening screen as the curtain rose on another day.

12

ENTIRELY MY FAULT

THE THING ABOUT YOUR SECOND SET OF MONKEY BITES IS, THEY'RE A lot like your second child. With the first one, there's a lot of fanfare; everyone comes to see, you take too many photos, and everything it does is cause for discussion. But by the time your second rolls around, it's old hat. You wash it by yourself. You're lucky to get a single picture. Your daughter doesn't faint. No big deal.

I was heading over to the tour grounds to start the day and was maybe a hundred yards down the beach when I happened to glance behind me. I was thinking maybe Logan would be there, he was running a little late that morning, but Sweetie was there instead. When she saw me, she stopped and we just looked at each other. On the wide expanse of sand, she appeared tiny, like a kid at the beach looking for her mom. But after a few seconds, she headed back toward the Human Kitchen and disappeared into the trees. I turned and continued on my way.

Thirty seconds later, as I walked carefully over the damp rocks in my sandals (a path we used at low tide), Sweetie appeared out of nowhere and climbed up on my chest. This was our typical greeting: I extended my hand, she took it, swung herself up, and put her face a few inches from mine. Her expression looked fierce, as if she was pissed off: She squinted, puffed out her lower lip, stuck her chin forward. And she made a quick chirping sound that seemed to say "Where do you think you're going?" but that really just meant "Hello."

The only problem was . . . I really didn't want Sweetie at the tour grounds with me anymore; she could be a bit of a playful pest over there and didn't allow me to get anything done. So, for everyone's sake, I decided to carry her home. Back over the slippery rocks I went, step by step, letting Sweetie use my right arm as a perch.

What happened next was entirely my fault. My sandals were made of leather and were not ideal rock climbing gear. Since I was concentrating on my feet, I didn't see an overhanging branch that had dropped low across the path. I hit it so hard with my head that I lost my footing, and when I lurched forward to keep from falling, Sweetie got scared and flipped out. She bit me on the left forearm and—in violation of all monkey codes—I pushed her off me, practically threw her.

"I didn't do it on purpose!" I shouted. "Please!"

Sweetie wasn't listening. Like a spring-loaded set of teeth with arms, she dived back at me in a single bound, ripped open my left triceps, then chomped into my left elbow. A stream of blood dripped onto the rocks at my feet.

It's a curious bit of primate programming, but spider monkey bites always come in threes. And they don't just snap their jaws and bite-bite-bite, either. Each bite is more like rapid-fire gnawing that lasts for maybe two seconds. Once the bite switch is thrown in their brains, the monkeys appear to be on autopilot, totally absorbed in their work, unable to stop. Their bodies stiffen, their strong fingers grip, and off they go.

Unlike the first attack, I was all alone for this one. When she was done, Sweetie sat down placidly on the rocks and looked at me; she wanted to climb back up, started toward me—but my legs were shaking and I didn't trust them to carry me, and her, safely to the sand. "Stay! No! Give me a minute!" I begged, and she did. But if Sweetie had wanted to climb up, I couldn't have stopped her. Hell, if she'd wanted to lick my bleeding arm, there's not a thing I could have done about it.

Pincho arrived at the perfect moment. Pincho was one of the sanctuary workers, and he was amazing with the animals. He walked into cages where I would be shredded, cuddled carnivores like pets, and wrangled even the most dangerous monkeys without consequences. He was a small Costa Rican man with dark skin, a thick black mustache, and a smile that lit up his whole face all day long—though he was not smiling as he stepped onto the rocks. When he saw my arm and sized up the situation, he knew just what to do. Without a word, he grabbed Sweetie at the base of her tail, swung her over his shoulder like a bag of belligerent laundry, and hauled her away.

Thankfully, the bites were not as deep this time, and after the cleanup, it really wasn't so bad. I guess your second set of bites really is like your second child: As long as all fingers and toes are accounted for, you feel pretty lucky.

13

THE LAST PARAKEET

It might not seem like a deep revelation, but being in Costa Rica reminded me daily that life is both incredibly fragile and amazingly resilient.

Traca lived this truth hour by hour in her epic mothering mission with the baby parakeets. Despite her best efforts, two more of the little peepers were dead, leaving only two of the initial seven. Based on their different physical sizes, Traca named her two survivors Little and Big. Why were they dying? It wasn't for lack of attention, that's for sure. Traca doted on these guys all day long. Every few hours she mixed fresh food, cooed to them, washed their mangy young feathers, soaked their green poop-encrusted feet. Without a doubt, no birds ever, in the wild or in captivity, were as loved and honored as Traca's little brood. Yet still they died.

I held one of the fading members of the flock in my hands one night as Traca changed their bedding. While it was technically alive, the little parakeet was barely clinging to its perch here on earth—eyes closed, breathing labored, fragile as rice paper in the rain. With the least force I could manage, I supported its head with a fingertip and willed it to live. I could feel the heat, the energy, streaming from my body and I imagined it was a miracle I was sending to this little creature . . . but nothing I or Traca could do could keep him alive till morning.

In contrast, all around us, life burst forth in amazing abundance, variety, and power. When I tossed a mango seed into a small compost bucket by the Human Kitchen sink, I found a six-inch mango sapling a few days later, reaching for the sun beyond the windows. Hothouse temperatures, high humidity, lots of rain; conditions for fecundity were perfect.

To experience the full force of nature in all its vibrancy, Logan and I liked to slip off the trails and disappear into the dense over-growth. We did this every few days to check the hidden cameras we had set in the jungle. At Carol's request, we were attempting to catch a puma in the act of cattin' around. Puma numbers are critically low, so finding tangible proof of one could mean additional research funding for the sanctuary. Unfortunately, we didn't have much luck. We photographed many perfect night shots of absolutely nothing, one wild kinkajou, a bunch of agoutis (like hairless, stick-legged hamsters on steroids), and one picture of Pincho with his shirt off. Still, it was fun to venture out into the thick of the rain forest and see what we could capture.

One day, we went farther than we'd ever gone before, following an overgrown jungle creek for an hour or so, moving deeper and deeper into the untouched forest. At times we climbed over massive fallen trees that were so rotten, we feared they would crumble beneath us. We inched through narrow rock passes, hands on one side, feet on the other, lunging for horizontal limbs growing out from the banks. It was slow going and it was hot. Logan handled it without much effort, but I created a new colloquial expression for extreme perspiration, as in: sweating like a pig, sweating like a river, sweating like John in the jungle.

Step by step, drip by drip, it felt as if we were moving back in time, as if we were the first humans to explore this uncharted land. Trees towered over us, two hundred feet or more into the canopy; green plants extended leaves as wide as card tables; a million shades of green overlapped, each more vibrant and alive than any plant I have ever watered. Giant golden orb-weaver spiders set traps for the humming-birds that filled the air. Iridescent whip-tailed lizards ran from our stumbling feet. There were bushmaster snakes out there, vipers of all sorts, and a camera-shy puma or two. But we saw none of them. We were left to pass undisturbed, just two more bits of creation in a team-ing, timeless tangle of life.

Whether it was the heat or the soul-stirring beauty that surrounded us, I came to see even Sweetie's bites as a source of inspiration. Not a blessing, exactly, but not a curse, either. Though I was tired of being treated like a rottweiler's chew toy, Sweetie did remind me that I was alive. Simple as that. There was blood in the sheath of skin I called home, and it hurt when you ripped it open, and it healed by itself after you cleaned it up. Like the jungle, it wanted to live, but it would not live forever. So each day was precious, a chance to explore, to sweat, to move a little farther up the stream, reaching, looking, hungry for the light.

Returning from our epic trek, Logan and I stepped out of the jungle and found Jackson sunbathing on her own private beach. I hate to say it, but she looked bored. She was certainly the least happy member of our family, still tethered to her friends and her life back in Gorham. It took her twelve days to say she wanted to go home for the first time, but I could tell, right from the start, that the trip was hard on her. Lacrosse season was starting soon. Auditions for *Fame* were taking place back at school. Mostly, she just missed her friends like crazy, writing daily letters that she had no way of mailing. "I'm homesick," she admitted one night, her head on the Human Kitchen table, at a loss for what to do about it.

At the risk of insulting her and having these pages burned in our woodstove, I think Jack was going through a bit of Internet withdrawal, too. Back home, whenever life got slow or offered a quiet moment, she logged in to her phone and started the chatter. "Go play with a monkey," Traca was quick to suggest at the sanctuary, offering the most alluring alternative to the Web that we would ever have. Even so, I often found Jack sneaking online like a teen alcoholic taking a quick shot.

All right, I admit it: I brought a laptop with me on the trip. I went back and forth on it, but in the end, I bought a tiny netbook computer and stuffed it in my pack. In spite of my "unplugged" goals for the journey, and recognizing that it would provide Jackson with an all-too-tempting portal through which to disappear for a while, I thought it would come in handy for research and planning (which it did), as well as help the kids meet their school obligations (which it did). But just as at home, the real problem was how to police it, because Jackson *did* have an online journal to keep for school, and the Human Kitchen *did* have Wi-Fi when the generator was running, so Jack *could* hide behind her "I'm doing my homework" ruse to get her texting-chatting-Skyping fix even in the middle of the rain forest.

I'm not against all computing, even the pointless stuff. I think it's fun to surf the Web. I love a mindless YouTube binge every now and then. It's just that I want so much more than that for my kids.

There's a story I read once about Hermann Hesse, the German writer. He was riding a train when he saw a beautiful child, a young boy, across the aisle from him. The child had golden hair and seemed almost angelic, filled—in Hesse's mind—with all the limitless potential a human life could hold. As he watched this boy, "the Mozart Child" as he called him, he began to cry, because he knew that the world would dull and stifle the child, as it does nearly everyone, filling him with empty pleasures and numbing distractions and—though he could not have foreseen it at the time—Facebook.

Of course, it wasn't all homesickness and withdrawal tremors for Jackson. She was up more often than she was down, doing her share of work without too much complaint. We usually volunteered together for tour detail each day, keeping an eye on the crowds and learning Earl's spiel word for word in case he ever needed us to fill in for him. The tours were two hours long and absolutely packed with info—but we were getting it down pretty well.

One night as we were walking on the beach at sunset, just the two of us, Jackson and I started to ping-pong random facts back and forth at each other, little Earlisms that were worn into our brains by sheer repetition. (For the record, a collared peccary is the wild, bristly pig of Costa Rica.)

Jackson started things off. "Did you know that our collared peccary is named Leno?" she asked.

I knew exactly what came next. "Yes," I said. "He was named after our smelliest worker, who thought it was a compliment."

"Did you know that the collared peccary is a geophage? That means they can eat *dirt*," Jackson clarified.

"Did *you* know that they can digest botulism?" I asked.

"Did *you* know that they eat raw, wild cashews by the bushel even though the skin is the same as eating poison oak?"

"Really? Did you know they can eat dieffenbachia, also known as the mother-in-law plant?" I volleyed.

Jackson was just getting started. "Did you know there is a species of frog that only lives in the wallows of peccaries?"

And on down the beach we went.

Jackson was cracking herself up with how much she knew, and the longer we bantered like this in the fading Osa sunlight, the more I could see the little Mozart Child inside her starting to shine a little brighter.

It was a few days after this that Logan and I stepped out of the jungle and found Jackson sunbathing alone on her private black sand beach. By then, the Mozart Child magic was long gone.

"I'm starving," Jackson griped like an entitled resort guest.

"Where's your mother?" I asked.

"Sleeping," Jackson said, pointing toward our cabin. She never looked up as I walked away.

I found Traca lying down for a nap, but as soon as I walked in, she sat up, agitated. Without her having to say anything, I knew she was thinking about the parakeets. She looked like a mother whose children were dying. She seemed fragile, on the verge of tears. I hugged her.

"It's probably useless," she said softly, "but I've got to try."

"It's not useless," I said. "It's not useless at all. It's the whole mission around here."

Traca smiled up at me, closed her eyes, and cried against my chest. In that moment, I hoped she was drawing strength from me, that together there was nothing we couldn't do. . . .

But we weren't enough. The next morning, after many careful feedings and hours of energy healing, Traca opened her birdcage and found Little lying dead on a soft blanket. She held him in her hands, looked at me, and smiled a sad smile, her eyes brimming. "He tried so hard," she said by way of eulogy, then cried large tears onto his small green lifeless head. I cried right along with her.

"Are you crying, Dad?" Jackson asked in disbelief. Then, softening: "Oh, great. Now *I'm* going to cry."

It may sound trite, but at the sanctuary it felt very real, like a new colloquial expression for the things that matter most:

Precious as this life we live. Precious as our time together. Precious as the last parakeet in the cage.

14

LET 'EM BITE AND SIT TIGHT

WHAT'S THAT OLD SAYING? BITE ME ONCE, SHAME ON YOU. BITE ME twice, shame on me. Bite me a third time . . . I clearly have no instinct for self-preservation.

Here's the thing about monkeys: They are not humans. They look like little versions of us. Their eyes sparkle with intelligence. They are playful, emotional. They communicate. They're extremely social. But they are also unpredictable. Concepts like territory and dominance are the stuff monkey life is built on, so to play house with them is to play by their rules, even when those rules are undefined, mercurial, or—at least to my human mind—downright arbitrary.

After my second set of bites, I wasted no time getting back in the saddle, or more accurately, letting Sweetie get back on the saddle of my head. I wasn't afraid this time—okay, maybe a little. After a couple of days' healing, I just went outside, supplicated myself like a good horsey, and got back to work. Still, things were different. Sweetie was much more possessive of me (Carol used the word "empowered"), and it usually started first thing in the morning.

My post-second-bite routine was to leave our cabin and walk straight to the beach. I didn't look over at the Human Kitchen. I just booked it to the sand and beelined for the tour grounds. If Sweetie happened to be on some other part of the property, I got a free pass. If she was waiting for me, Earl or Carol would distract her with some food, buying me enough time to make the walk in peace. When the tide was low, I cut across the rocks. At high tide, I took the jungle path. Both routes were a challenge to navigate in my sandals—either the steep up-and-down root-covered trail or the slippery, uneven oceanside rocks. Whether Sweetie was actually coming or not, I always felt I was being chased, and I was happy every time I reached the flat solid ground on the other side of the property without a small black hand reaching up for mine.

One morning, as I cleared the tricky stretch of my route and was walking on a raised plank path that led to the start of the tour, Sweetie came tearing around the corner at top speed. In one bound, she leaped onto a tree stump beside me, grabbed my shirt, and stopped. It was a little scary. She was completely out of breath, panting like a track star and covered with sweat. I might be putting too much of a human spin on her behavior, but as I thought of her sprinting after me, pushing her little fifteen-pound body to exhaustion in the desire to hold my T-shirt again, I started to feel more like an obsession than anything even remotely resembling a friend.

A day later, I was raking out the red-lored parrots' cage when Sweetie showed up out of nowhere and slipped past me through the open cage door. I was sure she would emerge shaking a couple of dead-lored maracas, but there was nothing I could do. The birds were squawking, Sweetie was racing around the inside of the cage like a hairy tornado, and all I could do was walk away, hoping she'd follow. My heart was pounding. I felt powerless. But what really scared me was when I looked back and saw Sweetie racing toward me, launching herself into the air and landing—in a jump that would have made Michael Jordan jealous—on my six-foot-two-inch-high head! I nearly squawked myself.

What made this episode even scarier in a way was what happened next. I carried Sweetie down to the beach and waited until we had both calmed down, but even then I could not coax her off me. Ten minutes passed. Twenty minutes. Usually she lost interest before too long, but now she clutched my head like a monkey hat. No matter what I tried, she would not budge. Out of ideas and sweating in the hot sun, I simply sat on an overturned rowboat and gave up. "Okay. You win," I said, "but I'm not going to move until you get down." Then I closed my eyes, took a deep breath, and prepared to wait her out. Five seconds later, maybe sensing her total dominance over me, Sweetie climbed to the ground and walked slowly down the beach without looking back.

Being a rational human being, I talked at length with Earl about all the scenarios to watch out for, triggers that might set my little time bomb off again. Jealousy was one, as with the first bite. You play with another monkey, or another human shows you some affection or touches you in any way—*bam!* Get ready for the nibblin'. Sudden shocks were another, as with the second bite. Slip on the rocks, conk your head, accidentally sit on a tail—*bam!* Unleash the teeth! One overweight male visitor before me had a plastic deck chair collapse while he was holding Sweetie. Though his bites would eventually heal, Sweetie never forgave him, becoming extremely aggressive toward him, driving him from both the troop and the sanctuary before his stay was up. I was hoping to avoid that.

With ten days to go before our departure date, my biggest concerns were things out of my control. What if a hawk flew overhead and spooked her? Or a snake slithered past? Or a wasp stung her? Or stung me?

The morning of bite episode number three started out normally. Six A.M. Straight for the beach. High tide. Take the jungle trail. Up the steep slope, root by root. Quick look back. No Sweetie. Around the first corner. Out of sight. Home free—

Ten paces later, I heard feet scrambling through the leaves on the path behind me. By the time I turned around, Sweetie was only a few steps away, running at full speed. I welcomed her as I always did: hand out, come on up. We chirped and she climbed onto my shoulders, standing up behind my head. No big deal. But I wasn't going to carry her any more than necessary, and I certainly wasn't going to risk navigating the entire length of the tricky up-and-down jungle path with her perched behind me like a *really* critical backseat driver. What I planned to do was ease back down the slope, taking my time. Then, once on solid ground, I'd scratch her for a bit, call for Earl, and get back to work.

"I'm going as carefully as I can," I said as I started down, holding trees for support, stepping as gently as possible. "We're just going down to the beach. Nice and easy." Another step. Another step. Sweetie had her soft hands resting on my temples, which was not unusual, but she was also hopping up and down and seemed agitated about something.

When I reached the ground, I stepped onto the black sand with a huge sigh of relief. I had planned to walk along the shore to the patio, a typically safe neutral zone—but the tide was really high. Looking back at that moment, I wish I had just walked right into the water. I would have had wet sandals and wet pants, but that would have been the end of it. Sweetie would have jumped off. Earl would have strolled down. Something other than what actually happened would have happened. Instead, I walked toward the Human Kitchen, ducking slightly to clear a natural arch of jungle overgrowth. I didn't trip. There was no danger. I was speaking as you might speak to a baby. "Let's go find Earl. Okay?" I said sweetly. "He'll have some raisins. Would you like that?" I took maybe two steps, and for no reason I can identify, she bit me.

The first bite was on my head, just below my hairline above my left eye. Right away there was blood or scalp or brains (I think I was in shock) obscuring my vision and everything seemed to slow down. Sweetie moved to my elbow, chewed up the back of my left triceps, and reopened my old elbow bite in the process. Then, to complete the triptych of bites, she launched onto my back, bit through my shirt, and left two canine puncture wounds directly on my spine. At this point I must have been yelling because Earl was running toward me and his instructions were crystal clear.

"Run!" he screamed. *"Run!"*

That got my attention.

All of us animals have two options when being attacked. If we don't know them instinctively, we learn them in elementary school science class or on the playground. Two words: fight or flight. We either stand our ground or we run like hell. This is the natural order of things. But when you're a large white male and you ask to live as part of a monkey troop at the Osa Wildlife Sanctuary, you're told not to show any aggression or fear—an extremely unnatural response that might be called the "Let 'Em Bite and Sit Tight" strategy. The trouble is that this goes against everything your body is telling you to do. Believe me, no one wants to stand there and let a monkey gnaw on his forehead. So when Earl gave me the green light to flee, three weeks of pent-up instinct suddenly ignited in my body like a grease fire, and my legs instantly charged forward.

I wish someone had been filming my dash for freedom because I'm sure it was a Scooby-Doo moment. My legs probably windmilled in the air for a few seconds . . . my entire body had great intentions of sprinting to the beach . . . but I lost my balance almost instantly, launched into midair, and landed face-first in a muddy drainage ditch with a pathetic splat. Wet, my thumb sprained, bleeding, heart racing, I looked around frantically to see where Sweetie was.

Not far from my head, I found her standing safely on the ground with a puzzled expression on her face that seemed to say: *What the hell is your problem?*

15

THE OUTSIDE OF THE CAGE

TWELVE NOON. THE SECOND TOUR OF THE DAY WAS UNDER WAY AND Logan was over at the tour grounds assisting Earl with that. Winkie was there, too. Carol was on the other side of the Gulf, picking up a few supplies, and Traca and Sweetie were doing a little yoga up at our cabin. As for Jackson . . . I wasn't sure. She'd just been eating a huge plate of pasta (in an effort to "feel full," as she said) before offering me the last few bites (in an attempt, I suspect, to have me wash the plate). Now she was somewhere outside and I was sitting at the end of the Human Kitchen table, alone. Well, sort of alone.

On the table before me, a few random creatures were keeping me company. Traca's last remaining parakeet, Big, was doing well, filling out his fancy green pantaloons nicely, resting in a small pet carrier. Farther down, another cage held a baby jaguarundi, like a small black house cat but with sharp claws, a desire for raw meat, and a vicious if squeaky little growl. The final tabletop residents were also our newest arrivals: two baby owls who were delivered to the sanctuary a few days back.

When I was a kid, my mother collected owl figurines. I think mothers start collections like this to give their kids an easy gift idea, and it worked like a charm for my brothers and me. Virtually every Mother's Day, birthday, and Christmas, all three of us dutifully (and cheaply) handed over the big-eyed goods until she had a display case aviary with well over one hundred specimens. Having seen so many garish cartoon replicas, I wasn't prepared for how much more garish and cartoonish baby owls were in real life: huge staring eyes, odd panting beaks, and funky rhythmic head bobs. In honor of my mom's interest in and devotion to all things owl, we named one of these intense little fluff balls Esther.

Outside the Human Kitchen, it was the kind of day the office of Costa Rican tourism likes to brag about: blue sky, warm sun, tropical perfection—but I was sitting this one out. Since my third set of monkey bites, I had decided to make the remainder of my stay a monkey-free zone. Pitiful, yes, but much less stressful for me. Each morning I stayed in my bedroom-cage until breakfast. Then Traca took Sweetie for a walk down the beach. When the coast was clear, Jack or Logan gave me the signal and I ran like hell to my kitchen-cage. After that, I just repeated the process every time I needed to go anywhere all day: no jungle paths, no carefree excursions out in the open, no monkey contact of any kind, period. Honestly, I couldn't take it any more. I had PTSD: posttraumatic Sweetie disorder. Though the bites weren't life-threatening or really even all that painful, I found myself reliving the attacks again and again. I dreamed about them. I saw monkeys in the shadows of our cabin at night. I even started bawling like a baby while listening to my iPod one afternoon. It was Sara Bareilles singing "Gravity," a beautiful song with piano and cello. And the lyrics, a desperate plea from a powerless lover:

> *Set me free. Leave me be.*
> *You're on to me, on to me, and all over me.*

Maybe it was the haunting mix of keys and resonant strings. Maybe it was the message. Maybe I was just ready to snap. Whatever the trigger, I fell apart. Without restraint, I released all my pent-up fear and sadness into that song, squeezing years' worth of therapy out of a single four-minute ballad. I cried for feeling trapped and vulnerable; for being scared to go outside; for growing old; for wasting so much time disconnected from Traca. I cried for how much I loved my kids and for how much I would miss them when they were gone. I even cried for the childhood cat my parents made me take back to the animal shelter after she clawed up all our window screens. It was not an organized grief; I was all over the place. But when the song ended and I pulled myself together, I knew one thing for sure: I was done with the monkeys. If I needed to cower in a cage to avoid another Sweetie bite . . . so be it.

The good news was—at least from what I could observe from inside my various cages—my new isolation was working out just fine for the troop. After three days of self-imposed exile, the sanctuary was at peace; no fighting, biting, or bleeding. And while it sucked to be essentially another animal in a cage, there were so many great things happening in the free world, I was content for the moment to let Traca and the kids have all the fun.

Though I missed my time exploring the jungle with Logan, I was thrilled that he was now on camera trap detail with Pincho. Pincho knew the rain forest better than anyone else, and he taught as they walked, all in Spanish, which was even better. They wielded machetes, tracked agoutis to their dens, drank with leaves from mountain streams, and generally acted the way real Costa Rican men of danger were supposed to act. To see Logan emerge from the jungle at the end of these treks, sweating, triumphant, and smiling from ear to ear, was an image that was easily worth a couple of monkey bites to me.

Jackson, meanwhile, was really starting to embrace her time with her monkey sisters, especially Winkie. They played a new game that was pure comedy. I'm not sure why or how it worked but it went like this: Jack cornered Winkie and made the typical monkey greeting face—squinty eyes, chin out, kissy lips. Then, for some reason, Winkie reacted like a silent movie comedian. She fell back, stumbled, threw her arms up, staggered, backed into the wall, desperately lunged for the window cage wire in front of me, then flopped to the floor, crawled like a snake, and on and on. Jack laughed nonstop through the whole performance, and so did her monkey friend—all of which was unplugged music to the ears of the Attacked White Male nearby.

And Traca was practically family to these little hairy children, if not a mother, then definitely a favorite aunt. In the exact opposite way that Sweetie enjoyed chewing on my extremities, she unconditionally adored Traca. They even shared the same T-shirt at times, presenting a human and a monkey head out the same neck opening like some freaky two-headed science experiment gone wrong. It looked like my worst nightmare come to life, but for Traca, it was a beautiful dream come true.

As for Traca and me . . . we were getting there. As expected, in spite of all the drama, life was easier for us on the road. With so many new, exotic distractions, our tired old domestic patterns felt silly, dissolving away like jungle mist, leaving behind the two friends that we've always been. We talked, laughed, and seemed to move a little closer every day. After my third set of bites, when I stood up from the drainage ditch, I staggered into the ocean where I knew Sweetie would not follow. I was shaking and scared, and Traca met me there. "That's it," she said protectively. "We're not doing this anymore." She looked me in the eye, all barriers gone, and stood beside me, knee-deep in the water, ready to take on the world together.

It was my decision to finish out our commitment at the sanctuary, even though it meant my hiding in the Human Kitchen like another exhibit on tour. So while the rest of the family enjoyed a carefree, once-in-a-lifetime experience, I just waited and watched and learned what I could. If nothing else, my life in captivity did give me a complete and thorough understanding of why Carol and Earl work so hard to release animals back into the wild.

Bottom line: It's *way* more fun on the outside of the cage.

16

AS POLITELY AS POSSIBLE

As with many pivotal moments, nothing unusual led up to it. The day started out normally: The howler monkey alarm went off at 5:00; we harangued the kids to wake up; Jackson barely moved until six o'clock, grumbling like a teenage ogre and generally being unpleasant. Traca was always the first one out, Logan was second, Jack staggered down eventually, and I waited to be called like the hiding, cowardly pomfretphobic (someone with a fear of monkeys) that I had become.

Around ten that morning, I was sitting in the Human Kitchen feeding Big. I'd just gotten back from snorkeling with Logan—Sweetie was over on a tour—when Earl walked in. He was red in the face, sweating, and right away I could tell that something was wrong. His opening phrase was another indicator that the shit was about to hit the proverbial jungle fan.

"I'm going to say this as politely as possible," Earl began. "This is not working. For Logan to be snorkeling in the middle of the day when there is work to do is unacceptable. You're here to work. This is not a vacation." And then he really got rolling. "Your kids arrive late every day. Jackson sits there on the computer all afternoon doing nothing. I can't get either of them to fill out their feeding logs properly. And today I need everybody helping. Everybody!"

By "everybody" I knew he also meant me, but as I've said, I was done being a monkey snack. "I'm sorry, Earl." I explained again. "I wish I could be out there—"

"Well, you could," Earl interrupted. "You could. And if you're afraid of the monkeys, you probably shouldn't be here."

Earl was under an enormous amount of stress at that moment. Carol had left town a few days earlier for a rare visit back to the USA, which meant Earl was not only running the sanctuary alone, he was also the alpha, the highest-ranking member of the troop. Adding to his responsibilities on that particular morning, a camera crew was over at the tour grounds preparing to film the release of a ferocious ocelot named Lily, with state and park officials on hand to witness the event. At the same time, Pincho and several other staff members were attempting to maneuver Georgia, the dominant capuchin monkey, into a transport cage for relocation. (Georgia was a wild, aggressive female who once bit Carol so hard on the foot that she snapped off one of her eyeteeth in Carol's anklebone!) At the same time, tour groups were arriving early, wandering on the beach and into the sanctuary. One obnoxious visitor was heard saying, "I'm gonna go over there and *hug that monkey.*" Naturally, Sweetie, Winkie, and Poppy were insanely curious about all the goings-on, and the last thing an ocelot release party, a capuchin containment crew, or a bunch of uninitiated visitors needed was an amped-up group of spider monkeys tossed into the mix.

Just before Earl read me the riot act (as politely as possible), he'd completed something like fourteen trips back and forth along the jungle path, rounding up monkeys, directing traffic, trying to keep all primates—including the monkey-hugging jerk on the beach—from getting hurt. I just happened to be the one sitting around to bear the brunt of his frustration.

Hours later, after Lily the ocelot, Georgia the capuchin, and all the tour visitors were safe and getting on with their lives, Earl and I talked at length. He was embarrassed and apologetic at first, backpedaling for losing his temper . . . but I stopped him. It wasn't fun to listen to, but I had to admit that his rant was pretty much right on the money. Our kids had not been what you'd call motivated workers. Yes, they were doing it. They were technically going through the motions, but they were also complaining a lot, rolling their eyes, showing up late, half-assing their way through the day. While I hated to admit it, Jack *did* spend too much time on her Facebook page, even when told not to; and Logan *didn't* fill out his anteater log, even when asked repeatedly to do so; and I *was* afraid of the monkeys!

But it wasn't all bad.

There were moments on our trip that we will never forget. Some of them inspired us with a power and beauty we couldn't have imagined. Others were horribly sad or painful, life-changing in their own way for the impression they left on our hearts. Still others, like the tongue-lashing from Earl, taught us an unexpected lesson at exactly the right time. For the kids, at least, when I relayed Earl's message in graphic detail, I think it was just what they needed to hear.

The next morning, when the howlers sounded the 5:00 alarm, the kids got right up. Not a word of complaint. They may have been tired and grumpy but they didn't show it. For the first time all trip, they got to work by six. They fed their babies and filled out their feeding logs without being reminded. No Facebook. No sitting around. After breakfast, they offered to rake the jungle path together without being asked, just to be of use.

Then Logan assisted Earl on the first tour of the day without an eye roll or a yawn, no slacking, full-assed, so to speak. Then Jackson gave her first *solo tour* at the sanctuary; two hours of info to seventeen tourists, all by her fourteen-year-old self! Traca acted as her crowd controller and said Jack was absolutely fantastic, a wealth of free-flowing facts. I only wish I could have been there to see it.

The final issue to resolve was me. As Earl said: If I was afraid of the monkeys, I probably shouldn't stay. So we decided to go. With eight more days before our scheduled departure flight out of San José, we were catching an early boat the next morning and heading up to another rescue center in the north: the Rainsong Wildlife Sanctuary on the Nicoya Peninsula. Earl had connections; he made a call and we were in. It would be a brutally long day of travel but that was just fine with me. As Earl said while we were making pizza dinner on our last night: "This is your adventure. You don't want to spend it in a cage, do you?"

17

ESCAPE FROM MONKEY ISLAND

We woke up at 3:30 a.m. We got our things together by headlamps, trying to make a four o'clock boat for a five o'clock bus.

It was pitch-dark as we walked to the Human Kitchen, and our headlamps didn't help much. They almost make things worse in the jungle, casting dark shadows that move like stalking predators every time you take a step. It may sound overly dramatic but my heart was pounding. I was walking fast, making a lot of noise in the silent morning, unable to see or hear what was around me. I passed the anteater's cage. Nearly there. A few more steps when—

"There are monkeys here!" Earl shouted from somewhere in the darkness.

I could see shapes approaching. They were fast, already on the bars of the kitchen windows, running sideways, coming toward me. Traca had the kitchen door open and I lunged to get in when a gentle black hand reached out of the darkness and touched my cheek. At that moment, everything slowed down the way people report after experiencing trauma. I saw the hand beside my right eye. I felt all four fingers as they brushed the length of my face. I was sure—positive!—the monkeys would be on my backpack when I got inside . . . but they weren't. The door latched. Somehow I was safe, for the moment.

Of course, no one else felt any of this. Traca and the kids were all out in the dark, outside the cage saying goodbye to their hairy pals. Not me. I had only one thing in mind, and I asked Earl if it was possible. "Is there any ironclad guaranteed way I can get to the boat without interacting with a monkey?" Earl lured Sweetie to him with some raisins, then walked off. He stopped maybe thirty feet away. I could see Sweetie looking at me like a child being left at day care. She was too close. When I left the safety of the Human Kitchen, she could be on me in five bounds if she wanted to.

"The boat's here," Logan said. I didn't know what to do.

I stepped outside and started to run, then stopped and stood my ground. I was both fighting and fleeing, torn, frozen. I almost started to run for the pitch-dark jungle trail, for no reason. Finally I just ran for the beach. Logan later said he was sure I was going to trip or slam into a tree. I had lost my headlamp. I was moving blindly toward the black Gulf like a man on fire, my huge backpack on my back and my smaller pack in my arms. When I reached the water, I splashed right into the surf up to my knees and tossed my gear into the boat. Moments later, at a leisurely and far less frantic pace, the rest of my family climbed on board. We shook Earl's hand. Then we shoved off, motoring away into the dark morning.

The Osa Wildlife Sanctuary is an amazing place. Thousands of people come through on tours every year, learning the importance of conservation and interacting safely with the curious monkeys who usually swing by to check the tours out. Carol now runs the sanctuary by herself (she and Earl had a parting of ways), but the setup is still the same: a rehabilitation/rescue/release center on one hand and a unique human/spider monkey troop on the other. They could have tossed all the monkeys into cages; it would certainly have been easier for them, less disruptive, safer for the visiting white males like me. But to see Sweetie, Winkie, and Poppy interacting with wild spider monkeys who passed through the property, to watch them swing through the trees, foraging for food, harassing the slow-moving howlers and simply being free . . . it's hard to imagine that cages and bars would be an improvement.

Right before we arrived at the sanctuary, Poppy (the oldest female) had been pregnant. It was unplanned, no invasive breeding program or sperm on ice needed. Poppy just saw a cute wild male spider monkey at the top of a mango tree and slipped off for a little monkey business. Sadly, she lost the baby, but she'll try again. The boys will be back. And life, as it was always intended, will continue.

In the wild, when spider monkeys have their first baby, they leave their natal troop and find a new one. What this means for the sanctuary is that Sweetie, Winkie, and Poppy will not be with the Crewses forever. So if you'd like to meet them, you'd better hurry.

Before we leave the Osa, I want to make one final pitch for this amazing organization. If I have given the impression that I do not endorse Carol or her work or that I consider the operation unsafe, listen up:

The monkeys are not a danger on tours. They're territorial around the Human Kitchen, but that's on the other side of the property. During tours they are docile and inquisitive, sometimes standoffish, sometimes extremely engaged. If you are lucky, one of them will choose you from the crowd, maybe take a raisin from your hand and hang out for a while. If they do, don't squeeze them, grab them, pull their tails, or tease them in any way. Just let them climb you like a tree and be amazed. Look into their intelligent eyes, study the skin of their wrinkled black palms, feel the grip of their otherworldly prehensile tails, and spend a few moments connecting with them before they choose someone else and scamper away. If you follow the *maaawn-kay* rules (and they are explained at the start of every tour), you will be fine. You may have your glasses or your camera stolen if you get careless, but you and your skin will be safe. Even you big white males.

Looking back on it now, in spite of all the teeth that found their way into my flesh, we had an incredible experience at the sanctuary. It's remarkable what you can learn in a month.

We learned the gecko's seven-note song. We learned how to pick a toucan out of the jungle choir. We learned what a sloth's tiny humanoid ears look like. We learned the sound a baby kinkajou makes during his midnight feeding . . . and the sound Jackson makes when it's her turn to feed the baby kinkajou at midnight. We learned that owls grow to full size in forty-five days and will eat most anything you dangle in front of them. We also learned that parakeets—at least the brood we inherited—are not very hardy. (Sadly, Traca's last parakeet, Big, died a few days after we left the Osa. We were told he just sort of gave up the will to live, but I suspect it was Traca's will for him to live that had kept him alive so long in the first place.) We learned that taking an outdoor shower in the jungle late at night can be both terrifying and thrilling. We learned that even card games can make you sweat. We learned that a single brownie cut into four small pieces can be the most delicious thing in the world. Most of all, we learned that with full attention, you can be ready for the miracles (or the monkeys) that are lurking around every corner.

Still . . .

When that morning boat set out across the Golfo Dulce and I was on it . . . it felt like a prison break, like I was an innocent man leaving his cell behind for good. The stars were thick above us, a billion billion lights, and the spray from our boat was alive with green phosphorescent sea life. As we began the forty-minute trip back to Puerto Jiménez, I watched the sanctuary recede into the darkness until Traca took my hand and Logan read my mind.

"It's okay, Dad," he said. "Sweetie can't swim. You're free."

Part Three

WWOOF

I learned the value of hard work by working hard.

—MARGARET MEAD

18

RAINSONG

OUR TIME AT THE RAINSONG WILDLIFE SANCTUARY—IN THE SLEEPY Costa Rican town of Cabuya—is worth mentioning, if only to illustrate how misleading Internet-based research can be when you're looking for volunteer opportunities. It's like online dating in a way. With the right profile photo and a few well-chosen words, everyone can look like Mr. or Ms. Right. But once you meet them in person, in the harsh light of day, the truth can sometimes be a bit of a disappointment.

If you check out the Rainsong website, it might look as if you've found volunteer heaven. In addition to helping rescued and injured animals, the site suggests you will join in such activities as "tropical gardening, camping and trekking, identification and gathering of exotic fruits, guided nature tours on horseback," and so on. They boast of butterfly gardens, a living insect museum, sloth search and rescue (whatever that means). And they have pictures showcasing private waterfalls and communal meals, even a group shot of a dozen happy young male and female volunteers in bathing suits, like a *Survivor* cast party photo.

"Ooooh. They have a hot tub," Jackson said, checking out the cute guys, no doubt picturing herself in her bikini smiling back from some future photo gallery highlight.

At $40 a week per person, it seemed too good to be true—which, of course, it was. When we actually stepped inside the Rainsong gate, what we found instead of paradise was a small roadside zoo with animals in tiny cages, all of it badly in need of cleaning.

Rainsong was the brainchild of Mary Lynn Perry, a heavyset woman in her early fifties with long gray hair that was usually tucked under a baseball cap. Mary started the sanctuary in 2005 after poachers shot her favorite horse, a horse that had been grazing at the time . . . at night . . . in its own corral! I remember a similar story in Maine one deer-hunting season about a *bulldog* being shot in its backyard . . . on a leash . . . wearing a hunting vest . . . so I guess hunters' stupidity is not confined to any one border. In any case, waking up to find her beloved stallion lying dead on the ground somehow inspired Mary to take action in behalf of all animals, and thus Rainsong was born.

I'm sure it was founded with the best of intentions, but when we arrived, there was definitely an air of neglect at the sanctuary. For one thing, we didn't see Mary much over the course of our seven-day stay. After she took our money, she left to work on a turtle preservation project up the coast. As a result, Rainsong felt like a ship without a captain, with untrained volunteers like us basically running the show. On our first day, we worked alongside a cute twentysomething couple from Spain, two guys from England, a seventy-two-year-old retired schoolteacher, his sister-in-law from Virginia, and several college girls from all over the United States. Without supervision or specific standards to strive for, most volunteers stayed for a week or longer, paid their money for the privilege, then did what needed doing and tried to make life at the sanctuary a little nicer for everyone involved. Have an idea? Go for it. So that's what we did.

As a first order of business, we raked. When we got there, the pathways between cages were completely obscured by a thick blanket of leaves, giving Rainsong an abandoned look. It took our family the better part of two days to get the place looking spiffy again. Then we focused on the anteater cage.

Back at the Osa, they had an anteater named Tank. The kids loved him. Tank was a vibrant, solid, playful animal who was constantly in motion. When Logan or Jackson entered his cage, Tank practically jumped into their arms, gripping them with his hooked claws. He loved to be held, hated to be put down. And though he wasn't fast, he was hard to get away from. He was enthusiastic. He was also a voracious eater, drinking greedily from a bottle with his long thin whiplike tongue and ripping into termite nests like a child opening presents. Of all the animals we met on the Osa, Tank was one of our favorites.

But all anteaters are not created, or treated, equally.

At Rainsong, their anteater was named Anti. While she was roughly the same size as Tank, like a football with a thick bare tail, the two animals could not have been more different. Tank was vivacious and thriving, Anti listless and thin. She paced in her bare cage as if she realized how pointless her pacing was. She lapped reluctantly at the sickening gruel we were given to feed her. She had no spark, no pep. The first time I picked her up, she just hung limp, her rib cage fragile in my hands. When I took her out of her cage and set her down for a walk, she managed two tentative steps, then sprawled on the ground as if waiting for death.

"Anti needs enrichment!" Logan proclaimed, quoting one of Carol Crews's favorite buzzwords.

So we gathered logs for Anti to climb on and built a section for dirt in her otherwise cement cage. Logan came up with the sandbox idea and took great pride in hammering and filling this stroke of brilliance into existence. On a roll, we cut up oranges and squeezed them in her new playpen to attract ants. Then Logan grabbed a machete and hacked down thick branches filled with green leaves to add a wilder feel to Anti's sterile enclosure. We added a potted plant, cut down termite nests. We let her forage for longer periods in the open air. And we encouraged her. In every way we could think of, we loved her.

Traca also took a special interest in two sad birds: a beautiful male toucan and his next-door neighbor, an aracari. Aracaris are a type of toucan with black plumage and a black bill. And while they're exotic birds compared with any bird back home, they seem almost common next to a full-blown Technicolor keel-billed toucan—the way Doug Pitt probably looks standing next to his famous brother, Brad.

As we learned from Earl back at the Osa, a toucan's skin color is actually a brilliant lime green, though this is visible only around their eyes, and their feet are an equally brilliant baby blue, a color that makes no evolutionary sense in the lush green jungle where they live. Most spectacularly, a toucan's bill is a rainbow of swirling color that looks more like an oversized tropical Popsicle than anything resembling a useful mouth.

"Did you know that a toucan's nostrils are on the top of his beak?" Jackson asked me facetiously one day, back in tour guide mode.

"Oh, really? Did *you* know that in heavy rains they look up to keep from drowning?" I retorted, never tiring of this game.

At Rainsong, the aracari and the toucan were both cooped up in enclosures no bigger than broom closets, but Traca made a few home improvements just the same. She gathered fallen palm fronds and built simple roofs for the otherwise exposed cages, creating some much-needed shade in a land of almost constant sun. She also spent time lavishing the birds with hose baths, a ritual that both she and the birds seemed to thoroughly enjoy.

"Imagine being able to fly and ending up in there," Traca said to me one afternoon, smiling as she watched the birds flapping in the falling water—beaks open, heads up, in no danger of drowning.

For the record, we found no tropical gardening at Rainsong. No gathering of exotic fruits or horseback tours. And unless you count the spiders that filled every corner of the place, there was no living insect museum, either, nor any butterfly gardens. No communal meals or sloth rescue work or private waterfalls that any of us could find. No hot tub, much to Jackson's disappointment. But one final image does stand out in my mind, though it may never make the splashy photo gallery on the sanctuary website:

As our time at Rainsong was nearing an end, I checked in on Anti the anteater and found her asleep, in her little triangle of ground that Logan had built, under a hanging branch of green leaves, nose in the dirt, with ants crawling all over her fur. She looked happy. It wasn't much, but it felt like something, having left a small corner of a life a little better than you found it. Maybe that's all volunteering is.

19

FOREIGN TRANSPLANTS

BEFORE WE LAND IN NEW ZEALAND, WE NEED TO TALK A LITTLE BIT about WWOOFing. For those of you who have never WWOOFed, WWOOF stands for Willing Workers on Organic Farms, and it's an international movement that is particularly popular Down Under. To get involved, you first need to go to the main WWOOFing website: www.wwoof.org. Once there, choose a region of the world, then click the WWOOFing country of your choice. In the Asia-Pacific category, for example, WWOOFers can choose from Australia, Bangladesh, China, India, Japan, Kazakhstan, Korea, Nepal, New Zealand, the Philippines, Sri Lanka, and Taiwan. If you select New Zealand, as we did, it costs $30 U.S. for one year of access to their database of available hosts, and you can pay online. After becoming a member, you set up a profile, post a picture of you (and your family, if applicable), write a little bit about who you are and what you're looking for, then search the areas you'd like to visit and send out email requests to various farms that look interesting. Our biggest challenge was finding places that would accept four people at the same time—but they were out there, and that's where we were headed.

Choosing New Zealand as our next stop was a no-brainer. It's gorgeous, English-speaking, notoriously friendly—and monkey-free, which endeared it to me right away. True to form on our rambling seat-of-your-pants tour, as we prepared to land, we weren't 100 percent sure where our first New Zealand stop would be. We had two prospects in the Auckland area that were open to the idea of family WWOOFing. One was a small goat farm, the other a large retreat center. Both said, "Yes, it will probably work out," but neither had officially accepted our request. So after fourteen hours in the air and probably eight hours of sleep among the four of us, we landed at

Auckland Airport, dog-tired and disoriented, but delighted to learn that someone named Rahaman was coming to pick us up. In the brief email message we found waiting for us, Rahaman was described only as "an older man with a gray ponytail," but this snippet hardly begins to capture the remarkable, complex person who would be our host for our first Kiwi week.

Rahaman was born plain old David Brown in conservative old England sixty-odd years ago. In his twenties, he was a self-described "righteous hippie," taking LSD to expand his consciousness and serving time in jail for all the expanding he did. It was a crazy period and a wild ride, but David wasn't in it for the high. He was seeking a direct experience with God, and this desire would ultimately take him to every corner of the world. He studied in Afghanistan with the Sufi mystics, spent four years at an Indian ashram studying under the renowned guru Osho, and lived with the Dalai Lama in Dharamsala. He traveled for years into the most remote parts of the Amazon basin to learn from the indigenous tribes of Brazil and explored Native American spirituality in the American Southwest. He took peyote with the Lakota Indians every day for years (until the smell of the stuff made him physically sick) and became a sacred pipe holder in the tribe's sweat lodge ceremony, and on and on and on. It was the Sufis who gave him the name Rahaman, which means "compassion" in Urdu, and—after a lifetime of searching—it is with the Sufi order that he feels most closely aligned. "It's all Sufism," he once told me, rather cryptically, referring to a belief system that is tolerant of all faiths, accepts all holy books, and values personal experience over dogma. It's also the reason he showed up with his gray ponytail, loaded us into his shell of a van (no backseats, just a bunch of blankets), and drove us to the tiny town of Tuakau, south of Auckland, for our stay at the Sharda Centre.

The Sharda Centre is a Sufi retreat founded in 1989 by a sweet and fiery woman named Helima MacEwan. Helima's vision was to create an international center where tolerance and peace could flourish. When this goal was more or less achieved, she further dreamed of building a magnificent temple, a Peace Dome that would bring believers of all faiths together. Well into her eighties, with pure white hair and a believer's conviction, Helima worked tirelessly to drive her temple idea forward. She had plans drawn up, space cleared, fund-raising under way; but some dreams take more than one lifetime to achieve. Helima died in 2005, and when we arrived five years later, the Peace Dome was still only a blueprint on the shelf and a cleared spot of ground on the Sharda property.

Because it was the off season, there were no other WWOOFers or guests waiting for us at the Sharda Centre when we stumbled out of Rahaman's van—which meant we were the only people staying in a huge dormitory. After a month of one-room living, this sudden abundance of space was a welcome gift, allowing the kids to have their own rooms and all of us to enjoy some much-needed privacy.

One practical matter to contend with while traveling—particularly with four people, more particularly on a budget, and most particularly with your family—is the tight living quarters typically encountered. Logan, Jackson, Traca, and I often shared a single room on the road, so we needed a few ground rules everyone could agree on, the most basic of which concerned nudity.

Dressing or undressing in mixed company was a daily challenge—at least our two teens thought so—so we quickly developed a way to create a semblance of privacy with very little lead time. The system was simple. If you wanted to change at any time of the day, you announced to the room in a clear, full voice: "Changing in three, two, one . . . ," at which point you were free to strip down and get on with it. As everyone's desire not to be seen naked was exceeded only by everyone's desire not to see one another naked, you could be sure by the countdown's end that no one would be looking your way. This became so automatic that before long, Logan reduced the warning to "Changing . . . now!" with equally successful results. Or maybe we all just stopped caring so much.

In addition to putting on and taking off clothes, you also have to deal with broader personal space concerns like . . . not having any personal space. When you are sleeping side by side, eating every meal together, riding the same buses, breathing the same air, it's natural to want—and necessary to create—a little time apart. If and when this doesn't happen, you will learn how patient or impatient you are, how kind or unkind you are, and how much you love or how suddenly you can grow to loathe your fellow family members.

If the idea of taking your teen children on a prolonged and overly close family vacation seems only slightly more desirable than, say, welding yourself into a storage shed with sleep-deprived cougars, you are not alone. Many parents I talk to about our trip wonder if all the intense togetherness would elevate their children's natural tendency to get on each other's nerves into something bordering on mental break-down, if not homicidal rage. We saw some of this on the road, at air-ports and bus terminals, where other parents were dragging their teens off on vacation and the kids were complaining about everything, snapping at one another like pampered, inbred show dogs. In the worst cases, the kids seemed half crazed by all the family time, the parents had sunken, despairing eyes, and everyone looked pissed off and in need of some private time.

Before we got to that point, Sharda gave us separate rooms, and for that alone we were more than willing to work for them. But with no organic farm on the property that we could see, and no guests who needed tending, we had no idea where or how to start our WWOOF-ing careers.

WWOOFing is essentially a barter arrangement; organic farms on the list need help, willing workers offer to help. In exchange for an agreed-upon number of hours of labor each day, free lodging and three daily meals are offered. There is no set length of stay required. WWOOFers can hang out for a few days or a few months, so long as all parties are cool with the deal. For travelers on a budget like us, it seemed like a wonderfully inexpensive way to see an otherwise expen-sive country.

Our first day at Sharda was spent weeding. When the Brits landed in New Zealand way back when, they brought with them much more than just a bland and uninspired culinary tradition. They also brought invasive plants: privet and barberry for hedges, wandering jew, aspar-agus ferns, and my least favorite: jasmine. Jasmine grows in long, tough nodes that spread out like an aggressive cancer across the ground.

"Pull it all out," Rahaman said with a smile, then left us on a hill-side that appeared to be covered with nothing but weeds.

There was lots of weeding to do at Sharda, sometimes close to the retreat center, sometimes out in the bush. In New Zealand, "the bush" is the native forest that once covered most of the island. When people showed up, about a thousand years ago, the bush was dense and dark, like a prehistoric jungle. So, naturally, it had to be cut down. With persistence and the usual endless human capacity to transform nature into something that can be sold, farmed, or developed, much of the natural vegetation was wiped out, leaving small and precious tracts to be protected.

At first it seemed futile, pulling small clumps of weeds in a vast tangle of sprawling wilderness. Standing in the bush is like taking part in a giant diorama about the dawn of the forest. Sunlight barely penetrates the dense canopy. Ferns and vines thrive. Mosses and liverworts (like a green seaweed) blanket the ground. The bush around Sharda was like that for acres on end, yet there we were, pulling three-inch weeds. Was this not the very definition of pointless?

Rahaman didn't think so. If left unchecked, he said, the weeds would choke and destroy this one pocket of native New Zealand. But if the invaders were systematically removed, even if it took a long time, this pocket would be preserved. So we pulled.

It wasn't exactly monkey wrangling, but it was about all we had the energy for on that first day; we were practically delirious from sleep deprivation. In no rush, the four of us just sat on a hill under an apple tree, slowly pulling jasmine out by the roots. And though we managed to amass a small green mountain of the wicked choking weed, we all eventually fell asleep in the sun, just four more foreign transplants soaking up a warm afternoon.

If you drilled a hole from our home in Maine through the center of the earth, you would end up not far from where we were sleeping. As a result, everything was backward for us in New Zealand. While springtime was beginning at home, fall was just getting started at Sharda. Drivers used the left side of the road instead of the right. Water spiraled down the drain clockwise instead of counterclockwise. Rugby was by far the most popular sport instead of being a game used as filler on ESPN2.

But some things remained the same.

At the end of that first day, Rahaman took us for a ride to Sunset Beach, a beautiful stretch of New Zealand shoreline on the Tasman Sea. The kids immediately fell asleep on the sand, their jet-lagged bodies demanding rest, while Traca and I headed for the setting sun, jumping into the sea together. Just as in Maine, the water was freezing, an icy shock of pure aliveness—and that shock, that breathless shout that Traca and I shared, reminded me of one of the reasons we had left home in the first place. Like Helima, like Rahaman, like all the mystics from every tradition throughout history, we were all just looking to connect with life as directly as possible.

20

THE SWEAT LODGE

To the Lakota Indians of the American plains, one of the most sacred rituals is the sweat lodge. Using heat, steam, and smoke, the lodge is designed to purify your body, mind, and spirit—or at least clear your pores out really well. Traca's been to a few of these and raves about them, but the kids and I were completely new to the experience. So it was with some apprehension that we all accepted Rahaman's invitation to attend an authentic sweat lodge ceremony at the Sharda Centre.

On a purely physical level, taking part in the ceremony is a challenge. For one thing, it requires you to sit on the ground inside a small domed space, surrounded by intense heat and total darkness for three hours or more. As someone who finds it difficult to get comfortable in my reclining coach-class seat (sipping ginger ale and watching in-flight movies), I had my doubts that sweat lodges and I were going to be new best friends.

If you've heard about people dying in sweat lodge ceremonies, it has happened. In the most notorious and recent case out in Sedona, Arizona, two people died and many more became seriously ill while participating in the same ritual Rahaman was planning. I asked him if there was any actual danger and he smiled.

"Not for us," he said. "They used plastic tarps in that tragedy, yeah? Plastic doesn't breathe. We'll be using canvas. Blankets and canvas only."

True to his word, he spread only broad sheets of canvas and a patchwork of colorful blankets around a curved tree-branch frame outside the center. At sunset, it was time to get started.

The ceremony began with a proper smudging; Rahaman burned

sage and wafted it with an eagle feather around each of us. Next we needed to heat the rocks that put the sweat in the sweat lodge. The Lakotas refer to these egg-shaped lava rocks as "stone people," and they were baked in an intense outdoor fire for over an hour. By the time we were ready to enter the lodge, there were nineteen of us, a full house for this small space. Most of the participants were local Kiwis who came for a cleansing each month. There was also Rahaman, a few other newly arrived WWOOFers, the ready-to-sweat Marshall clan, and an intense-looking Maori warrior, his face covered with swirling patterns of dark tribal tattoos.

The Maori are the indigenous people of New Zealand, and like the Lakota, they were royally screwed over by the invading Europeans. Though they once ruled this gorgeous part of the world, today it's rare to see one of them with full face tattoos out in public. It's even more rare, according to Rahaman, to have one of them attend your sweat lodge ceremony.

When the sun had disappeared behind the tree line, we crawled into the lodge on all fours, first the women, then the men. Logan was right beside me as we took our spots, shoulder to shoulder, around the pit where the stone people would attempt to make my previous epic jungle sweating look like a mild case of granny perspiration. Once we were in position, ritual items were passed around the circle without explanation. First cedar branches, then deer antlers. Then one by one, the stone people began to arrive. An assistant delivered them on their own set of antlers and they were blazing red, so hot they were almost translucent. After half a dozen trips back and forth to the fire, the assistant sealed the tent flap behind him and Rahaman took over: chanting prayers, tossing water on the stones, filling the space with steam, and plunging us into total darkness. I was breathing like a fish out of water, sweating with an urgency I had never experienced.

Wankan Tonka . . .
Wankan Tonka . . .
Wankan Tonka . . .
Wankan Tonka . . . hey hey.

We called out to God, the Great Spirit who is in all things. We welcomed all our ancestors, those living and those who came before us. We chanted at the top of our lungs, completely invisible to each other in the utter blackness. To a night-vision camera, we would have made quite a sight: nineteen mostly naked people barking out Lakota prayers, sweating as if we were all trying to wring a cup of water out of our underwear.

Three times during the ceremony, the tent flap opened and water was brought in, cooling things off a little. In any other context, I would have considered the communal wooden ladle we passed around to be a petri dish of liquid contamination. But in the sweat lodge, I just drank it. Rahaman referred to it as "the Sacred Water of Life," and that's exactly what it felt like to me. The fact that it touched every sweaty hand and sweaty mouth on its way around the circle to my sweaty hands and lips . . . I tried not to think about that.

Once we were all watered and ready to go, more stone people were brought in from the fire outside. Then the flap was sealed . . . water on the stones . . . into the void . . . *Wankan Tonka*.

It's disorienting, being suspended in total darkness like that. At times, I couldn't sit any longer, so I moved onto all fours, my face a foot from the stone people, chanting into the steam-filled space loud enough that my relatives in Denmark—living and dead—could hear me. It felt like dissolving. Unable to see boundaries of any kind, your voice mixing with so many others like a single sound, your mind completely absorbed in heat and vibration and blackness . . . it was transcendent. There was no me. There was only us.

The grand finale of the whole affair was the pipe ceremony. Two pipes were passed around the circle near the end and everyone had a chance to smoke them. Rahaman made a short speech about the sacred nature of tobacco inside the lodge and the dangers of tobacco on the outside. He told me later that he had said this for Logan and Jackson's benefit, but he needn't have bothered. Neither kid took a puff of a communal pipe when they found themselves holding it in the dark. Or so they said.

All told, it was a powerful experience that ran the gamut from the sacred to the ridiculous. At one point, the group was set loose to pray and chant at will, and the guy next to Logan held nothing back. In addition to blessing every deity from Allah to Zeus, every tree spirit and star nation, every housefly and dandelion, he ripped off a bizarre litany of sounds, like speaking in tongues or baby babble. Whatever it was, I'm sure it was not an earthly language. *"Foopa. Swaa. Swoopano. Fubano-swapa-tawny-wabban. Foopa!"* He shouted in this way for a solid ten minutes.

Logan sat beside me, invisible, gone . . . but I could *hear* the smile on his face. I could *feel* him choking back the laughter. When it finally erupted, softly, politely, just a burst of unrestrained delight that only I was listening for, it sounded to me, at that time, in that place, like the kind of prayer the Great Spirit would enjoy.

Traca said, when it was all over, that she'd barely been present for most of the chanting, so caught up in the ceremony that she all but disappeared in the steam. As for the kids, they probably won't be doing another one anytime soon, but they made it. After four hours, through the heat and haze, they crawled out with the rest of us and rose up into the night. By then it was after ten, and the contrast between inside and outside could not have been more stark. Our skin was hot and drenched, our scant clothing soaked. But the New Zealand air was cold and crisp, the sky vast and arched overhead, the stars thick as ancestors above. It felt like rebirth, every inhale a deep grateful gulp, every exhale a sigh of release.

21

WILLING WORKERS

ONE OF THE COOL THINGS ABOUT WWOOFING—AND THIS MAY SOUND counterintuitive—is the work. Especially if you have kids who might be categorized as less than "willing workers" back home. (Without any official data to back me up, I'm guessing Traca and I are not the only parents in this category.) To be fair, I have seen our kids work. It's not that they're lazy. They would simply prefer to do anything other than work whenever work is suggested. Ask them to rake leaves? You're lucky to get a half hour of lackluster effort. Stack wood? Same response. Insist that they keep their rooms clean? Prepare for a constant battle that will never be won and that will drain the joy out of the entire house. They've gotten a little better as they've gotten older, but long-standing patterns remain. Asking them to work for a solid hour at any task at all is like asking for an organ transplant, a major sacrifice accompanied by much groaning, grumbling, and frequent requests for the time, as in:

> ANNOYED CHILD: "What time is it *now*?"
> ME: "It's only been fifteen minutes."
> ANNOYED CHILD: "Ugh. I hate my life."

I remember asking Jackson to do the dishes one night before we hit the road. We don't usually ask the kids. I typically do them if Traca cooks, and it's not a big deal. We have a dishwasher. But that night we asked Jack to help out, and she reacted as if she'd been ordered to dig the Panama Canal by herself with a trowel. "What about Logan?" she snapped, shocked at the unfairness of it all. When we did not relent, she huffed, stormed to the sink, loaded one single dish, then looked back at us with complete contempt. "So you guys are just gonna sit there while I do these *all by myself*? Seriously?"

Have we spoiled them? Perhaps. Chores have been spotty. Demands, few. Consequences, fewer. But in New Zealand, because it was part of the deal and because they were not working for their unfair parents (maybe because of Earl's shaming tirade back at the Osa, too), they—for the first time in their young lives—worked hard, rarely complained, and even got into it from time to time.

I can't tell you how proud it made me to see the kids working—not like slaves, just like workers—and it happened every day at Sharda. When the center needed to be prepped for an arriving group of visitors, there was none of the moaning or stalling that usually accompanied work requests back home. Everyone, kids included, just started doing what needed to be done. Traca scrubbed the kitchen as if preparing for a military inspection, Logan and I scraped and painted a peeling outbuilding, and Jackson single-handedly prepared the dorm like a little Martha Stewart in training. She swept and dusted, made beds, and created flower arrangements for the guests, matching each small bouquet to the color palette of each room. She even ironed! That's right: *ironed,* all the bed skirts in all twelve rooms, marking not only the first time she'd ever ironed a bed skirt but the first time she'd ever ironed, period. (Okay, maybe we *have* spoiled them.) Best of all, she did it with a certain flair, a willingness even. After all the rooms were ready, she gave me a tour, pointing out the way the wildflowers on the nightstand matched the trim color in Room 4, or the way the lavender in the hollyhocks matched the window treatments in Room 9. She was playing around, not bragging at all, but there was also a real sense of pride shining in her eyes. Though I wanted to hug and kiss her with a pride of my own, I resisted and just said "Nice work," so as not to shatter the beautiful spell that a job well done had cast on her.

When all the cleaning was finished, the workday continued back in the bush with Rahaman leading another weeding raid. This time we were armed with gloves, cutting tools, and squeeze bottles of some kind of natural poison. As we walked single file into the overgrown acreage surrounding the Sharda Centre, the sky was overcast and the

bush was more forbidding than usual, a dark tangle of untamed wild-
ness.

"Are you kidding me?" Jackson said softly, holding up a small pair
of pruning shears as if they were the most ridiculous item on earth.
"This whole *place* is a weed."

Our enemy for the afternoon was privet, a plant best known for its
orderly hedges, now uncharacteristically running loose in the bush. It
wasn't hard to find; it was everywhere—so we just chose a starting
place, sat on the ground, and started working. For the less stubborn
specimens we encountered, we yanked them, roots and all, into the
air. When this was not possible, we used saws to cut the invaders
down, then put a dab of poison on what remained. It was tedious,
endless, but we were not in a hurry.

At one point, while the kids went off on their own, no doubt avoiding all privet pulling wherever they were, Traca and I worked side by
side, yanking and sawing and dabbing, systematically reclaiming one
tiny patch of ground at a time.

"There," Traca said after managing to pull a particularly obstinate
plant from the ground. She held it up triumphantly, its roots like a tiny
claw. "I think that's the last of it."

"Yeah," I agreed. "Only ten square miles to go."

Traca smiled and looked at the weed in her hand. It seemed to be
telling her something, and her smile faded as she listened. "Why can't
we do this to our relationship?" she finally said. She wasn't being critical. She was just wondering.

"Weed it, you mean?" I asked.

"Yeah. Leave all the good stuff. Pull out all the bad."

"Do we dab poison on the roots?" I asked.

"Just your roots," Traca said playfully, then got back to work.

We followed our own paths of privet for a while, eventually moving apart. And while I weeded alone, I wondered: *What are the bad
parts that need pulling?* It was hard to say anymore.

When we first met, Traca used to love my sense of humor, at least
she appeared to. At dinner parties, when I told a funny story, she was
the one laughing the loudest. But now . . . would she pull that part of
me out if she could? *She doesn't laugh like she used to,* I thought. *Some-*

times she even looks annoyed. At one of our last dinner parties before leaving Gorham, I noticed her yawning in the middle of one of my stories that had everyone else laughing. I asked her about it later when we were alone.

"What were you thinking just then?" I asked, taking her back to the table and the joke.

It was late and Traca was too tired for anything but the complete truth. "I was thinking: I wish you'd give someone else a chance to talk," she admitted.

What were the weeds that needed pulling? What would I pull from Traca?

I used to love her passion for anything alternative, but now, if I was honest, I resented a lot of that. The yoga, the meditation, the shamanism. Though it was good for her, it had been bad for us. Certainly bad for me. She'd return from long retreats feeling refreshed and energized, but it never brought us closer. If anything, it seemed to highlight how different we were, how distant. But would I pull that out of her even if I could? No. The answer wasn't to weed the other person but to somehow clear out the choking patterns that had been growing between us for so many years. Maybe the way forward was just one small reclaimed bit at a time.

"How's it going?" Rahaman shouted. I'd worked my way near to his private patch of privet and he waved me over. He was dressed in a red flannel shirt and shorts, looking like a friendly garden gnome with his wild gray hair and welcoming smile. We worked side by side, eventually talking about the things privet pullers talk about: women, love, loss.

Rahaman had been married once, for five years, but it didn't hold together. He'd known lots of wonderful women in his life, but by his own admission, he didn't yet have them figured out. "I'm probably the last one at the bottom of the glass you want to ask about that," he said. Even so, I ended up telling him a little about Traca and me. Not the whole story, but enough to ask if he had any suggestions.

"Not really," he admitted. "Sometimes things just change."

As I dabbed a bit of poison on a severed stalk, I mentioned how Traca had been exploring so many new areas, changing quite a lot.

"That's the thing, yeah?" Rahaman said. "One person is a bit further along with the change than the other." He pulled a wicked shoot of privet out of the dry soil, its roots helpless in the air. Then he looked at me. "The trick is," he said, "can you work with that change together, or is it better to work on that bit apart?"

22

DIVINE GODDESS OF DISCERNING WISDOM

AFTER SIX DAYS AT THE SHARDA CENTRE, OUR TO DO LIST WAS MORE OR less done. I'd finished mudding and taping some drywall in a bathroom, Logan had wrapped up his painting project, we'd all helped build a worm farm and pulled enough privet to fill a cargo ship. We'd also explored the tiny town of Tuakau and the surrounding area, eaten a lot of Hokey Pokey ice cream, and seen glowworms at night. Jackson had even *reironed* the bed skirts after a weekend retreat wrinkled up the place. Though Sharda was like Traca's Disneyland (spiritual talks at meals, visiting shamanism groups to shaman with, yoga and meditation mornings down where the Peace Dome might one day be), we all agreed it was time to WWOOF our way down the road.

So how does one choose from the hundreds of farms on the WWOOF New Zealand website? Most potential stops have pictures showing off their welcoming hosts, spectacular views, or handsome sheep—a little local flavor to help you decide if you'd like to visit. But for our next stop, two hours north, we were flying blind. All they had on their Web profile were the words "No Photos Added," though beside the question "Kids?" they did have the words "Yes, please!" which we took as a promising attitude. It didn't hurt that they were near Bethells Beach, a spectacular bit of coast that was included on a few online lists we ran across as one of the ten most beautiful beaches in the world.

And so we piled into Rahaman's seatless van, sat on his sweat lodge blankets, and headed to the train station. When we arrived, we were a few minutes ahead of schedule, so we waited on the platform. There was construction everywhere—the station was being renovated—and Rahaman seemed a little sad as he looked at the tangle of planks and scaffolding.

"So much change happening, yeah?" he said. "All around. It's a wicked taskmaster, change. You can't stop it."

We agreed and thanked him for his hospitality. One by one we hugged him, then grabbed our things. Our train was approaching. But as I turned to go, Rahaman stopped me. For a moment we just looked at each other. His long gray hair was out of its usual ponytail and it was uncombed, wild; he looked like either a homeless man or a sage. His eyes were clear and unwavering.

"The best you can do," he said, "no matter which way it goes, is to go through it with as much grace as possible." Construction tools roared around us: drills, hammers, change. Rahaman smiled. "As much grace as you can for everyone, yeah? Don't forget."

I told him I wouldn't.

I joined my family on the train and we headed north, first through the urban sprawl of Auckland, then alternating between small towns and pastureland. In no time, we arrived at Swanson Station, where we were met by our next host, a spitfire fairy-gypsy named Sherab Palmo.

Sherab (rhymes with "cherub") was forty-eight, slim and small with bright blue eyes and long brown hair. A native New Zealander, she looked like a sweet-faced waif at first, but her name told a different story. In Tibetan, Sherab means "divine goddess" and Palmo means "discerning wisdom," so this was no ordinary chauffeur. As we soon learned, she could tear apart and rebuild her own bus engine, frame out a room addition, design her own clothing, whip up a meal for twenty, and still find time to politely rip into a lazy WWOOFer who wasn't pulling his or her weight. "I open my own jars," Sherab told me (not a bad title for her autobiography), but she said it with a smile. A committed environmentalist, a sincere Buddhist, and a mother of three, Sherab had a heart that welcomed the entire world and as many guests as her ramshackle house could hold.

While the Sharda Centre was quiet and restorative, Sherab's place was a hive of activity. It was a sprawling property built high on a steep hill; the ten acres of buildings, buses, and debris looked like a moderately organized junkyard. Though we would all grow to love this work-in-progress house, our first impressions were not entirely positive. Boards were rotting under the eaves, the smell of mold and stale beer greeted us in the basement. The pool was jet-black. The bathroom was accurately called the Long Drop, a simple outhouse with a view of the dense bush and flies as big as your thumb that liked to buzz out between your legs whenever you sat down to do your business. Beyond this, it was absolutely *packed* with people. In addition to Sherab; her husband, Jo; and their nine-year-old son, Tutira; there were four other WWOOF-ers (Jake from the United States, Hendricks from Berlin, Linnia and Sophie from Sweden), Nic, Kristen, Andy, and Jeff (all twenty- to thirty-year-old Kiwi boarders), Rana (Sherab's adult son) and his girlfriend who lived up the hill in a bus, and Vadra (another grown son) and his girlfriend who lived down the hill in another bus. Add the four Mar-shalls to the mix, and there were nineteen of us at dinner (a sweat lodge of a different kind), everyone drinking, laughing, playing musical in-struments, and talking about everything from politics to travel to the best way to get rid of parasites picked up on the road.

This is another cool thing about WWOOFing: Unlike ordinary travelers, WWOOFers get an instant connection to a home. Rather than staying in bland hotels, visiting crowded tourist attractions, and eating out at impersonal restaurants (and paying the costs associated with all three activities), WWOOFers are invited in with families, given worthwhile work to do, and fed home-cooked meals by local people who know the area and are happy to share their lives and infor-mation with you.

And it's free!

Our plan was to spend about a week with Sherab and her family and see how we could help. Of course, we'd be visiting the aforemen-tioned top-ten beach, but there were also great bush walks and some massive sand dunes not far away. There certainly was no shortage of jobs to do around the property—which is a little like saying there was no shortage of jobs to do around Haiti after the hurricane. We were even invited to attend a real live gypsy fair with Sherab in the pimped-out double-decker bus she'd customized by hand. Naturally, we ac-cepted.

Being temporary gypsies ourselves, we thought we'd feel right at home.

23

THE GYPSY DANCER

"Don't be alarmed, John," Sherab said. "This is just the start-up."

With that, she cranked the key on board her bus and it gasped to life, its old diesel engine grinding a dozen times before finally catching and settling into a deep-throated idle, like a dragon with a smoker's cough.

The idea of living on a bus has always fascinated me. When I was ten, a friend and I used to play in an old camper van that was parked in the back of a local gas station. In that dusty little enclosed space, we imagined ourselves to be explorers, living on our own, everything within reach. I'm not sure exactly why, but having our beds, our kitchen, our bathroom, and our action figures all in one place—and on wheels!—excited us so much, we naïvely asked the gas station owner if we could *have* the van. Not just play in it, actually *own* it. The fact that he basically laughed in our hopeful little faces did nothing to lessen the pull that van has held on me ever since.

Naturally, I liked Sherab's bus the moment I saw it. Whether you would consider it a work of art I cannot say, but it was definitely a work of imagination. From the outside, it looked much too tall; it was essentially two buses welded together. Painted the color of old parchment, it had a hand-carved Balinese door in the back and the promise of lush pink velvet visible through the windows. On the inside, there was a large common area with burgundy cushions on crates for sitting, a woodstove for warmth, and a small kitchen for meals. In the back, there was a typical RV bathroom, as well as an all-purpose space with supplies for art, medical emergencies, homework, flat tires . . . and a loft above with two beds for the kids. There was also a double bed at the front of the bus known as the Princess Loft, which belonged to

Sherab. Tutira, Sherab's youngest son, called the whole affair the Brown Potato, but Sherab called it the Gypsy Dancer, and it was our home for three days in April.

As we climbed aboard the bus, our plan was to drive three hours north to Whangarei (pronounced FUNG-ga-ray) and meet up with a traveling gypsy fair, a routine Sherab knew all too well.

Shortly after her second son was born, Sherab's long-term partner and the father of her children just up and left. How the birth of a new baby translates into a good time to break up the family is beyond me, but the fact remained: He was gone. After she processed the initial shock and landed on her feet, Sherab made a bold choice. Wanting above all else to spend time with her kids, she bought a bus, spent two years building it out, learned as much about bus maintenance as possible, then hit the road. For the next seven years, she and her kids traveled with a modern-day band of gypsies; no permanent address, no mortgage, no schools, no roots . . . just her boys, the bus, the open road, and a weekly fair to make some money. Though she's been off the road for many years, Sherab still sleeps in the Gypsy Dancer every night, gave birth to Tutira in the bus bathroom, and seemed totally in command behind the large steering wheel—fingerless driving gloves on—as we lumbered out of the parking lot.

Down the first steep hill, everything groaned and creaked. Cabinets rolled forward. Wind chimes and baskets swirled overhead. The woodstove door slammed open. A jar of kitchen utensils smashed over. The whole contraption seemed ready to tip . . . but it didn't, and I was loving it. We all were.

Before I get too wrapped up in the magic of being on board, I will say two practical things. First: The Gypsy Dancer was *slow*. At times, as we struggled in first gear to climb the steep New Zealand grades, we had a line of traffic backed up behind us that looked like a funeral procession for the prime minister. Five miles per hour is being generous, and that is no joke. Second: The Gypsy Dancer was *loud*. Everything vibrated, rattled, the diesel dragon hacked up a lung. We were conspicuous, to say the least. As we drove through towns or stopped at intersections, every face looking back at us had a smile on it. Every kid waved and wanted to be on board. We were a parade of one. A giant brown potato on wheels!

In her glory days as a gypsy, Sherab said it was quite a show. Everyone involved tricked out their buses and lived on them full-time. There were artists and craftspeople, jugglers, fire-eaters, dancers, stilt walkers, and tons of kids. Forty families in all, each choosing a life on the road over a house in the suburbs—just a loud, slow, raucous tribe wandering the whole of New Zealand. At the time, they were famous. The press wrote articles about them. TV crews followed them around. It was a wild ride, I'm sure. But no dance lasts forever.

The gypsy fair we took part in seemed like more of a weekend activity for most participants, a retirement hobby by the looks of the other wrinkled "gypsies" who turned up. Most buses were simply camper vans with awnings out front. No psychedelic paint jobs. No fire-eaters, unfortunately. The flash of the production was long gone, replaced by a few flags flapping in the wind and a single Maori lounge singer cheesing his way through the entire late-seventies sing-along book to attract shoppers.

"I like dreaming. 'Cause dreaming can make you mine."

He sang this song a dozen times over the two-day event.

Lame karaoke and unadorned RVs aside, the trip felt like a grand adventure. We pounded stakes like circus roustabouts, slept on make-shift beds like stowaways on a steamer, and stayed up late talking in the dark like kids at camp.

At the end of the first day, Traca fell asleep early, Tutira and our kids were out cold, and the Gypsy Dancer was dark and quiet. In the Princess Loft, Sherab looked down at me, her eyes sparkling in the moonlight. Fire sticks and stilts were strapped to the roof over her head. Fairy bells tinkled with every movement on board. In this way, we talked for an hour or more, trading stories. . . .

Sherab left home when she was just thirteen. Three years later, she met a man and they got married, staying together for nine years. Her life was different then. She and her husband were reps for a New Zealand company similar to Amway, selling products in a network marketing operation, building their down lines, racking up their residual incomes. Far from the dynamic, independent woman she would become, Sherab swallowed the hook of this life and followed her husband's lead. She had two children with him. She was fully on board. Right up until the day Deadbeat Dad left her and the kids and the house without even offering a reason.

On her own with a two-year-old and a newborn, Sherab needed to reclaim the power she'd given away. She felt weak and lost, unsure of herself, overwhelmed. She ended up in Indonesia, in Bali, floundering in a sea of doubt. How was she going to provide for her children? She had no money. She had no direction.

But hope can be found in the most unlikely places.

On a dirty, bustling street, Sherab ran across a destitute Balinese woman. This woman was beyond poor, filthy, begging for coins. In her arms she held a thin, sickly baby, clearly malnourished, probably dying. And for a few connected heartbeats, the woman and Sherab looked into each other's eyes. Though she had no money of her own, no financial help to offer this woman, Sherab suddenly recognized a wealth within herself that cried out to be shared.

Without pity or shame, without any self-consciousness, Sherab sat with this woman on the street, took this stranger's baby boy into her arms, and fed him from her own breast. "It was an act of connection that changed my life," she said. "I didn't feel powerless anymore. I felt strong and somehow I knew I was going to be all right."

Beside me, Traca rolled over, filling the Gypsy Dancer with the nervous laughter of the fairy bells. She was fast asleep, but I wondered if she was responding on some level to the "reclaim your power" message in Sherab's story. It had been Traca's mantra for years, what all the yoga and meditation and shamanism were really all about: living authentically, finding her voice.

"You two look beautiful," Sherab said softly, smiling down like the Cheshire cat. "Inspiring to me, actually." Then her smile faded. Her face looked almost worried.

"What's the matter?" I asked.

"I'm not sure," Sherab whispered. "It's just a feeling."

"About what?" I whispered back.

Sherab thought about her answer for a while, as if weighing her words, even though the idea in her mind was a very simple one. When she was ready, she said it. "Is she happy?" she wondered, her words barely audible.

"What makes you say that?" I asked.

Sherab forced a smile. "It's probably nothing," she said. "I don't know. Sometimes, she just . . . looks like a little bird with a shadow over her heart."

Sherab's words hung in the air long after she'd said goodnight and disappeared into the Princess Loft like a cat in a cave. When the Gypsy Dancer was perfectly still, I watched Traca sleep and thought about it: *Was* she happy? Were we? I knew without a doubt that we loved each other. I could feel it, but . . . something *was* different. This trip was different. We were not being swept away by any short-term passion this time. We were moving slowly as if working something out, changing in ways we probably wouldn't fully realize until later. Then who would we be? I honestly didn't know. When Traca rolled away from me and the fairies laughed in every corner of the bus, I closed my eyes and let it all rest for the night.

In the end, the trip was more or less a bust from a financial point of view. The Gypsy Dancer gulped fuel the way a whale eats krill, and after chugging up and back over the steep North Island terrain, Sherab's meager fair sale profits barely covered the gas bill. Even so, it was fun. We hit a skateboard park for Tutira, climbed to the top of Whangarei Lookout, and stopped at a hot spring on our way home for some therapeutic water from the center of the earth.

But the highlight for me was a simple thing, a non-moment that inched by, loud, slow, and unnoticed by anyone else. We were passing through the spectacular New Zealand countryside, the huge windows of the Gypsy Dancer filled with rolling green hills and distant blue mountains and the sea and the sky and a million sheep. I was sitting beside Jackson, sharing her iPod headset, listening to a song we both knew, singing loud, shouting above the roar of the diesel engine like bad karaoke singers:

I'm walking on sunshine. Whoa-oh.
And don't it feel good!

In that moment, on that bus, looking at my daughter's singing, smiling face, I realized something . . . *I* was happy. In a way that I hadn't been in a long time. I felt light and free. Honestly, I felt like the ten-year-old boy I once was, only this time, the owner of the RV I used to play in said, "Yeah, sure, kid. Take the van. It's yours."

24

TIRELESS ROBOT SLAVES

Back at Sherab's, I knew what my assignment was but I wanted to double-check just the same. Before I got started, I tracked Sherab down, found her wearing high black rubber boots, a long olive green barn coat, and a big smile. She's maybe five foot four, maybe one hundred pounds, but she was in full-on Mussolini mode that morning, leading a group of WWOOFers off into muddy battle.

"Hey. Are you sure you want me to start in the girls' dorm?" I asked. "I was thinking I could work on the bathroom or the gutters—"

"No," Sherab said, having already decided. "I've wanted that door moved forever." (She pronounced it fa-EH-va as is the Kiwi custom.) "Have at it, then," she added before launching into the day.

With my marching orders clear enough, I gathered up some tools, grabbed Logan, and headed downstairs to get started. To get to the girls' dorm, we passed through a large common room that was a disaster. The shades were still down. It was dark. Empty bottles and trash were everywhere. Someone was still asleep under a blanket on the couch. The room reeked of stale beer, cigarettes, pot, and mold. We didn't linger.

Next, we entered a dark hallway, the back end of which was piled to the ceiling with boxes, chairs, picture frames, mops, insulation, junk. It looked like a barricade, certainly a fire hazard. Our escape was the second of three doors.

The girls' dorm was nothing fancy: three bunks for six WWOOFers, an exit door to the outside on the left, a large window on the right. Though it was messy and cramped, it was also intact: Nothing leaked, nothing was broken . . . which was more than could be said for most of the house.

Upstairs, the bathroom was roughly framed out but unfinished;

the shower stall was just bare wood studs with a yellow plastic sheet tacked up for a modicum of privacy. Outside, the fascia boards under the eaves were mostly rotten and the gutters were useless, no longer directing water, just directing your eyes to the eyesores they had become. With a few materials, Logan and I could have replaced those boards, painted them, reattached the gutters, and actually left Sherab's home a little nicer than we'd found it. I wasn't so sure the same could be said for the girls' dorm project.

Sherab wanted the exit door on the left moved to the right and the large window on the right moved to the left. It was a feng shui decision, I think, but with so much more urgent work needing to be done, it felt a little like touching up your trim paint while your house was on fire.

Oh, well. If it made Sherab happy, we were happy, and so we got to work. We measured for the transfer, located studs, penciled on the cut lines, popped off trim. And as I watched Logan wielding a long level and scoring the drywall with a box cutter, I realized this was the first time he and I had ever worked on a construction project together.

When I was growing up, my father used to do a lot of work around the house. I watched him finish our basement, hang a suspended ceiling, fish a vacuum system through the walls, glue on laminate countertops, mess with plumbing and electrical wiring; but he almost never asked me to help him. Years later, when I got my own house and had to learn how to do all that stuff, I asked him why he never taught me.

"You only have one childhood," he said. "I thought you'd rather be outside playing."

Of course, he was right. At the time, I wasn't the least bit interested in building anything, but as I watched Logan prying nails loose and wielding a Paslode nail gun and a demonic Sawzall for the first time like a natural-born burly man, I couldn't help but feel I'd missed out on something with him, like I'd missed out on something with my own dad, too.

"Oh, crap," Logan said. "Ants!"

He'd just pulled a square of drywall loose and thousands of black carpenter ants were swarming the room. It's always that way with remodeling jobs: start to fix one problem and discover three more below the surface. In the girls' dorm, in addition to the mother lode of ants, we found the insulation black with mold and the inner wall laced from floor to ceiling with some kind of dry climbing weed. The whole wall cavity needed to be cleared out and scrubbed down before it could be repaired. It was a big job that took us two full days, but I didn't mind at all.

I'm not sure what it is about watching my kids work, but it's my new favorite spectator sport. More than when I'm cheering for a big race or a big game, when I see them doing any physical work, I want to applaud. I don't need them building the pyramids. They just have to work without checking a clock, without long distracted breaks, with any kind of enjoyment or passion or facial expression that is not a scowl. When they do this, and they did it a lot at Sherab's, they transcend every entitled-teen stereotype I've ever projected on them and it's all I can do not to break out into a sappy chorus of "These are the good old days."

One of our last jobs at Sherab's was to dig out the perimeter of her black lagoon of a pool. The idea was to make a level base all the way around, suitable for pouring concrete. It was hard work; the soil was wet clay, packed and heavy, and there were mountains of it to move. But the kids led the charge, digging, hauling, leveling. Even after the sun was gone and we could barely see, they goaded Traca and me to work harder, faster, really wanting to make a major dent in the project before calling it a day. It's not changing the world, moving buckets of clay from here to there, but I saw it gradually changing our kids. With every door we framed up, window we installed, garden plot we weeded, or load of manure we shoveled, our children were getting a crash course in manual labor, in taking pride in their work, and when necessary, in just sucking it up and doing what needed to be done.

At the other end of the productivity scale, Logan and Jackson were also getting some world-class examples of sheer laziness from most of the twenty-year-old WWOOFers we lived with. Drunk by noon, high most of the time, these slackers did as little as possible, ate as much as they could, then sat around watching *Dexter* DVDs until three in the morning.

I heard two of the worst offenders talking about a job they'd been

given; Sherab wanted dirt moved from one section of the yard to another. It was a straightforward assignment but a hard one, requiring a
few hours of strenuous labor. For the task, the boys were given a
wheelbarrow and a shovel. They were both strong, in their prime; but
rather than just do the job, they stalled like a couple of arthritic mules.

"Why do we have to move it from way over *there*?" one of them
moaned.

"This is bullshit," the other bitched. "It'll take forever."

"Let's just drag some from here and say we didn't know."

"Whatever's faster, bro."

And so they dug up a nearby flower bed that someone had filled
just a few days before. When Sherab saw what they had done and
ripped into them for being worthless, brainless freeloaders, they acted
shocked and tried to appear contrite—or at least as contrite as their
baked-drunk faces were capable of appearing.

By comparison, Logan and Jackson came off looking like tireless
robot slaves, and I think they liked that. I also think, if they ever head
off to do some WWOOFing on their own, they will have learned a few
unwritten rules that do not appear on the International WWOOFing
website.

The first is: If you're going to WWOOF, WWOOF hard—
especially if you're young. Many WWOOFing hosts Traca and I spoke
with said they were not crazy about accepting any WWOOFers under
the age of twenty-five because they ate more than their share and did
not pull their own weight. The conventional wisdom seemed to be
that young people are lazy and spoiled, just looking for free food and a
free bed.

Second: Don't be a pig. Offer to clean up after meals. Be respectful and aware of others around you. For example: Don't drag your
drunk girlfriend into the girls' dorm and start humping her when a
fourteen-year-old girl (such as Jackson) is sleeping on the bunk above
you.

Small courtesies like these will be appreciated.

So the work was good, but the time off from work was even better;
Sherab asked for four hours of WWOOFing each day, and once that
was done, we were free to explore the surrounding area. We checked

out Bethells Beach, which was, and is, beyond spectacular. We launched ourselves off steep sand dunes that surrounded a pristine nearby lake. We took more bush walks and felt wonderfully insignificant in the shadow of massive fifteen-hundred-year-old kauri trees. But like so much of what we found on the road, our greatest discovery was not something we expected to find at all. In fact, our greatest discovery on this particular stop—at least for the kids—was an old man who lived in a bus just up the hill beside the Gypsy Dancer.

His name was Bob Paul, and in all visible ways he was just an ordinary chap. He was in his seventies, with a thin, pinched face, a large nose, and a quiet demeanor. His body was long and lean, strong for his age, but his presence was not what you'd call commanding. He didn't open his mouth very wide when he talked, rarely looked at you when speaking, and trembled slightly, an affliction most visible in his hands. From the outside looking in, he was just another face in the background, a lonely divorced dude living in a plain blue bus. But that's not what the kids saw at all.

Back in the day, Bob had been a world-class runner. He won a silver medal at the Kiwi Nationals, specializing in 5K and 10K distances. He ran marathons well into his fifties, nearly made the New Zealand Olympic team, and still ran the rural hillsides just for fun. When he was no longer competitive, Bob became a successful coach, training many of New Zealand's top runners. Chat with Bob for more than five minutes and you'll realize he's an encyclopedia of running information, with story after story of races and records, injuries and crazy screwups on the track and in the field.

When Bob learned that Logan was one of Maine's top running prospects for the upcoming cross-country season (and that Jackson had a passion for running as well), he offered to coach them both, and the kids jumped at the chance. From then on, when we were not working or traipsing about, the kids were with Bob. He adjusted their strides, worked on their mechanics, wrote up training regimens, basically poured his vast experience into their eager feet and seemed to soak up their attention with equal delight.

On our last night at Sherab's, as dinner was about to start, the kids were nowhere to be found. They'd gone up to Bob's bus hours before—

many hours before—so that's where I went to look for them. I climbed the dirt path to the bus parking lot as dusk settled across the property, dissolving shadows into the gloom. Outside Bob's bus, I stopped. The place was a wreck. It was a long, plain touring bus without any of the Gypsy Dancer's style. Weeds were growing up around the tires. The blue paint was peeling. No lights were visible inside. To my screenwriter's mind, it looked more like a horror movie set than a place to hang out, and with that thought, uneasiness flared inside me. *What did I really know about this guy?* I knocked. No one answered. I knocked again. Nothing. I went in.

What I found was a party. Bob was sitting on a window seat, looking ten years younger, telling a story. His face was ruddy and animated and he appeared to be radiantly happy. Across from him, Logan and Jackson were enthralled, hanging on his every word. I said hello but didn't interrupt beyond that. I just watched my kids' faces as Bob's story went on, watching for signs of boredom. There were none. They were into this and so was Bob. It wasn't a horror film at all. It was a love story.

We left the next morning, hopped a quick flight to Christchurch in the South Island, spent the night in a hostel, then grabbed an early morning bus and headed north along the beyond-gorgeous coastline. The South Island of New Zealand is famous for some of the most beautiful scenery in the world and I knew we'd find that. But like the pleasure of a job well done or the value of an old man's life, the beauty around us was really just the start of all that was waiting to be found.

25

THE BIRTHDAY BATH

WWOOFING YOUR WAY FROM FARM TO FARM IS LIKE STARTING A NEW life every few days. Once you make your arrangements online and get to your next WWOOFing town, a new driver in a new car shows up and takes you to a new place, where a new set of people are waiting for you with new jobs to do and new things to see. On a practical level, it means waking up in a new room, on a new bed, with a new view out a new window. While it takes some getting used to and can leave you disoriented in the middle of the night, you certainly won't be complaining anymore about the dull sameness of life.

Our next stop was the town of Kaikoura, and according to our guidebooks, we were in for a treat. Kaikoura sits on the rugged east coast of the South Island and is blessed with a unique coastal-alpine setting: majestic mountains encircling a pristine shoreline. World famous as a destination for ecotourists, marine wildlife watchers, and anyone who enjoys the drop-dead-gorgeous outdoors, the promise of Kaikoura made us all eager to climb aboard when Liane Rumble and her gray Jeep SUV rolled up to cart us away.

Liane lived twelve kilometers north of town in an off-the-grid house she'd built with her husband, Rick. Their home was surrounded by organic gardens, chickens, roosters, guinea fowl, a small dog named Rio, a wonky-eyed goat named L&P, and a three-year-old boy named Jimmy, the Rumbles' only child. They also had a curved metal arc of a building out back, and this was where they put the WWOOFers. They called it the Hangar, and it featured two single beds on the first floor and one double bed up in a loft. To spoil us, it came equipped with a full-sized pool table and a woodstove. To keep us grounded, it also offered a lukewarm outdoor shower and a composting toilet. Out our new sliding door, the ocean was an easy ten-minute walk to the east and the Kaikoura Mountains—the northernmost extension of the New Zealand Southern Alps—were just across State Highway 1 to the west. We were surrounded by beauty.

We didn't do much that first day. After settling in and getting the lay of the land, a little light garden work was all we had time for. But the day does stand out in my mind for two reasons: (1) It was Traca's birthday, and (2) I nearly poached her to death.

A ritual bather back home, Traca had been missing her nightly soaks, and when I found a funky outdoor tub behind the Hangar, I decided to draw her a birthday bath she would not soon forget.

The tub sat in a clearing surrounded by gooseberry plants. It was made of white cast iron and was suspended over a blackened fire pit. You see these setups all over New Zealand, a bit of cowboy ingenuity to warm your tired WWOOFing bones. To operate, simply fill the tub about halfway with a garden hose, light a fire below, heat the contents to a near boil, then cool with more hose water until the desired temperature is reached.

By the time my fire had done its job, a beautiful nearly full moon had risen above the pines. With great excitement, Traca stripped down to her birthday suit, slipped into her birthday bath . . . and nearly parboiled her pale little birthday butt in the process.

"*Whoa!* That's hot," she said, clutching the rim of the tub with her fingers and toes in a pose that resembled an inverted cat trying not to fall in a bubbling soup pot. I tried not to laugh but I couldn't help it. Even as I added more cold hose water, the tub was still roasting; I think I started with *way* too much heat. And when the water began to overflow, the hot coals below sent billows of smoke into the air. For the next ten minutes, Traca dipped her feet in, then pulled them out, bright red and tender, steaming in the cool night air. It was ridiculous.

"It's nice to unwind, isn't it?" I said.

"It's so soothing," Traca agreed, daring to dip her entire bum into the liquid lava and counting to ten before pulling it out, looking like a baboon.

Eventually, the steam cleared and the water cooled enough for her to settle in. I sat at the head of the tub, rubbing her shoulders and looking up at the huge New Zealand sky. For all its absurdity, the bath evolved into a beautiful, intimate moment.

"Did you ever think, on the day we got married, that we'd end up here almost twenty years later?" I asked.

"Not exactly," Traca said, "but yeah, something like this."

"That seems like a long time ago," I said, remembering our wedding day.

"We're certainly not the same people we were back then," Traca said.

In the quiet that followed, I tried to picture our actual wedding ceremony, our vows, but the details had grown fuzzy over the years. Since we didn't videotape the actual day, we couldn't rewatch the event from time to time and refresh our memories. In fact, the only video we had was some grainy footage shot by one of my cousins on her bad VHS recorder. It's no more than ten minutes long and the quality is terrible. It briefly shows Traca walking down the aisle with her father, skips the entire service, then picks up again in jumpy cuts at the reception. The only unbroken scene is our first dance.

We danced to a song that I'd written specifically for the occasion. I'm not a trained musician but I'm pretty good with melodies. And though my kids accuse me of recycling the same four chords in every song I write, I didn't have those little critics back then. I just thought an original song would be more personal, so I wrote one.

I called the song "The Farthest Point," the metaphor being that marriage is like a boat that carries two people toward the horizon, the farthest point away. There's no rush because you'll never get there. Love is not where you're going, it's where you are. It's how you travel. So you ask someone to join you for the ride because it's more fun to float across the sea of life with someone you love than to do it alone.

We were living in Los Angeles at the time, so I recorded a rough version of the song on a cassette tape player, played the piano and sang along, then shipped it to our wedding band back in Maine. After that, I pretty much forgot about it until we were called out onto the dance floor.

In the video, we look painfully young, just twenty-four years old, like kids playing dress-up. We walk out on the dance floor hand in hand, our faces shining with perspiration, joyously happy. Traca looks gorgeous in her white gown, a halo of flowers in her hair, a radiant smile on her face as she looks at me. And I look like a dorky leading man, so happy to be marrying this beautiful woman, so completely lacking in fashion sense.

My black tux was a terrible fit, and that was my fault. When I went for the rental fitting, it was a scorching hot summer day and I never actually tried it on. As a result, my pants were too big, requiring last-minute safety pins bunched in the back, and my vest was *way* too small, revealing a dorky band of white shirt above my droopy waistline. Most dorky of all, my hair was cut and styled in a perfect mullet, the likes of which I have never worn before or since. It was slicked like a rubber wig and hung long in the back, with a few carefully pulled strands arranged to appear casual on my shining forehead.

You can't see any of these details in the video. The dance floor is dimly lit. The recording is handheld and shaky. All you can see are two young people in a familiar scene: their first dance as husband and wife, eyes locked on each other, with friends and family around them, waiting for the music to begin.

When the band started playing my song, I knew we were in trouble right away. From the very first beat, it was too slow, painfully slow. I'd written it as a midtempo number that wouldn't leave us dancing all afternoon, but the band was playing it as the slowest ballad ever written, over six minutes of plodding originality! And when they launched back to repeat the final two verses, a musical idea that worked fine on the faster version, Traca and I started laughing. I remember it feeling like slow musical torture at the time, but as I've replayed the tape through the years, I've come to see it for what it really was: the start of our life together, awkward and improvised as all lives are. We kissed and we turned, slowly spinning, frozen in time with all the promise and hope of eternal love waiting beyond that circle, that song. Any perils that awaited us, any problems that we'd face, would all come later. For that moment, we were united and whole. Our story was unwritten. Our love was untested. Our song, unfinished.

"There's no need to hurry," you can hear the ocean say.

The farthest point is still the farthest point away.

Twenty years later, in an outdoor New Zealand tub, the night air was getting cooler and steam was rising from the bathwater, drifting away like memory. Above us, the tops of the surrounding pine trees swayed back and forth, caught in an ocean wind we could not feel. Only the moon was still. And a single star.

"Make a wish," I said.

And Traca did, keeping it to herself.

26

OHAU STREAM WALK

A FEW DAYS LATER, WE WERE ALL DRIVING UP THE COAST WHEN WE passed a small sign that read OHAU STREAM WALK. If I had been the one driving, I doubt I would even have noticed it. The sign was plain and simple, no competition for the gorgeous South Pacific Ocean just off to our right. In fact, in an area famous for epic snowcapped mountain treks and deepwater dolphin encounters, killer whale tours and humpback breeching shows, a common stream walk might have seemed to me like the most minor of minor attractions. But like a banner reading BIG HOLE AHEAD at the entrance to the Grand Canyon, the understated OHAU STREAM WALK sign gave us no clue what to expect when we got out of the car in the parking lot.

It was Liane's idea. As part of our daily WWOOFing chores, she'd packed us all in her car along with Jimmy, hitched up a trailer, and tossed in some shovels, pitchforks, buckets, and ratty gloves for what promised to be a spirited game of "Gather the Stinking, Fly-Covered Sea Rot," otherwise known as collecting seaweed to be used as fertilizer in the Rumbles' garden. But before we ever reached the beach, the stream walk sign caught her eye and Liane made a quick detour. Such is the way with fate.

A few feet up the wholly unspectacular path, we found a fur seal sitting in shallow water. Signs all over town warned people to keep twenty meters (roughly sixty feet) from all wild seals. Seal teeth are like ice picks, and a bite can give a nasty infection—though clearly the little seal we found had not read the warnings. It was just ten feet away and quite interested in us, watching our every move. "Let's keep back, you guys," I said parentally, but the seal wasn't listening. He climbed the bank without much trouble and waddled right up to our feet.

I've seen plenty of seals in my day, in zoos and on TV and occasionally popping up like stray dogs along the coast of Maine, but I'd never been so close to one in the wild. This seal was a young one, not afraid at all, just taking us in with his large black eyes. And as I watched my own reflection in his dark alien orbs, they reminded me of something I had seen in a movie.

The Lord of the Rings gets a lot of attention in New Zealand; all the epic exteriors were filmed in various parts of the country, and you can still visit many of the sets. (At Sharda, we were a mere one hour north of the Shire!) As big *LOTR* fans, Logan and I couldn't resist posing for nerdy pictures whenever the backdrops inspired us, and we probably talked about the story more than Jackson or Traca or any non-nerd wanted us to. Anyway, if you have seen the films, you might remember that the bad wizard Saruman had a black crystal ball called a *palantír*. The *palantír* was like onyx, only a bit smoky, alive with some dark power. At the risk of sounding like a super *LOTR* geek, seal eyes have roughly that same quality. No whites, no pupils, just unreadable *palantíri* looking back without emotion at the world around them.

We hung out with this little guy for a while, tried to keep Jimmy from riding off on his back, and considered ourselves lucky to have stumbled upon him. Then, after five minutes or so, we continued up the stream path and into what might best be described as a seal convention.

Turns out the first seal was just a teaser, like finding a penny outside an open bank vault. With every step we took, we saw more and more of these flippered little fur balls. At first, they seemed confined to the stream. There were six, then ten, then maybe twenty young seals hopping from rock to rock, playing in the deeper pools. But after Jackson spotted one seal waddling through the trees . . . and then another . . . we started finding seals *everywhere*.

It was a little like finding goats on the ocean floor when you're out snorkeling—which is a weird way of saying that seals aren't the animal you expect to find in the woods, especially in New Zealand. Unlike Costa Rica, the New Zealand landscape is home to very few land animals. In fact, other than bats, New Zealand has *no* native mammal species whatsoever. (No snakes, either, Jackson was happy to learn.) Before humans arrived a mere nine hundred years ago, making New Zealand the last large landmass on earth to be inhabited by *Homo sapiens,* the island was mostly crawling with flightless birds; without predators to chase them into the air, even the bats spent most of their time on the ground. Naturally, human inhabitants soon sought to improve on this delicate ecosystem, introducing opossums, stoats, ferrets, deer, dogs, and other animals, quickly driving many native species to extinction. After years of conservation and an intense opossum/ferret/stoat eradication program, the landscape once again feels pretty empty. Traipse through the bush and you will find only birds. Cool birds, friendly birds, but just birds. Not a single furry, chattering, scampering thing. Even back in Costa Rica, where animals were plentiful, you never got the sense that the forest was *crowded* with wildlife. But the farther we went up the Ohau Stream Walk, the more crowded it got—bustling, rush hour, Times Square, three-ring-circus crowded. And we were right in the middle of it.

I'm talking hundreds, maybe thousands, of seals, everywhere: sleeping under branches, curled up under bushes, piled up like cordwood in the path, waddling through the ponga trees, clogging the waterways, barking and burping their deep guttural grunts as if to say, *Hey, guys. Welcome to the picnic. Did you bring the fish?*

Liane said this seal extravaganza occurs only a couple of times a year. She had no idea it was happening when we stopped; we just got lucky. For some reason that no one knows, the young seals leave the ocean and—accompanied by a group of graying adult seal chaperones—hit the bush for a raucous daylong playdate. Like a sold-out rave, every inch of the quarter-mile path was packed with revelers. But the real hub of the party, like a hot seal nightclub, was the gorgeous waterfall we found at the end of the trail.

Emerging from somewhere high above us (a distant source one hundred feet up that was no doubt crawling with seals as well), the waterfall cascaded into a dark pond that was alive with acrobatics. Seals jumped and flipped, barked and rolled, swam in teams that charged this way and that way, obviously having fun, happy to let us watch. Jackson couldn't resist and touched a curious pup on the nose while Logan posed beside the crowded pool as a dozen seals poked up to say "Cheese."

As I watched all of this, it made me realize: If we had stayed in Maine, I would have been at the office at that moment, probably sitting at my desk, on the computer, checking email, completely unaware that the semiannual seal party was going on without us.

But then, like Liane's decision to stop at the Ohau Stream Walk in the first place, sometimes one good impulsive decision can make all the difference.

27

MOUNT FYFFE

Of all the Kiwi hosts we met on our trip, Liane and Rick Rumble seemed to have the whole WWOOFing thing figured out. Unlike Sherab, who had lazy, half-cocked WWOOFers always descending on her kitchen, devouring every crumb in sight, the Rumbles had pretty much WWOOF-proofed their house and their lives. While they stayed in the main house, we were more or less confined to the Hangar. And though we occasionally ate with them, they just as often delivered food to us, a room service option that was both good and bad. Yes, it was nice to eat as a family for a change, but it did limit the *amount* of food we could eat at any one time. (Logan, the bottomless pit, was particularly concerned about this arrangement.) What it really meant was that if we ran out of milk or fruit or Weetabix for breakfast, we had to *ask* for more. Not that the Rumbles were stingy with the goods; they served us rock lobster and *paua* (abalone) for dinner one night, two delicacies that are more precious than gold in New Zealand. The difference was that the Rumbles were in control. There would be no invasion of the WWOOFing locusts at the Rumble House.

What's more, they expected us to do some serious work. Five hours a day. We built massive lasagna-style compost piles, constructed a mansion of a chicken coop, hauled debris, and weeded our fingers to the bone. ("I hate weeding," Jackson confessed on multiple occasions, making it abundantly clear that she would not be a professional weeder when she grew up—but also making her solid weeding efforts feel all the more deserving of a silent standing ovation in my mind.) We also tapped into our inner lumberjacks with a round of wood splitting that honed our ax skills while testing the limits of our lower back strength. Logan and I shared this manly task one afternoon from 1:30 to

6:00 P.M., which was roughly four hours longer than all his previous firewood chopping experience combined. He didn't complain, though. Hour after hour, he just took his turn slamming his ax into log after log, helping amass a small forest of ready-for-the-stove segments. By the end of it, my body hurt, my hands were sore, and I wondered how Logan was holding up.

"You okay?" I asked, expecting some kind of complaint.

"I'm doing good," he said. "But this log . . ." He shook his head ruefully and looked down at the next tree section on his chopping block, then glanced up at me for dramatic effect. "This log is doing *real* bad." Then he reared back with his ax and split that poor log with a full-body swing and a life-affirming shout that cracked both me and the log up. Liane and Rick were thrilled with the effort.

Which brings us to Lesson Number Three in the unofficial WWOOFing handbook: If you (A) work hard and (B) resist the urge to eat, smoke, and hump everything in sight, there's a good chance that (C) your hosts will go out of their way to make sure your stay is a pleasant and memorable one. At least that's how we ended up, on our last full Kaikoura day, at the base of Mount Fyffe.

It was Liane's idea. "Take the day off," she suggested. "I'll pack a lunch. You relax, spend some free time outdoors." When we didn't protest and demand more seaweed raking, she dropped us off early in the morning, gave us food and a cell phone, and agreed to pick us up when we called. All we had to do was climb the mountain.

Climbing Mount Fyffe is no walk in the park. Though the trail is essentially a crushed gravel road wide enough for a truck, it's also long and relentless, with each switchback revealing another switchback, getting steeper and steeper all the time. Ten minutes after we started to climb we were leaning forward like ski jumpers, plodding like turtles. The hike is posted as eight hours to the top and back, but Jackson's left ankle started to hurt around hour one. By the time we got to the midway hut for a lunch break, it had not improved. To make matters worse, we were completely socked in with fog, surrounded by a colorless world with no view whatsoever.

Views are something New Zealand in general and Kaikoura in

particular rightly boast of. Whether you're walking around the peninsula or walking to the outhouse, at any hour of the day, you are immersed in gorgeousness: the pink morning light on the mountains, the rising afternoon fog along the rugged coast, the sunset glow across the pasturelands. No matter where you point your camera, New Zealand is the supermodel of countries. It just doesn't take a bad picture.

But on Mount Fyffe that day, there were no pictures to take, no real fun in the air, only low clouds that clung to us like a wet blanket. As we sat down to lunch, we didn't talk much, just ripped into the food Liane had prepared for us: gourmet egg salad sandwiches, homemade scones, sweet apples, and dark chocolate, all totally delicious as usual.

Before becoming a mom and a self-sufficient homesteader, Liane had been a chef. Though she didn't brag about it, she had been the personal chef for former Beatle George Harrison in 1999, at the time that George was stabbed by a deranged fan in London. Back then, she worked at the Harrison estate with her husband, Rick, who became head of estate security immediately following the stabbing.

When that long and winding road came to an end, the Rumbles traveled the world, working aboard multimillion-dollar yachts and managing swanky resorts before finally settling down in Kaikoura to surf, start a family, and host WWOOFers like us.

But as another great English rocker once sang: You can't always get what you want. It ended up taking seven years to conceive their first child, and by the time Jimmy Rumble popped into the world, Liane was forty-two, Rick nearly forty. When we met him, Jimmy was a strong-willed chap who, even at three years old, used such expressions as "Don't look at me!" and "You don't talk!" and my personal favorite: "Don't do what I told you when I said!" All these commands were delivered with utter disdain and incredible gusto for one so young and—though he was as sweet as he was sour—we could tell it wore on Liane. Not so much that she lost her touch with the egg salad, but still, it took a toll.

It was like our world trip, in a way. At considerable expense, with the best of intentions, Traca and I hoped to give our children an amazing gift, a treasure box of experiences to take with them into life. But the night before we climbed Mount Fyffe, Jackson was up late crying big tears on Traca's shoulder, saying "I want to go home. I just want to go home!" She missed her friends, missed her life. She was tired of pulling weeds and sleeping in the same room with her parents. It didn't matter what our hopes were for her or what adventures might be waiting for us down the road. Sometimes the fog is too thick to see more than what's right in front of you.

After lunch, we continued up the mountain, dividing into alternating configurations of two, chatting away in the clouds. Gradually, just the smallest bits of white at a time, we began to find snow. Then, step by step, the snow got a little deeper. Higher still and the sun began to peek out from time to time, making our now snow-covered, evergreen-lined trail look like the entrance into Christmas Town. Until at last, the blue sky appeared as we stepped above the clouds.

For the final hour of our climb, the world below us was only clouds, a sea of cotton waves lit from above by a warm and brilliant sun. Jagged snowcapped peaks sharked up through the white for as far as we could see, etching a heartbeat onto an intense cobalt sky. It was like a dream, like heaven, as if we'd sneaked onto Mount Olympus and were looking off Zeus' balcony.

Sometimes there is a gap between what you wish for and what you get. You hope for a bundle of joy and you get a petty tyrant for a while. Or you hope to offer your child the world on a silver platter and all they really want to do is go home and eat at Gorham House of Pizza. The top of the mountain seems like a good idea when you're standing at the bottom. But then the weather changes, and your ankle hurts, and the fog rolls in, and the tears begin to fall.

As we stood on top of Mount Fyffe, taking pictures, feeling lucky, looking out at the cloud-covered world, our time in New Zealand was almost up. We had one more WWOOFing stop in Golden Bay, the little spit of land at the tippy top of the South Island, but after that I had nothing planned for our last Kiwi week. Like the sea of white that rippled out in all directions below us, it was all just a blank page that was waiting to be written. One minute it might be terrible; the next, it might be glorious. We couldn't stop it. As Rahaman said, the best we could do was to go through all the changes with as much grace as possible. For everyone.

"All right. I'm cold," Jackson said, changing again.

And just like that, we started down, stepping back into the clouds.

Part Four

VOLUNTHAI

In teaching you cannot see the fruit of a day's work.
It is invisible and remains so, maybe for twenty years.

—JACQUES BARZUN

28

SAFETY CONCERNS

WE THOUGHT A LOT ABOUT SAFETY ON THE ROAD.

I guess if we really wanted to be totally safe, we would have stayed at home. In Maine, there are no exotic diseases to speak of. The water is fresh and clean. The air is pure. No land mines or tanks. If safety were the highest goal, we would have stayed with the easy and familiar: the same job, the same house, the same street. Risk taking, adventure, the unknown . . . these are all just different words for danger, right?

I lived in Los Angeles during the Rodney King riots in the early nineties. For hours on end, Traca and I watched images of violence on TV: looting, lawlessness, even death. Black smoke and flames filled the screen and it felt, as we watched, as if the whole world were on fire.

It happened again as we waited in Melbourne.

Australia was supposed to be just a two-day stop, a brief "G'day" on our way to our next volunteer adventure. Through a U.S. organization called Volunthai, we were set to teach English in a rural Thai village. Logan and Jackson were told they might even be able to teach their own classes, which, though terrifying to them, sounded pretty cool to their parents.

But on the eve of our departure, after months of sporadic fighting in the Thai capital, the government tanks rolled in. It was a classic David and Goliath standoff. The Red Shirt protesters thought the new government needed the boot and were demanding that the president dissolve parliament, call for early elections, and step down. To make their point, they took up a position in the middle of the ritziest shopping district in Bangkok, barricading themselves behind a makeshift wall of bamboo and old tires. The government was trying to be patient, letting them have their democratically protected say. But as tourism numbers started to fall and the fighting intensified, official patience ran out and the military ran in. As we watched on TV, the tanks pushed into central Bangkok and the military scattered the resistance, arrested the leaders, and imposed a curfew across the city and many of the surrounding provinces.

Like the rioters in Los Angeles twenty years before, the vanquished Red Shirts raged, rioting in their retreat, setting fire to the stock exchange, a shopping mall, and dozens of government offices. Then the U.S. embassy closed, prompting an Australian newscaster to appear on the TV in our hotel room and report: "The government has raised the official travel advisory to: Do *not* travel to Bangkok." That seemed pretty clear. We called our airline and postponed our flight.

For three more days we waited. We visited the Melbourne Zoo and worked hard to attract the meditating koala's attention. We toured the botanical gardens and tried, unsuccessfully, to convince our kids that trees were a viable tourist attraction. We basically took a little break from volunteering and relaxed as much as possible.

Then, on the night before our rescheduled flight, we were back on high alert, scouring the Web, trying our best to evaluate the unfolding situation. From all accounts we could find on the ground in Thailand, the violence seemed to be confined to a small area. Most people were living their lives normally. Some even said they had no sense that there was any conflict going on at all, particularly in the countryside. We emailed other Volunthai volunteers already at schools in the region we were headed to, and they used terms like "beyond tranquil" and "deeply peaceful." In short, they encouraged us to come—though not everyone was so encouraging.

With our departure imminent, the fear really started flowing from home. Normally neutral friends and family pulled out all the emotional stops.

"A coup is likely," they predicted. "The violence will almost certainly get worse and spread. You will be a target!"

The conflict was more or less divided down economic lines, with the poor, rural Red Shirts seeking the removal of the elitist government and its wealthy supporters. We would be perceived— or so we were warned—as rich Americans and might represent some-

thing the rebellion didn't like. All scary thoughts. All meant to protect us.

In the end, I suppose it boils down to faith, odds, information, and
instinct. I remember watching TV all day back in Los Angeles and
feeling, really *feeling,* that the rioters were right outside our apartment. The news was filled with anger and danger, fueling a palpable
sense of panic. Hours later, when Traca and I dared to open our door,
we were surprised to find that the sky was blue and the streets were
quiet. For miles and miles in every direction, there were no signs of
danger, the birds were singing, people were helpful and unusually
open. Honestly, the city had never looked more beautiful to me.

Sensing that this type of localized media hype was probably happening again, I lobbied in favor of going to Thailand and—shortly
after midnight, after many last-minute Web searches—Traca agreed.
I could tell she wasn't fully convinced we were doing the right thing,
but either way, it was a huge relief to me when we turned off the TV,
powered down the computer, and curled up in bed having finally made
a decision.

Of course, nothing is static, not rebellions, not safety, not
certainty—and by the time we woke up, around six the next morning,
all it took was a single new email from home to toss our newfound
resolve into a tailspin.

The message was from our brother-in-law Tod. Under normal circumstances, Tod gives great advice. He's thoughtful, rational, a big-
picture guy, but as soon as I saw his name in Traca's in-box, I knew he
was not what we needed just then.

"Don't read that," I said. "We've already decided."

Too late. Traca opened it like Pandora's box and released all the
fear back into our room. With only two hours before we had to leave
for the airport, Tod suggested that we skip Thailand for a while, let it
cool down. Maybe go to Vietnam, he said . . . and just like that, Traca
started looking up Jetstar flights to Ho Chi Minh City.

What followed was a crazy hour of indecision, with the scales of
safety and danger tipping this way and that, with the clock ticking
louder and louder, until I found myself standing in our doorway, done
with all of it, needing and wanting to make a decision.

"Traca. Stop. Listen to me," I said. I was stressed and flipping out. I pointed to my foot inside the room. "With *this* foot, I will walk to my backpack and get ready for the Skybus pickup." Then I pointed to my other foot in the hall. "With *this* foot, I will walk downstairs and call the airline and change our tickets to Vietnam. Just tell me what you want to do."

Traca looked at me, not sure. All she wanted was to be safe.

Then Jackson walked in. "What's going on?" she asked.

We told her the high points: Vietnam, cool down, Tod's message, unsure . . .

"Are you kidding me?" Jack said, as if we'd just proposed going to Iraq or Darfur. "Vietnam is *so* much worse than Thailand. I'm not even *interested* in Vietnam."

It was a reaction based on zero information and even less analysis, but for some reason, it tipped the scales. Without any further discussion, Traca made up her mind.

"Okay. Let's go to Thailand," she said, and I walked to get my backpack.

I wish I could have said with complete certainty that there was no risk waiting for us in Thailand, but there is always some risk. Besides, we didn't quit our jobs, pull our kids out of school, rent our house to a total stranger, and carve out six months of new experiences because we were looking for a sure thing. We did it to be fully engaged in life, to step outside the narrow focus of fear, to put our faith in the goodness of local people, and to stand together, as a family, in the safety that we hoped like heck was waiting for us.

29

INVASION OF THE FALONG FAMILY

"Yaw name eez?" a girl said. She was dressed in a white short-sleeved shirt, blue skirt, and matching blue tie. Her eyes were wide with hope and she smiled like an adoring fan. Behind her, a dozen other Thai schoolgirls in matching uniforms looked on, too shy to approach, equally excited to hear the answer.

Jackson smiled back. "My name is Jackson," she said.

The girl's smile broadened and she took Jack's hand, pressing the back of it softly to her cheek. "You ah so bee-*you*-tee-fall," she said. "I love Jack*sun*."

I'm sure Selena Gomez gets this all the time, but it was a new experience for our little girl and one she had to get used to. Who knew living in rural Thailand meant instant celebrity status for both of our kids? It certainly was a far cry from the danger and violence we'd been expecting when our plane landed in Bangkok a few days before.

Bangkok is the capital of Thailand and a city of more than eight million people. As the most visited city in Asia, it has a reputation as an all-night party town, but none of its celebrated revelry was on display as we arrived. A citywide curfew was still in effect. And since our Thai driver did not speak or play the radio for the entire forty-minute trip into town, it felt as if we were being smuggled in rather than visiting.

After an uneventful drive down an empty freeway, we were dropped at the equally empty Suda Palace Hotel, where hundreds of large, blazing lightbulbs on the building's façade looked out of place, as if the management hadn't received the "under siege" memo. The night air was still and stifling, eerily quiet. And when we were shown to our room at the end of a deserted hallway, we immediately locked the door. By unanimous vote, rather than take any risks, we all went to sleep without dinner.

The next morning, to counteract the stress of the previous few days, we each got a Thai massage. It was offered in our hotel by blind male masseurs, and for five dollars a person, it was hard to pass up—though it did prove to be the very opposite of relaxing. Jackson and I went into the massage parlor together, lying side by side on parallel beds. The two blind Thai men who were assigned to us looked like twins; both were middle-aged, dressed in what looked like pale blue surgical scrubs, sporting the same bowl cut hairstyle and matching blue-tinted sunglasses. As they felt their way from limb to limb, often "looking" at the ceiling while they worked, their fingers were like iron rods, digging for pockets of tension as if trying to extract a confession. We never did scream out loud, but Jack and I shared plenty of silent laughing and facial expressions of pure mock agony throughout our hour-long sessions.

Twelve noon saw us running a little late, trying to catch a one o'clock bus to Chaiyaphum (pronounced chai-ya-POOM), a small urban center five hours northeast of Bangkok. From our hotel, we hired a couple of tuk-tuks (three-wheeled taxis) and set off into the bustling traffic of the capital city. With the curfew lifted, the streets were now a logjam of cars, rickshaws, trucks, and bicycles . . . but no tanks and no Red Shirts. Without incident, we arrived at our first real obstacle: Mo Chit bus station.

Mo Chit is not laid out like any bus station I've ever seen. While endless buses idle around the perimeter, the main building has multiple floors of small ticket windows, hundreds of individual clerks selling a myriad of different bus lines, all with routes advertised in utterly incomprehensible Thai. To say the Thai written alphabet is different from its English equivalent is like saying peacocks are different from toads. Thai letters are ornate and cryptic, like abstract calligraphy, every character sporting a fancy curlicue as if showing off for the king. To make this lettering even more confusing to Western visitors, Thais use fifteen vowel symbols that are placed above, below, to the right, or to the left of any of the forty-four basic consonants. In other words, reading was not an option.

As I stood on the first floor wondering where or how to begin, a group of four Thai boys approached me. They were maybe ten years old, dressed nicely, unchaperoned as far as I could see. "What your name?" the boldest boy barked at me. "My name Baa," he said before I could answer.

"Hello, Baa," I answered, and all the boys laughed.

"Baaaa," they all repeated like a paddock of sheep.

"Baaaa," I echoed, and everyone laughed twice as hard. Now, I'm a pretty good mimic, so I tried again while the sound was still fresh in my mind. "Baa?" I asked.

I had them rolling in the aisles with that one, huge laughs and big smiles all the way around. "No," the bold boy said when the hilarity had passed. "Iss *Baa*. Not *Baa*!" Then they all scrambled away from an approaching security guard, laughing louder and louder as they ran.

Mercifully, there were a few English-speaking bus reps wandering around Mochit—which spared me the indignity of mispronouncing the word "Chaiyaphum" to all four hundred agents—and we made our bus on time. Five hours later, we reached our destination, where no fewer than twelve people were waiting for us, including the director of the school we were headed to. His name was Mr. Mongkut and he was a serious man, in his mid-fifties, stout with short hair, wearing a crisp white uniform. He stood at the end of a long receiving line and shook our hands with great solemnity, as if greeting us at a funeral.

"You come now," he ordered, pointing toward a waiting white van, and we followed obediently. I thought we were going to spend the night in Chaiyaphum. At least that's what our contact at Volunthai had told us. New teachers usually get one full day of teacher training before heading off to their assignments. But for reasons that were never fully explained, Mr. Mongkut wanted us to go immediately to his village and teach the next morning. (Clearly, he was eager to obtain—and vastly overestimating—our English teaching skills.)

In the van, our driver was a polite thirty-year-old man named Lek who spoke limited English but was constantly smiling. Beside him, a hip eighteen-year-old girl named Ban acted as our translator, when she wasn't texting on her smartphone. "You need make stop?" Ban asked before we pulled out into traffic.

"Actually, yes," I said, remembering. "We need to get some clothes."

In Thai culture, appearance is everything. How nicely you dress will determine how much respect you are given. Thais like you to be clean, well dressed, and full of easy humor. Meet these three requirements and you will be loved to bits. After nearly three months on the road, however, our clothes were far from clean and hardly what you'd call nice. So we pulled in to a Chaiyaphum department store for a little shopping and our first real dose of regular Thai life.

A few things stood out right away. For one, most items were very inexpensive. At thirty-one Thai *baht* to the American dollar, even the nicest clothes cost less than five bucks. For another, there was not a single pair of shoes in the shoe department that was ever going to fit on my huge American feet; even the largest size was five sizes too small. But the thing that stood out the most, beyond small shoes and cheap clothes, was . . . *us*. In the bustling store full of people, we were the only Western faces, and all eyes followed us. One little boy simply could not contain himself when he saw me.

"Falong! Falong!" he shouted. His face was surprised and excited. He jumped up and down, laughing and screaming, pointing his finger at me. *"Falong! Falong!"*

(To be technically accurate, the word the boy was shouting was *farang,* but I'll be writing it the way it was pronounced. After hearing it so many times, it's hard for me to think of it any other way.)

"What's he saying?" I asked our translator, Ban, who was beside me on her cell phone.

"No problem," Ban said. "Means 'foreigner.'"

"Falong!" the boy screamed at the top of his voice. Then he hugged my legs and ran beside me, clapping his hands, utterly blown away by the fact that I was there at all. *"Falong! Falong! Falong!"* he blared like a siren.

Ban smiled. "We no get much visitor," she explained.

Eventually we made our purchases, hopped back in the van, and set off for Nong Kha, a tiny village in the countryside about one hour north of Chaiyaphum. A local family had agreed to host us for the next month, and the homestay house we were taken to looked promising. It had two stories with lots of room, just off the main road behind a sturdy metal fence. After greeting our homestay family, we were given the entire second floor with two large separate rooms—kids in one, adults in the other—and an open-air porch overlooking a rustic chicken house, green rice fields, and distant mountains. Each room had powerful fans to blow away the oppressive heat and new micro-screens in the windows to keep out the oppressive bugs. Beds were comfortable. Our first home-cooked meal of pad thai was delicious.

Our new housemother was a powerful fifty-year-old woman named Fang. Fang was a teacher at the school we were headed to, and she took in boarders from time to time to supplement her income. She was a serious woman, always dressed and made up as if going to the office, even on her days off, even in the stifling heat. She shared the house with her first-grade granddaughter and her bedridden husband, both high-maintenance members of the family. As a result, Fang was a blur of activity, completing an endless daily To Do list that now in-cluded "Feed hungry Americans."

"You like meat?" Fang asked as we were getting ready for bed on our first night.

Traca, being both a strict vegetarian and a polite houseguest, tried not to be difficult. "Don't go to any trouble," she said.

"Okay. Chicken?" Fang pressed. "And fish? No problem."

The next morning, after a good night's sleep and a breakfast of chicken *and* fish (along with fresh vegetables and fruit, which Traca ate), we put on our new clothes and walked a quarter of a mile to the Nong Kha School. When we stepped into the courtyard, we found many students cleaning the grounds, sweeping, picking up trash . . . but as soon as they noticed us, they all stopped whatever they were doing to *wai* us. A *wai* is a Thai greeting: palms together, hands below the chin, bowing slightly, huge smile on face.

"Good mawning, tee-chas," they all said. Girls giggled. Everyone looked happy.

After checking in at the office, we were whisked back outside for the morning assembly. I was hoping to ask the staff a few questions, maybe get some language games or basic English teaching tips to start with, but everything happened too fast. In no time, first period was starting and Traca and Logan were led away to teach Patom Three: third grade.

"Where should we go?" I asked Por, our handler at the school. Por was maybe thirty, neat and smiling, not a wrinkle on her crisp military-style uniform.

"No room now. You teach hee-a," Por said, pointing to an empty cement volleyball court. "Iss easy, yes? You go." Then she left us with twenty-five students, sitting on the ground, no chalkboard, no supplies, no nothing.

It was hot, nearly one hundred degrees, and I was already sweating through my new button-down shirt.

"What do we do?" Jackson whispered.

I had no idea. I looked out at the eager sixth graders, then back at Jack. She just shook her head and pointed at me as if to say: *This one's all yours.*

"Okay," I said. "Hello."

"Good mawning, tee-cha," the students all said in unison. Clearly, they had done this before.

"My. Name. Is. John," I said, enunciating each word. Then I pointed to Jackson.

"My name is Jackson," she said, playing along.

We were twelve seconds in.

"What. Is. Your. Name?" I asked the group, pointing to the first student in the semicircle.

"My name iss Pee-ta," Peter said.

"Hello. Peter," I said, relieved to be communicating even in this small way. I had no Thai to fall back on or translator to turn to. It was English or nothing. I pointed to the next student.

"My name is Chimlin. Nickname Jim," a cute little girl said.

"Hello. Jim," I said. I had twenty-three to go. "And. What. Is. Your. Name?" I asked the next girl in line.

"Name is Baa," the girl said.

"Hello. Baa," I said, and everyone broke out laughing.

What we learned in that first hour-long class was that the students already knew every word and every possible thing an untrained English teacher might instinctively try to teach them. They knew the alphabet. They knew the ABC song. They knew the days of the week, months of the year, body parts, colors, things outside: house, sky, tree, rock, grass. Then I opened my backpack and asked them to identify every item I pulled out: pen, paper, passport, pencil, book, you name it. After this, I started drawing pictures in a notebook and discovered they also knew every animal I could think of, every fruit, every object.

"What. Is. This?" I asked, sketching quickly.

"Iss spoon," they all said in unison.

"Yes. And. What. Is. This?" I asked, more sketching.

"Is faurk," they said.

Jack chimed in when I floundered, and together we made it. When the period mercifully ended, the students stood up happily. "Sank you, tee-cha!" they all said, smiling, *wai*-ing. Then Jackson and I retired—like soldiers in retreat—to the tee-chas' lounge to regroup.

Things got a little easier after that. Our next class was taught in an actual classroom with books to read from and props to hold up. We weren't the Berlitz family, but we got better all the time. And no matter what we did, the students seemed beyond thrilled just to have us in the room. They especially loved Logan and Jackson.

Without exaggeration, our kids were treated more like visiting pop stars than untrained volunteers. Jackson often posed for pictures after class and signed autographs for her adoring fans, while Logan had a teen idol effect on the young Thai ladies. They shrieked when he looked at them, screamed "I love you!" when he passed by. One girl was so nervous around him, she peered over a sheet of paper the entire class, afraid of what direct face-to-face contact might do to her. It was crazy.

But it did make one thing very clear: The fear we had felt before arriving in Thailand was long gone. Our new village was peaceful; the villagers were kind. Near as I could tell, the greatest risk we were facing would not come from angry protesters. But if it was possible to be killed by adoration, the kids needed to be very careful.

30

SOUR TEA CRAP

WHEN YOU BUY SOMETHING IN THAILAND, YOU MIGHT ASK, *"RAK-KAH, tow-rai?"* Which means, "How much is it?" So long as you really drag out and swoop the *o* in "tow" from high to low, and roll your *r*'s so they almost sound like *l*'s, you stand a pretty decent chance of being understood. But since you have very little chance of understanding the answer you'll receive, you might consider following up automatically with *"Dai-mai kee-an long hai?"* Which means, "Could you please write it down?" At least that's what our little Thai phrase book said.

I was practicing these two sentences in preparation for a trip to the market when Por, our teacher friend from school, dropped by. Por spoke the best English in the village and was constantly asking me for help with her pronunciation. When I asked her to give me some feedback on the Thai I was working on, she was thrilled to switch roles.

"Dai-mai kee-an long hai?" I said, proud of myself and expecting approval. Por just stared at me, not a single glimmer of comprehension on her face. I tried again, less certain. *"Dai-mai kee-an long hai?"* Nothing. At this point I just figured—as I've always known—that I suck at this, and all, languages. So rather than prolong my listener's confusion, I showed her the book with the phrase printed out in Thai characters. Right away she understood.

"Oh," she said. "Iss not right. You say: *'long hai.'* But iss: *'long hai.'*"

That was it. My *hai* swooped down. Her *hai* swooped way up. Everything else was fine but she'd understood none of it.

Such is the way with Thai. In tonal languages, inflection is critical. Take for example the word *mai* (pronounced my). If you say it flat, it means "mile." Say it low, it means "new." Say it high, it means "right?" Swoop it from low to high, it means "silk." And if you swoop it from high to low, it can actually mean two things: the most basic word, "no," or the verb "to burn." Sheesh. What if you want to say "We don't want to burn a mile of new silk, right?" It boggles the *mai*-nd.

At first, I found all this high and low stuff to be ridiculous. I mean, come on: One wrong swoop and you can't understand *anything* I'm saying? But then I had a chat with a local girl named Bè-oh and I realized communication is tricky no matter what language you're using.

It was after a Buddhist ceremony that we all attended in the next town over. In honor of the day the Buddha reached his enlightenment, some local monks were saying prayers and passing out blessings. Food was prepared. Everyone in the area turned up. When the monks finished chanting and the crowd began to head home, I took a walk through the town, just looking around. As I came to a corner, Bè-oh was standing by the road and she called to me.

"Tee-cha, tee-cha," she said.

"Hello. Bè-oh. How. Are. You?" I asked.

"Am fine, sank you," she said. "Where you go?"

"I. Am. Walking," I answered. "What. Are. You. Doing. Today?"

Bè-oh's face flashed concern. Quickly, she opened the English book she was holding. She was probably thirteen, but her book was a first-grade reader. Still, she flipped though the pages, wanting to answer me, desperately looking for the words.

"It's. Okay," I said. "No problem."

But Bè-oh kept looking. She flipped faster, glanced up at me, more pages, more glancing, then she made a decision and took a shot.

"When do we go . . . abore?" she said.

She smiled. I smiled. But I had no idea what she meant. Her smile dimmed and she looked down, reading more carefully. "When do we go abore?"

Wanting her to succeed but still totally lost, I stepped closer and took a look at her book. The page she had decided upon was titled "Transportation" and the first line was printed under a picture of a plane. "When do we go aboard?" it said.

I have no idea why she chose that particular sentence. Obviously she didn't understand the question. Or maybe she just panicked.

Whatever the reason, I gave her an A for effort, knowing firsthand how stressful it can be to try at all.

Even nonverbal communication proved to be a challenge in Thailand. There was a seventy-five-year-old man named Paa who acted as a caretaker for our property. He was a small man with a deeply wrinkled face, neatly combed silver hair, and a gentle smile. I'm not sure exactly what Paa did at the house when we weren't around, but I usually found him sitting out on the front patio, dressed in shorts and a tank top, resting in a large carved teak chair that looked like a throne. I tried to talk to him from time to time but Paa spoke no English at all. So once my limited Thai skills were used up (which didn't take long), we'd resort to pantomime. The problem was, at least as far as I could tell, that Paa's signs and gestures were mostly random. He'd hold up two fingers, point to me, put his hands on his hips, pretend to be reading a book, throw a few punches, hold up one finger, answer an imaginary phone, dig with an imaginary shovel, point at me, and then wait for my reply. Completely lost, I usually just threw a few punches and dug a few holes myself. In this way we passed the time.

When I was in eighth grade, I got a D+ in Mademoiselle Gosselin's French 2 class. It would prove to be the lowest grade of my academic career, and it says something about my ability to grasp foreign languages. It's not just that I find them difficult, which I do. I'm simply not all that interested. Whereas Traca is fascinated and motivated by the challenge a new language presents, the whole process just makes me tired. All those irregular verbs, the masculine-and-feminine nonsense, the future tenses. I'd rather just take my D+ and go home.

But with Thai—and this came as a total shock to me—I was actually having fun learning a language for the first time in my life. I can't explain it. Maybe because it was so impossible, because I was so certain to fail, I just relaxed and made a game out of it. I don't know. It really didn't even feel like a language to me. It was more like a random string of sounds that meant nothing unless I related them to word pictures in my mind.

And so I pictured a cup of Sour Tea Crap when I needed the Thai greeting for "hello" (*Sa-wat dee, krap*). Or I pictured a raccoon eating some rye bread when I wanted to ask someone's name: *Kun cheu a-rai?*

(Coon chew a rye?) Attila the Hun eating his chow reminded me of the Thai word for "breakfast," *ah-hahn chów* (a Hun chow). Naturally, potty humor is the most effective way to remember anything, so I'll never forget the words for "Sunday" (*wan a-tít*), "butterfly" (*pee seu-a*, or, to me, "pee sewer" with a bit of a Maine accent), "pink" (*see-chom pou:* see chomp poo), and the word for "corn": *kau-poon*, which sounded enough like "cow porn" to make me smile and spark my memory.

Was it possible to reduce an entire language to a series of ridiculous English word pictures? Probably not. But I had four weeks to try.

Luckily, to say "four weeks" in Thai, you say *see a-tít*, and who can forget that?

31

ONE THAI DAY

Each day began at 4:15 a.m. with roosters.

Before the sun was even a promise in the east, every rooster in Nong Kha began screeching, competing to announce the morning. These were the ferocious Thai fighting cocks that strutted around our yard like pimps, keeping their many mangy ladies in line. Curiously, as decked out as these loud dudes were, the hens they lorded over looked positively plucked, like freaky living-dead chickens, bald and ready for Paa's pot. Maybe they were molting or had feather mites. I never did find out. Whatever the reason, as the cock-a-doodling began each day in earnest, we couldn't see any of them. Sunrise was more than an hour away.

Once we got used to the raucous pimp chatter, we usually slept until six. Then Logan and Jackson would hit the country roads together and burn up some miles, while Traca and I would either run, meditate, or do a little yoga. However the morning got started, we all reconvened for the first shower of the day around seven. Thais are very clean, and it was expected that we would take at least two daily showers. Actually, it wasn't just expected, it was requested.

"You wheel tack showa een mawning and in eve-a-ning. Okay?"

We heard this from three separate people the night we arrived. As for the actual showering part, it was a little more involved than hot and cold knobs and a directional showerhead. In the bathroom, there was a large basin of standing water, a plastic bowl, a slightly sloped tile floor, and a hole at the base of the wall for drainage. To wash up, you filled the bowl with water and dumped it on your head until sufficiently wet. Then, you lathered up and repeated step one. The basin was filled with rainwater and it was a little cold, but that was fine. By seven o'clock, it was already eighty-five degrees in the house, on its way to one hundred or more, so a cool dip/dunk was always a good thing.

Breakfast was served at 7:30. We usually had rice, cooked Thai vegetables, eggs, fruit, sometimes meat if Fang wanted to pamper us, and always hot sauce. "If not spicy, it not Thai," Fang was fond of saying as she served the daily mounds of food. I'm not sure what kind of ogre family she thought we were, but most days we managed to eat only about half the food we were given—even with Logan, the bottomless pit, on our team.

Eight A.M. and off to school. We looked like dorky missionaries, but that was the dress code. For the men: pants, collared shirts tucked in, and shoes, not sandals. For the women: long skirts and high-necked shirts, showing as little skin as possible. Thais are very conservative and modest in all aspects of life, even at the public pool. We went swimming one day to beat the heat, and every Thai swimmer, from the youngest to the oldest, wore knee-length shorts and a T-shirt. One teenage girl even wore sweatpants to splash around in. I'm telling you, Speedo is not getting rich off the Thai market. By comparison, Jackson looked positively naked in her bikini, but she simply could not conceive of a world where you swam in wet clothes. To her credit, she did wrap herself from neck to knee in her sarong as soon as she stepped clear of the water so as to avoid an international scandal.

After a morning assembly in which we sang the Thai anthem to the king and said prayers to the Buddha, classes started at 8:40 A.M. Classes were fifty minutes long and we taught three of them spread out over the day. Class sizes ranged from six to twenty-six in grades one through twelve. We saw every class at least once over the course of a week. As for the actual job, I can tell you this: Teaching English without a translator to a group of kids who really don't speak English is not as easy as I thought it would be. For some reason—and this is probably because of my complete lack of experience—I thought we'd show up, start talking, act words out, clown around a bit, and somehow, magically, we'd have everyone reciting Shakespeare in no time.

But this was not how it shook down. What we discovered was that these kids knew a lot of words, every obscure thing you might find on a flash card, like unicorn, X-ray, yo-yo, and zebra. But they did not have a single clue about how to put a sentence together or ask a simple question. They were also soft-spoken and shy, especially some of the girls, so conversation was often an exercise in embarrassment. And some of the boys were simply not trying. After all, if you were going to be a rice farmer like your father's father's father's father, why did you need to know what color some *falong*'s socks were? In English?

In all honesty, there were days when we felt completely unqualified to pose as teachers, finding the students struggling with the most basic concepts and feeling as if fifty minutes were an endless chasm to cross. Other days, we found our stride, taught a lesson that seemed to work, saw real learning going on, and the time flew. As I'm sure every real teacher knows, it was fun to see the children getting excited in class. One student walked out of one of our best classes with a huge smile on his face. He was bursting at the seams to say something, and he paused in front of Jackson and me to express his feelings.

"I . . . am . . . *happy!*" he said.

I was thinking the same thing.

When school ended, around two o'clock, the rest of the day was ours. We walked home, bought a cold drink on the way, usually took shower / dunk bath #2, and then set out to explore. The kids liked to hit the town and play soccer with local friends, or ride the house moped up and down the main street, or wrestle with the gaggle of young schoolkids who stalked their every move. Traca started teaching yoga to a small but passionate group of local women. Or she and I would practice our Thai together or walk through the gorgeous, endless rice fields, down unmarked roads, through one village and then another. Many times, we heard the ubiquitous *"falong falong"* from all sides, but even that was changing. In our village, as we took a stroll one afternoon, we noticed the greetings were different. "Tee-cha!" we heard. Or better still: "Hello, Jawn. Hello, Tray-sa." Nearly every home in Nong Kha had a child we were teaching, and as we walked by, parents came out, smiling, waving. Which, I must say, felt pretty good.

Dinner was served at seven o'clock. More delicious Thai food. Then another shower before bed. Unless there was some special event, a visiting guest to dine with, or a trip to town planned, we were almost always in bed before nine. And with good reason.

Each day began at 4:15 A.M. with roosters.

32

WHITE GLAMOUR

For every shy American boy who could use a boost to his self-esteem, might I suggest a vacation in rural Thailand?

Places like Chiang Mai in the north and Phuket in the south have been crawling with tourists for years, but in Nong Kha and the surrounding countryside, the sight of a large Caucasian boy is still a rarity and has the power to get the local people—particularly the ladies—excited. To give you an idea how Loganmania played out in our day-to-day lives, how's this for an ego stroke?

Logan, Traca, and I were sitting up on our porch one afternoon, resting in the hundred-degree heat while watching storm clouds form over the mountains, when Jackson came running up the stairs.

"Logan," she said. "You have company."

"Who is it?" Logan asked, expecting some of the young neighborhood boys who followed him around like rambunctious puppies.

"I don't know," Jackson said. "It's girls. And they're not from school."

No, they were not. They were from the next town over: four seventeen-year-old girls who had heard about Logan through the Thai grapevine and came to see what all the fuss was about. In the fifteen minutes that these total strangers were with him, they posed for camera-phone pictures, swapped emails, asked every question their smattering of English would allow, and basically basked in Logan's presence for as long as possible. Add this to the continued autograph signings in class and the general pie-eyed mooning that followed him around school, and we had the makings of a teen idol sensation.

Seriously, I was thinking about putting up a little souvenir stand by the road featuring POM ♥ LOGAN T-shirts. (*Pom* means "I.") Jackson thought we'd make a killing.

In her own way, Jackson was also adored—but Thai boys were not the type to show up at your house, unknown and unannounced. Though they often shouted "I love you!" from a safe distance and even wrote it on the floor in spilled rice one day, they were usually respect- ful and—I suspected—a little intimidated by our brash and powerful young lady. I saw this in class all the time.

One of our simplest English class exchanges was a common back- and-forth conversation that went like this:

"Hello. How are you today?"

"I'm fine, thank you. And you?"

"I'm fine, too. What is your name?"

"My name is [*insert Thai name*]."

"Hi, [*Thai name*]. My name is John. Nice to meet you."

"Hi, John. Nice to meet you, too."

Not exactly Oscar-winning dialogue, but it got them talking. So we'd go around the room and play out this scene with each student, usually shaking hands at the end. But one day, when I told the twelfth- grade class that Jackson (a ninth grader) would be the one walking around to speak and press the flesh with them, most of the boys cow- ered, scrambling to the back of the room and huddling around the rearmost desk. All the girls thought this was hilarious, and many of the boys were laughing, too—but I could tell some of them were gen- uinely nervous. One poor guy, who clearly would not be taking my daughter to the Thai prom, grabbed his books and walked, stone- faced, out the door when Jackson got a little too close for his comfort.

I've wondered about this crazy adoration and I see a few possible explanations for it. For one: Many commercials I saw in Thailand were really just corporate American spots overdubbed in Thai. So the faces the local kids saw on TV day after day were beautiful U.S. teens, happily hiking through the Rockies or enjoying an ice-cold Coke in the Los Angeles sunshine. As I watched these ads in the context of rural Thai life, I could see that Logan and Jackson appeared to have stepped right off the set and into the Nong Kha School. So maybe that's why the girls swooned and the boys trembled.

There was also a cultural fascination with white skin. When the TV wasn't showing happy American kids selling chewing gum and

soda, the stations ran an endless litany of ads for skin-whitening products. To drive this "White Is Right" mentality home, all the popular
TV shows featured incredibly pale Thai actors, and the models in the
magazines were also all bleached out, like perfect shells on the beach.
It was a little creepy, actually. In the bathroom at our homestay, there
was a brand of lotion from Lux called "White Glamour" and it promised: "fair and admired skin." It went on to say: "With skin so allur-
ingly white, you will be empowered to unleash and enjoy your feminine
spirit." Because, of course, who could unleash their feminine spirit
without a nice white face? Traca talked about this with Aud, a female
teacher at school with perfectly even, beautiful brown skin, like a
mocha latte come to life. When Traca asked why anyone would ever
want to lighten such a wonderful color, Aud blushed. "Oh, no," she
said, shaking her head, embarrassed. "I black. You bee-*you*-tee-fall."

Fair skin is not a modern fascination, I'm told. For centuries it has
signified high social status. That is, if you are rich enough to stay out
of the fields and out of the baking hot sun, your pale complexion and
lack of wrinkles will tell the world all about it. But as we looked around
our school at these kids with their perfect brown skin, the kind many
American teens flock to the beach to achieve, the kind the entire tanning industry is built on, we just wished there was an ad campaign
telling every Thai child how bee-*you*-tee-fall they all were.

As for the crazy adoration, our housemother, Fang, explained it
like this: "Iss easy," she said with a big smile and a thick coat of white
makeup on her face. "Thai woman laav *falong*. Much much mah-nee!"

Which did explain all the fat, balding, older white guys we saw
with hot young Thai wives. But it didn't explain Logan. Not yet.

Whatever the truth, our kids loved all the attention. Each day
after school, Logan and Jackson rode the house moped over to a neighboring village and met up with a dozen girls and boys from all over the
area. They converged to play soccer and hang out, or at least that's
what they were physically doing. Jackson told me Logan had his eye on
this one certain girl, and Logan did not deny it. Her name was Sumalee and she was a beautiful, soft-spoken seventeen-year-old with a
constant smile and eyes that lit up whenever Logan was around. Traca
and I weren't invited to these gatherings, but I liked to picture Logan

and Sumalee, after the game broke up, working hard to communicate, walking off into the emerald-green rice fields as the sky surrounded them with brilliant pink and red. I'm sure it wasn't about money or skin color or any of that.

It was just a shy Thai girl with a shy American boy, both getting a little less shy all the time.

33

MEET THE RENTER

LIVING IN NONG KHA, IT WAS EASY TO FORGET THE WORLD. WE NEVER watched the news. We couldn't read the local newspapers. Other than a painfully slow dial-up modem at the school, there was no Internet access, so we mostly stayed off the computer. If we had to log on for one reason or another, we watched the pages load the same way everything in the village happened: slowly, at its own unhurried pace. Once we got into the rhythm, it was a peaceful way to live.

One afternoon, with a break in my schedule, I decided to do a little Internet research for our next stop; we were hoping to do some volunteering in India, but nothing had been arranged yet. Before I launched into my search, I checked my email out of habit and found the real world, the life we left back in Gorham, waiting for me in my in-box.

The note was from Joyce, our renter, and it was a long one. Apparently, her computer had crashed and she could not restore it, which meant—since she was a bookkeeper—that she could not work. Which, of course, meant she would not get paid that month. Which was really just a long-winded way of saying she would not be paying the rent anytime soon.

It took my slowed-down brain a few minutes to process the rambling excuse, but then, like a dial-up modem making a connection, I remembered all the reasons I never should have rented to this woman in the first place.

Joyce had responded to our House for Rent ad on Craigslist. In retrospect, Craigslist was probably not the best way to handle an out-of-the-country, long-term, last-minute rental search. We should have gone through a real estate agent who would have done proper credit checks and could have handled any problems that arose while we were away. But in an effort to save money, we posted a free ad and hoped for the best.

To its credit, Craigslist did provide us with a steady stream of interest, though I suspected much of it was thinly veiled attempts to scam us. The most transparent was a note I got from a desperate woman with weak English skills who wrote: *"I am in urgent want for to buy your vehicle 4BR FULLY FURNISHED HOME. AVAILABLE NOW!!! This is just the model I've must to buy."*

I wanted to write back: *"Dear Urgent Want. I don't think our home is as mobile as you are suspecting. You're welcome to come take it for a test drive but I've got to warn you, it hasn't moved an inch since we bought it."*

A few legitimate renters looked promising for a while, but as our departure date neared, we made peace with the idea that we might not find anyone to pay our mortgage while we were away. Even so, we were committed. We had plane tickets. We were going this time. In the real estate world, I think they call this being a "motivated renter," and I'm sure Joyce could sense that.

Just before she pulled in to our driveway, I called my friend Lisa, who was a landlord herself, and asked for some advice about screening potential applicants. "How do you know who to rent to?" I wondered. Lisa's answer was simple:

"Go with your gut," she said. "If you like the person, trust that. If you have a bad feeling, walk away."

With that in mind, I sat across from Joyce and took her in. She was somewhere in her forties and she looked haggard, even haunted. Her face was thin with dark circles under her eyes and her skin was marked with open sores that she said were from mold poisoning in her blood. "I got it from my last rental," she explained. "It was growin' under the couch."

It was the first red flag of many that day. *Who sits on a moldy couch long enough to absorb the spores into their bloodstream?*

Joyce tried to laugh her condition off in a "Can you believe it?" kind of way, then started coughing with the vigor of a lifelong smoker, a stinky habit we were hoping to keep out of our home.

"Just so you know, we don't allow smoking in the house," I said. "I want to be clear about that."

"Oh, no," Joyce said, once she got her hacking fit under control. "I never smoke. None of us do. That's something we do not do. That's for sure. No way."

Red flag. She's protesting too much. Walk out to her truck and check her ashtray.

I never did check, but I really didn't need to. Honestly, you didn't have to be a psychic to pick up a shifty vibe from this woman. It even crossed my mind that she might be on crystal meth. She was a single mom, self-employed, with two teenage kids. She didn't strike me as an evil character, more of a woman with a hard life; but there was something else . . . some unnameable gut warning that rang clear as a bell.

I'm sure there are many different levels of creepiness to pick up on. A serial killer might make your skin crawl off your back, a con artist might register as a vague case of the willies. But Joyce was definitely registering somewhere on the chart for me. She was saying all the right things. I just didn't believe her.

Over the course of our one-hour meeting, Joyce pulled a wad of cash from her pocket and offered to pay prorated rent we were not asking for . . . *red flag* . . . then produced a printed lease and placed it on the table with all our terms already typed up . . . *red flag* . . . agreeing to pay every single utility without negotiating in any way . . . *red flag.*

The biggest red flag of all came at the end. When we told her we needed her first and last month's rent, payable before we left on the twentieth, Joyce looked worried.

"The twentieth?" she said, clearly struggling with this deadline. "See, 'cause I don't get paid until the twenty-*second*. I can pay you then, no problem. But before that . . . it's a little tight."

Red flag. Are you kidding me? She can't pay until two days after we leave the country for six months? Beyond fishy.

When her interview was over and Joyce had driven off in her truck, no doubt smoking like a chimney, Traca and I weighed our options. We both saw the warning signs, we just interpreted them differently.

"She wants to do the right thing," Traca said, seeing the good, as usual. "She just needs a chance. I say we give it to her."

"Can I say I told you so when she starts a meth lab in the basement?" I asked, not kidding at all.

The fact that I signed her lease—after I read it over several times to make sure there wasn't a clause in it that said Joyce now owned our souls—is a testament to just how badly I wanted to get out the door at that moment. Without storing much of anything, without even insisting on our security deposit, we left our house spotlessly clean and utterly Joyce's.

Three months later, we were in Thailand, eighty-five hundred miles away from our home in Gorham. After reading Joyce's epic excuse and kicking myself for not trusting my instincts, all I could do was type up an encouraging, hopeful reply and send it.

Maybe she really is having trouble, I thought. *Maybe she'll pay.*

Then I logged off, shut the computer down, and decided to let the world back home take care of itself for another three months.

34

UNINVITED GUESTS

To cook or eat anything in rural Thailand means spending time with flies.

That's just how it goes. Flies find food and hang out. Whether you're chopping or chewing, flies will crawl on the lip of your wok or the lips of your face if you let them. And what exactly were they doing with all this crawling around? I wondered. If they were wiping their nasty little feet on the rim of my glass or laying eggs in my pad thai, it was not obvious. Near as I could tell (and I watched them pretty closely, which was not hard to do with so many around), they seemed to be . . . licking. More accurately: They were placing their freaky retractable mouth apparatuses on anything that could eat or that could be eaten—a thought that did not, I assure you, enhance my desire for the tomatoes I was chopping into salsa one afternoon after school.

The salsa was part of a dinner party Traca and I had decided to throw. Initially, the guest list included four teachers from school, the three members of our homestay family, plus the four of us, for an ambitious table of eleven. It was to be a Tex-Mex extravaganza featuring, among other things, guacamole, refried beans, cheese, and salsa—all things not found in the typical Thai refrigerator. To pull it off, we bought supplies on a day trip to Chaiyaphum, and we were set to put it all together on party day.

The only trouble was that once word of our soiree spread around the village, we discovered that there's no such thing as a private party in Nong Kha. First, guests asked to invite friends. Then those friends invited friends. Then children and grandchildren piggybacked on invitations. Apparently, everyone wanted to see what the giant *falong* family ate for dinner, and frankly, it had us a little concerned. With fewer than six hours till guests were scheduled to arrive, it looked as if we'd be having somewhere between twenty and forty visitors. Which meant we needed more food.

In the middle of the school day, with two free periods before us, Jackson and I hopped on the house moped and set off into the hundred-degree day. Our plan was to buy more of everything and add potatoes to the menu. Many Thai friends we spoke with thought American food meant french fries, and we did not want to disappoint. Since the closest potatoes that anyone could think of were twelve miles away at the Ban Huayangdam public market in the Nong Bua Daeng District (I can't pronounce it, either), Jack and I hit the road to make some tracks and get more snacks.

Rural Thai markets are fun. In addition to the color and the commotion, you can buy just about anything that can be eaten: fat live toads, live eels, bugs, huge sad fish swimming in shallow tubs of dirty water, octopuses on a stick, whole pig heads, or, if you so desire, a local delicacy made up of a pig's ear and a strip of skin leading to an intact snout—which we did not buy. You can also—by being an American— get all the attention and assistance a person could possibly want. As Jack and I walked past the simple stalls, inspecting the heaps of local produce and edible curiosities, all eyes were glued on us, following our every move.

At first I thought it was just the *falong* phenomenon, but after a few minutes I realized that something felt different. The women in the market did not look happy. They whispered to each other. They furrowed their brows as we approached. Eventually, a bold woman from the legion of female vendors stepped in front of me, blocking our path. She was at least sixty, tiny and wrinkled, and she pointed her tiny wrinkled hand at my chest. Then she pointed at Jackson . . . back to me . . . back to Jack . . . raised eyebrows but smiling. Her expression said, *Explain this, please.* So I did.

"*Korng pom look sow.*" My daughter, I said.

The woman beamed, her face a riot of happy wrinkles. "*Look sow?*" she said, overjoyed. Then she called out: "*LOOK SOW! LOOK SOW!*"

What followed was a chorus of *Look sow*s as every woman in the market told her neighbor that I was not, thank goodness, married to Jackson. I was in fact her father.

Supplies in hand and relationship clear, Jackson and I booked it back to school, taught our last class of the day, then headed home to get cooking for the masses. I started chopping the aforementioned tomatoes, put some beans on the stove to boil, and threw our house-keeper, Boon, into a culturally induced panic in the process.

Boon was in her forties, a solid country woman with a round face and a gentle smile. In spite of the heat and the tedium, she worked hard all day long and always looked happy. My appearance in her kitchen was the only time I ever saw her frown.

Two things about Thai cooking (other than flies): It's quick, and men don't do it. So as I stood in the kitchen endlessly boiling and chopping, Boon wasn't sure what to do. She tried repeatedly to take the knife from my hand, looking me in the eye each time like a sym-pathetic nurse helping her delusional patient. And she simply could not stop turning off the burner the beans were bubbling on, bringing me bean samples at two-minute intervals. Each time she'd appear, holding one mostly raw bean in her hand, I'd inspect it and politely say: *"Mai, Boon. Rórn mahk."* Literally, "No, Boon. More hot." Boon would groan a soft sound, imploring me to reconsider. When I in-sisted, she'd reluctantly return the bean to the pot, fire up the stove, and show up a few minutes later with another uncooked bean for me to reject.

Eventually it was showtime and the guests started to arrive, in cars, on mopeds, on foot. Traca and I have thrown many dinner par-ties in our twenty-plus years together, but I feared this one was going to be a colossal international flop. As we scrambled with last-minute preparations, our friend Por poked her head into the kitchen, sampled the guacamole we offered her, and screwed up her face, the universal symbol for "Yuck!"

"Thai no like weg-i-tables," she said. "Like meat."

Damn. We should have bought some of those ear-snout appetizers after all.

In the end, our party won't be remembered for the food. Some people liked it. Some didn't. Most of it was eaten by the time we went to bed. It won't be remembered as a wild shindig, either. We sat on the floor, politely chatting. Many people stayed for less than an hour. For me, though, the evening will forever be enshrined in our Dinner Party Hall of Fame for an event every party planner fears. I'm speaking, of course, of the cloud of inch-long flying insects that descended on us precisely at the moment I delivered the final bowl of beans to the feast.

Thai houses are open. Windows often have no glass, ceilings and walls have large gaps, doors are rarely closed—so the swarm that invaded our village had no trouble getting in. I'm not kidding. This was a full-on, repent-for-your-sins, holy-mother-of-God plague in our kitchen, and our living room, and our guacamole, and our salsa—all of which appeared to have grown wings.

In fact, wings—and the creepy bugs they flew in with—were everywhere: in my hair, down my shirt, sticking to my sticky skin. Traca and I were hysterically laughing at the sheer absurdity of it all.

"What does Emily Post say about plagues?" I wondered.

Logan was running around with a broom and a smile, attempting to single-handedly beat back the apocalypse, while Jackson also found the whole thing wildly funny, which was not the reaction I'd expected from her. At another time and place, certainly at the start of our trip, it was not hard to imagine Jack being horrified by the bugs, seeing them as more than enough reason to go home and griping about the whole affair long after it was over. But as the swarm swirled around her, Jack was cracking up, covering her mouth to keep the invaders out, nearly losing it when she saw a foot-long lizard run across the floor with dozens of wings sticking out of its mouth.

"Godzilla just ran into the kitchen," she said, gasping for breath, her hair crawling with insects. "And I think he's hungry."

It lasted for about ten minutes, and then, just as suddenly as it began, it was over. I have no idea how or why it happened, but as if on cue, every member of the swarm fell to the ground and vanished. The floor was littered with wings, thousands of wings, everywhere, but the insects were gone.

In the aftermath, we finally got to sit down as a family and have some food with our guests, none of whom were bothered in the least by the invasion we'd just witnessed. Naturally, the houseflies were there, licking my bowl, my spoon, my arm—but I barely noticed them, focusing instead on Por, who was sitting beside me fishing some trapped, struggling insects out of the black beans.

"You can eat," she said, holding one up for me to see. It looked like a gigantic carpenter ant. "Fry. You like. Many protein."

35

ENGLISH TEACHERS

YOU MAY BE ASKING YOURSELF AT THIS POINT, HOW AND WHY DOES somebody get to teach English in Thailand without any formal training or an ounce of experience? For that matter: How do a fourteen-year-old girl and a seventeen-year-old boy get to tag-team their own classes when they haven't even graduated from high school?

The simple answer is: We were better than nothing.

With all due respect to Por and the other Thai English teachers at the Nong Kha School . . . their English was not so hot. Yes, it was better than everyone else's English in the village, but being able to play "Chopsticks" on the piano only qualifies you to teach "Chopsticks" to others, so to speak. We loved them, we could understand them (most of the time), but like one generation passing down broken dishes to the next, their pronunciation alone was more than enough reason to have us there.

I sound like an English snob, I know, and who am I to judge? After all, I'm the guy who breaks into a sweat when ordering *agua* in a Costa Rican restaurant. The same guy who asked a local Thai farmer in a jungle plot one day, *"Tam ling nee?"* I was curious to know if there were monkeys in the surrounding trees, so I pressed the point. *"Tam ling nee?"* Nothing. I pointed, pantomimed, spoke slower, louder. *"TAM. LING. NEE?"*

The man stared blankly at me and never said a word. It was only later that I realized what I'd actually been saying.

"Do monkey this?" I'd been shouting. Then slower, louder: *"Do. Monkey. This?"*

But speaking English is something I, and the whole family, can do effortlessly. At the Nong Kha School, even without any proper teaching techniques, we could speak correctly throughout every class. We knew when to add pronouns, how to articulate the letter *r* and the letter *d*. Without even trying, we could serve up full, slow sentences on a silver platter for our students to sample, and this continued outside the classroom as well. Simply by being in the village, we were a rolling English lesson all day long. As we walked and stopped to chat, we were ambassadors for the language in a place that saw virtually no tourist traffic at all . . . which really brings us back to the heart of the original question: Why and how were we there?

The real answer is: Michael Anderson.

When Michael graduated from the University of Texas in 1999, he was sick of school, bored, wanting a little adventure. So he went to Thailand. After bumming around for a few months, he happened upon a rural village where a few eager students encouraged him to come speak at their school. Like us, he was a huge and instant sensation, one of the first *falongs* the area had ever hosted. Following his brief school appearance, the principal humbly asked if Michael would stay on and teach English for the semester. They couldn't offer him money, but they could give him food and shelter. His decision to accept not only changed the course of his life but planted the seeds that would one day grow into Volunthai.

Michael spent the next six years in Thailand. He married a local girl named Ae, and they now work to attract English speakers to many tourist-free corners of the country they both love. To accomplish this, they set up a nonprofit based in Washington, D.C., that is not like most overseas teaching gigs. You don't need any ESL training or qualifications. As it states on their website, you may apply if you meet at least six of these seven requirements:

1) Have a college degree (or are still in school)
2) At least eighteen years old
3) Have some teaching or volunteer experience
4) Don't drink or smoke every day
5) Likeable personality and tidy appearance
6) Outgoing, creative, and independent
7) Willing to adapt to another culture

In short, you need to look good, dress well, smile, make jokes, and go with the flow. Have a little education and don't be a drunk. If only all amazing jobs had requirements that were so easily met.

It cost $375 per month to be a Volunthai volunteer, and that figure drops to $200 for each additional month you stay. This fee covers your room and board and gives you the opportunity to add English Teacher to your résumé. Get yourself to Thailand and you can live, eat, and work for little more than $12 a day.

Thailand isn't for everyone, of course. We met an American man from Alabama who couldn't stand the place. "It's so hot," he said, visibly sweating. His name was Glenn and he was a big guy, in his late thirties, fat, with a big mustache. Glenn worked for the U.S. Department of Defense in Iraq, making more than $300,000 a year as a procurement officer. "Just jerkin' off in the sand," as he described it. "I hate those people," he added, referring to the Iraqis. He didn't care much for the Thais, either. "People are nice," he conceded. "Just stay away from the retards, you know? I don't even try to speak to 'em. If they start jabbering away at me, I just hop on my bike and ride off. 'Learn English!' I say." Naturally, he had a beautiful young Thai wife.

I think it's safe to say that Glenn will never be a Volunthai volunteer (or an ambassador for U.S. tolerance and goodwill), but he did illustrate a point. If you resist Thailand, attempt to conform it to your culture, and choose air-conditioning and motorcycles over the slow, steamy pace of simple, rural Thai life, you will forever remain an outsider, just another loud tourist passing through. But if you simply show up and relax and let the land of a thousand smiles welcome you, you'll not only enjoy yourself more, you'll be exactly what Michael and Ae and Volunthai are looking for.

As for teaching, it was a mixed bag. Some classes were fun. Others seemed to drag on without end. We were the only foreign teachers at the school that month, so we had only each other to learn from. When ideas worked, we shared them after school and duplicated them the next day. When they didn't, we discarded them and brainstormed better approaches at night as we gathered on our open-air back porch. Our main goal was to get the students conversing, not just repeating, and so we asked a lot of questions.

"What. Color. Is. Your. Shirt?" we'd say, pointing to a boy's white uniform top.

"My shir iss whyyt," the boy would respond.

Or: "How. Many. Books. Do. I. Have?" we'd ask, clutching a small stack of four first-grade English readers.

"You haav faa buks," another student would say with a big smile on her face.

We played hangman on the chalkboard, spelling out propaganda like SCHOOL IS FUN and WE LOVE THAILAND. Or we pushed desks to the side and taught the concepts "Stop. Go. Fast. Slow. Walk. Run" to ecstatic fifth graders. On days when even these failed to excite, I also had a secret weapon in my notebook that became an instant and sure-fire hit.

Since our arrival at the Nong Kha School, I started learning to sing the Thai national anthem. Each day after morning assembly, I asked our friend Aud to teach me a few more verses that I phonetically wrote down. Even word by word it was difficult to put on paper, but I forged ahead, eventually springing it on a class one day during a low point in the lesson.

"Prà-thet thai ruam lueat-núea chat chuea thai," I sang, with seven more verses to follow. I was butchering it but the kids loved it, hysterically laughing until the final refrain. From then on, they called for it all the time. "Sing *prà-thet thai,*" they'd shout, already cracking up.

Hey, whatever keeps 'em interested, I say.

Did I wish we had some actual training or tools or a single clue among the four of us? Yes, I did. Am I glad the lack of these did not stop us from giving teaching a try? Without a doubt, I am.

During a free period one day, I checked in on Logan and Jackson; they'd started teaching classes together and I wanted to see how they were handling things without a parent in the room. At first, I thought pairing up the kids was a bad idea, worried their combined star power would simply be too much, like having Justin Bieber *and* Taylor Swift on the same stage. But when I found them, they were working with the rambunctious sixth-grade class and they had everything under control. Logan was taking the lead, doing most of the talking, but Jack was engaged, too, chiming in as needed, holding her own. At one point, they arranged the students in a circle on the floor and passed a crushed paper ball around the group.

"What. Do. You. Like?" Logan asked before tossing the ball to a girl across from him. The girl caught it, a little embarrassed, then began to think.

"I liiike . . . cat," she said softly before tossing the ball to a boy who was excitedly waving for it.

"I liiike fuuball," the boy said proudly, then lobbed the ball to his friend.

"I liiike snake," the next boy joked, and everyone laughed.

From the door, I watched the smiles on my own kids' faces and matched them with one of my own. While their friends were back home compulsively texting or mindlessly Facebooking or shooting each other in a virtual war online, Logan and Jackson were here, teaching these kids, learning from them, laughing along with the group.

"What do *you* like?" Jackson asked when the ball was passed, encouraging a shy student to offer her answer.

Had the crushed paper ball rolled over to me at that moment, I knew exactly what I would have said.

36

MANY RICH

I KNOW THERE IS TECHNICALLY A NATIONAL TEACHERS DAY IN THE United States (it's the Tuesday of the first full week in May, in case you've forgotten), but having put two kids through the U.S. public school system, I can say it was never a big deal in Gorham. When Logan and Jackson were younger, I remember sending them to school one year with small gifts and cards to pass out, but that was pretty much it. Over time, the occasion just came and went with all the fanfare of Arbor Day. Now, I suppose it's possible that some school districts make a big production of Teachers Day . . . but I'd be willing to bet that even the most lavish American celebrations pale in comparison to the heartfelt extravaganza the kids at the Nong Kha School put together for us.

Teachers Day in Thailand is really a three-day event. At least it was while we were there. The first day was rehearsal, and on that particular day it was hot. How hot? If the small travel clock / temperature gauge I carried with me was to be believed, it was 50 degrees Celsius in the sun. That's 125 degrees Fahrenheit! To put this number in perspective, the hottest temperature ever recorded on earth is 134 degrees, or just nine degrees warmer. In the shade where I was sitting, it was 110 degrees, which made it by far the hottest ambient indoor air temperature I had ever experienced.

Into this heat, all 280 students were called to an open assembly hall. The hall was really just a supported roof with a half wall all the way around and no windows; it was used as a common area for gym class on rainy days and for the occasional all-school meetings. The kids sat on the cement floor, lined up in neat rows from grades one through twelve, boys on the left side, girls on the right. On the stage before them, there was an elaborate Buddhist altar and a row of chairs.

The chairs were where Traca and I and a few other teachers sat, surrounded by electric fans.

What followed was an intense, earnest scene that I seriously doubt many Western schoolkids could duplicate without a stack of discipline problems or possibly even open rebellion. After a lengthy lecture on the importance of Teachers Day, the Nong Kha students came forward, youngest to oldest, in groups of eight. With painstaking precision and sincere little faces, the students practiced how they would prostrate themselves before a statue of the Buddha. Then, shuffling on their knees along a woven banana leaf runner, they moved in front of us, their teachers, where they practiced another very specific supplication before offering us their gifts, which for the moment consisted of slightly embarrassed imaginary hand gestures. This went on for four hours.

The next day there were no classes. It was an entire day set aside for the students to work, unsupervised, on their offerings. The idea was to make an elaborate, stylized creation out of clay, fruit, and real flowers. It was a contest, and near as I could tell, there were no guidelines. The kids just shaped and sculpted and crafted their works of art, gathering in small groups all over the school grounds. We, the teachers, basically hung out all day. We didn't have to look over the kids' shoulders and keep them on task. They weren't being graded on this. They just worked on their own. One group was up until midnight that night completing their masterpiece.

The third day was Teachers Day. No classes. Showtime.

Every student who had been in need of a haircut came to school that day sporting a crisp new do; many young boys looked like monks with their freshly buzzed heads. All clothes were cleaned and pressed. Everyone looked happy. We assembled in the hall, kids on the floor, teachers and Buddha on the stage. When everyone was in position, the bowing, prostrating, and gift giving got under way.

The creativity was incredible. While the youngest Thai kids offered simple arrangements of wildflowers wrapped in palm fronds, the older students went all out, creating complex and beautiful designs, each more original than the next. There were multilayered towers of golden bowls filled with cascading flower garlands. There were intricately folded banana leaves curved like wings on the back of an ornate dragon carved from a pineapple. The offerings were like mini Rose Bowl parade floats, vibrantly colorful with thousands of tiny petals. They were also painfully temporary. In the intense heat, these arrangements would not last the day.

Flowers aside, the real stars of the show were the students. As usual, they were well behaved, but it was more than just their ability to sit still. Maybe I'm giving them too much credit, but their little scrubbed faces were shining with what looked to me like reverence, a sincere, humble respect for their teachers, for my family, and for me. They were bowing at our feet, every last one of them.

When it was all done, one final floral creation was placed in the center of the hall. I thought it was for the winner of the Offering Design contest, but it wasn't. It was for us. "You like," Aud told me with a smile. "Go sit."

Traca, Logan, Jackson, and I sat around a low table as a local priest recited an ancient incantation, designed—I was later told—to keep us safe on our journey and bring us luck in our lives. As he did, the students and the teachers formed a ring around us and a roll of string was unwound, tied to the flower centerpiece and extended until it encircled the entire group. I could not understand the rapid-fire Thai blessing we received, but the feeling in the room was clear. *We honor you,* it said, *and we hold you, for this moment, at the center of our lives.*

When the prayer ended, the priest closed his book and tied a small string around each of our left wrists. It's a tradition in Thai culture. They do it at weddings—all the guests offer strings of luck to the bride and groom—and the sentiment was the same for us. By itself, a single string didn't look like much, just a white line across the brown of my skin. But a single string was not what our friends had in mind.

We were moved to four chairs, and one by one, in a beautiful receiving line of smiling familiar faces, the staff and kids came forward to honor us, each with a collection of strings to offer. Some boys gave Jackson an actual bracelet, quickly slipping it on her wrist and whispering "I love you" before hurrying triumphantly away. Others attached penny candies to their strings. Most strings were the traditional white yarn that the local monks made, blessed and sold in the village temple. Others were pink. Some were baby blue. As they tied them, they also offered us blessings in their best English. Things like:

"Many luck."

"Many many maah-nee."

"Happy happy . . . everything!"

"I love Tee-cha!"

"Good aftanoon. Many rich!"

It may sound like a simple gesture but it was incredibly touching. Traca was in tears for most of the ceremony, basking in the generosity and heartfelt kindness of these people. Actually, it didn't take much to push her over the emotional edge. She was experiencing a kindness overload at the time. Her little cabal of female teacher friends surprised her with a custom-made Thai coat, created specifically for her by a local tailor, then presented her with an elaborate fruit carving one afternoon just because they loved her. With those as primers, a parade of more than two hundred sincere well-wishers easily filled her heart to overflowing. But I suppose that was the whole point of Teachers Day to begin with.

37

THE ANTS AND THE WING

A FEW DAYS LATER, TRACA AND I HAD AN ARGUMENT. WE'D JUST GOT-
ten back from a trip to a local mountain with Por and Aud, and apparently the way I'd been goofing around with Logan and Jackson did not
sit well with her. "In fact I found you rather rude, if you want to know
the truth," she told me. This triggered the defensive kid in me, which
escalated the whole disagreement and ended with our spending some
time apart.

It was an old pattern for us, our most common source of conflict
back home. Traca wanted me to be more considerate of her feelings. I
wanted her to be less judgmental of my behavior. Whenever we engaged each other from these two positions, it never ended well, leaving
us in a loveless stalemate that was hard to get out of. Luckily, we rarely
played this pattern out on the road, and in Nong Kha, I knew our spat
was only temporary.

The next day, the school held another assembly. With our post-
argument funk still lingering, I went to the hall without Traca and
listened to three monks make a presentation. The monks were bald
and dressed in traditional saffron robes, but they were also sporting all
the latest technology. Two of the monks sat at a table onstage, one
talking into a microphone, the other controlling a video projector on
his laptop. The third monk roamed through the crowd snapping pictures on his digital camera. I sat in the back of the hall, behind all the
students, just taking it in. The microphone monk spoke in rapid Thai,
so his message was mostly wasted on me, but the projector monk's
video message was crystal clear: Don't sell drugs in Thailand. To get
this point across, he played a short film that dramatized the following
scene: A drug dealer gets busted by the police in the middle of the
night and is dragged from his home. The cops are not kidding around.

They haul the man like trash into an open courtyard and tie him to a post. The villain is not defiant. He is screaming, begging for his life, but it's no use. There is a zero-tolerance policy for this kind of criminal, and as the Nong Kha students all watched, the policemen raise their guns, take aim, and blow the drug dealer away.

Don't sell drugs in Thailand. I certainly got the message.

After that, there was more monk talking and I zoned out, focusing instead on four ants that I spotted on the low cement half wall beside me. The ants were trying to carry a long insect wing, one of the discarded millions left behind by the dinner-crashing swarm that had invaded the entire village. The wing was awkward for the ants to maneuver; they were barely moving, nearly falling off the edge of the wall at times, but they soldiered on, step by step. It was an epic struggle and I was into it, following their progress for a few grueling inches, when suddenly, two of the ants dropped the wing and simply walked off. Left behind, the two remaining ants continued the mission as best they could, dragging their dry, lifeless prize behind them.

I felt a little like God looking down at this tiny drama, marveling at the futility of it all. The wing was a husk. Why did they even want it? And why were they up so high on the wall? Where were they going? What was the point?

Then I laughed to myself. It didn't take a poet to see the symbolism here, and the longer I watched the two ants working way too hard, the more I wondered whether Traca and I looked like that sometimes. What was God thinking, looking down on us? And after Logan and Jackson—*our* two baby ants—left . . . what then? If it got to the point where Traca and I were dragging around our own lifeless husk of a marriage, would we know when to let it go? Would I?

As I watched the ants and the wing, I could relate to their tenacity. I knew that the idea of quitting, of walking away, was just not in my makeup. In spite of our ups and downs and our momentary friction, I was committed to carrying my end of the wing, so to speak. Traca had her own view of commitment that had evolved through the years. It was no longer the strict "Till death do us part" kind of vow we'd made to each other on our wedding day. Now she was more committed to growth, to joy, to making the most of the short lives we had to live. "I want passion," she was quick to say during our least passionate times, but that's really not what we needed. Passion is like spice, and no one eats a bowl of spice, even in Thailand. Commitment is the meal. Passion, like an argument, is only temporary, after all. Only commitment can carry the wing from one side of the wall to the other—a fact that was driven home to me every day back at our homestay house.

Our housemother, Fang, was married; her wedding pictures were proudly displayed all over her home. In the photos, Fang and her husband look to be in their early twenties, the groom handsome and strong in a crisp military uniform, the bride dressed in white and stone-faced, more solemn than celebratory. If they were happy on their big day, it doesn't show in their portraits. But as dour as they appear, I'm sure neither of them had any idea of the cruel fate that love had in store for them.

I hate to admit it, but I never learned Fang's husband's name. I never even spoke to him. I'll call him Saa-me, which means "husband" in Thai.

However it happened, Saa-me had a stroke many years ago, leaving him bedridden and virtually helpless. He could not speak or move much. He lay on a bed to the side of the living room, usually dressed in a white sleeveless T-shirt and covered with a thin sheet. In the heat, he sometimes moaned softly, his frail legs bent, his adult diaper visible. Once, I saw him looking at me, and when I met his eyes, I smiled, but he did not smile back. He just stared out at the world from his blank limbo, while the strong military man he used to be kept watch over his wasting body from the many photographs around the room. And though the rest of the household came and went as if Saa-me wasn't there, Fang stayed with him. She fed, changed, bathed, dressed, and carried her husband, all without fanfare or complaint.

Divorce rates in Thailand are low; there is still a stigma attached to separating, though that is changing in the big cities. The most recent numbers I can find show six out of every hundred Thai marriages legally end in divorce, compared with the fifty-fifty split found in the United States. Yet even these figures don't tell the whole tale. One study suggests the rise of Thai divorces is due in part to the many

START OF THE TRIP: The Marshall family on their way to the airport. It's the first time any of them have worn their fully loaded packs.

COSTA RICA: Traca and John with Carol Crew (now Carol Patrick) practicing the Alpha Shout on their way to the Osa Wildlife Sanctuary.

COSTA RICA: The Human Kitchen, the center of all Sanctuary operations and the space where the spider monkeys were most territorial.

COSTA RICA: John and Sweetie during their first meeting.

COSTA RICA: Jackson with Tank the anteater. Tank never wanted to be let go.

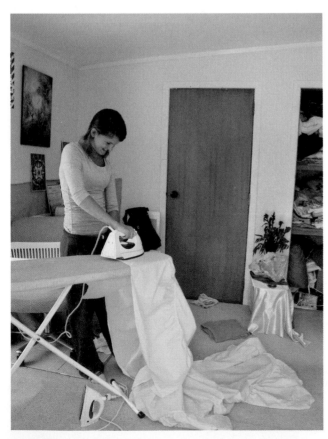

NEW ZEALAND: Jackson ironing for the first time at the Sharda Centre.

NEW ZEALAND:
Sherab's bus, aka the Gypsy
Dancer or the Brown
Potato.

NEW ZEALAND:
Logan helping to
move the window
in the girl's dorm
at Sherab's place.

NEW
ZEALAND:
The birthday
bathtub behind
The Hangar at
the Rumble's
house.

NEW ZEALAND: Traca loving the view above the clouds on Mt. Fyfe, Kiakoura

NEW ZEALAND: Logan, Traca, Jackson, and John at the top of Mt. Fyfe.

THAILAND: Logan and Jackson with a group of adoring students.

THAILAND: Several girls from nearby towns surprised Logan one day, stopping by to talk and take pictures.

THAILAND: Jackson during recess with three of her most persistent admirers.

THAILAND: Lining up with the other teachers at Teacher's Day.

THAILAND: Jackson's hands at the end of our reception. So much affection in those little strings.

INDIA: After chasing the water buffalo out of John's path, Job turned to scream in triumph.

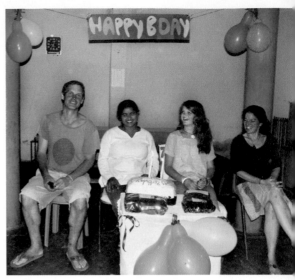

INDIA: The seats of honor at Jackson's fifteenth birthday party. One of the Older Girls April, shared the same birthday.

INDIA: Clifton Shipwa and a few of the childrer he is raising at the Good Shepherd Agricultural Mission.

INDIA: John helping out in the laundry, something that always embarrassed the Older Girls.

LADAKH: Khen Rinpoche with Logan and Jackson on a hillside above Stok Village.

LADAKH: Maya on the streets of Leh, offering her strings of necklaces. "My dear! I am here!"

LADAKH: A view of the mountains and the new Golden Buddha statue in the Nubra Valley.

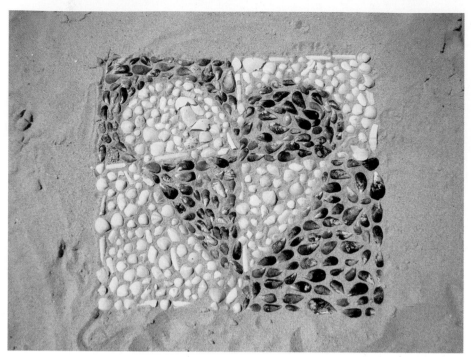

PORTUGAL: The heart mosaic on the beach in Salema, Portugal.

PORTUGAL: The last day. At the Lisbon airport, ready to fly back home.

Thai–*falong* marriages that are becoming more common. In fact, one report from a study done in 2008 found that *all* divorces filed in a one-month period were from mixed couples, tangible proof—as if it was needed—that unions built on "mah-nee" and "bee-*you*-tee" are even shakier than those founded on love. For couples that endure, at least to my way of thinking, it is commitment, in one form or another, that gets the credit. Certainly, it's commitment and commitment alone that keeps you changing your partner's adult diapers year after year.

But what are Traca and I committed to? Are we committed to being together forever at all costs? Is that what marriage is? Or is that kind of love an anchor, as Traca sometimes suggests, stifling growth and trapping people who might otherwise feel called away? How does "forever" accommodate change? And what happens if you're the last ant holding the wing?

I sat at the back of the assembly hall, listening to more microphone monk and watching the ants. They hadn't quit, but they were virtually standing still, one pushing, the other pulling. Progress was minimal. And then, for a reason only the heart knows, one of the remaining ants opened its mouth, let the wing drop, and scurried over the edge of the wall out of sight. Seconds later, probably sensing the futility of it all, the last ant let go and hurried off in the opposite direction.

38

GOODBYE, AUM

WHEN OUR LAST DAY AT THE NONG KHA SCHOOL WAS OVER, AFTER 280 *wai*s and an equal number of *Sa-wat-dee, krap*s (it also means goodbye), we were given a raucous farewell karaoke party by our fellow teachers. The next morning, Fang made us one final pad thai breakfast, and then Aud drove us to a nearby bus stop and made sure we got on the right Bangkok shuttle.

Back in the capital city, the violence and protesting were long gone, and we were shown the royal treatment by a surprise tour guide named Pim (not her real name). Pim is a diminutive woman in her sixties, impeccably dressed with a regal demeanor, who attended college many years ago with Traca's aunt Patsy. Born into the Thai royal family, Pim now acts as one of the king's personal assistants and as such is showered with immense respect wherever she goes. It's sort of like fame by association, but it's much more than that. The king of Thailand, Rama IX, is the longest-reigning monarch on earth and the most beloved figure in the country. To be connected with him in any way vaults you beyond mere celebrity status into a stratosphere of reverence that is hard to imagine but fun to experience. So after a Traca–Patsy–Pim email exchange, Pim treated us to, among other things, a private tour of the royal palace, a private boat to escort us to an exclusive and equally private restaurant, and a visit to my new favorite museum, the throne room at Dusit Palace.

It is impossible for me to adequately describe the masterpieces contained in this collection. The brochure lists them blandly as examples of "traditional Thai arts," and if that is true, then the Taj Mahal is an example of traditional Indian architecture. How can I possibly convey the beauty of a silk screen made by one hundred and forty-three craftspeople who worked for four years on nothing else, weaving two hundred and fifty shades of silk into a twenty-seven-foot-long by sixteen-foot-tall tapestry? Or a teak carving created by seventy-nine master carvers, all working for over one thousand days to produce a solid wooden wall, ten feet wide by twenty feet tall, with the most intricate trees, vines, elephants, gods, and temples, each figure a miracle of subtlety and skill and all of it blending together as if by magic into a unified whole? To call this collection breathtaking is an understatement. It is a testament to the heights human creativity and patience can reach, offering visitors the chance to stand surrounded by pure genius for a while before heading back out into the heat and hustle of Bangkok traffic.

With our Thai visas about to expire and our royal tour concluded, it was time to continue our way west. But none of us were eager to leave Thailand. After nearly four months on the road, the slow, settled feeling of village life with its comfortable routines and predictable schedules felt surprisingly good. Logan and Jackson had loved being around kids their own age, and they had blossomed in the warm glow of so much adoration. And Traca and I had managed to generate a little warm glow of our own. Though there was conflict between us at times, and moments that felt like setbacks, there were easy times, too. We relied on each other in Thailand, teaching together toward the end, wandering through the rice fields in search of nothing in our free time. We even managed to slip off for an actual date on our last night in Bangkok, disappearing into the electric carnival of Khao San Road. The kids were exhausted that night, and after dinner they just wanted to go back to our hotel and watch TV.

"You guys go," Jack said. "You need it."

So after tucking them into their beds and locking them in their room, we hit the town. We laughed and shouted over the blare of bad bar music, cheered with random World Cup fans who were gathered around TVs at every market stall, then went back to our room and made love as temple bells rang out in the distance.

We stayed up late that night, talking in the darkness, listening to the city noises outside. At one point, I was watching Traca's face when she closed her eyes and slowly began to smile.

"I had a dream last night," she said softly. "I was flying. And I was good at it. Soaring through the sky. So free."

Her face looked rapturous, as if she was reliving the flight. "I had a dream, too," I said, remembering. "I dreamed I had a deep, slow kiss with Angelina Jolie."

Traca laughed and opened her eyes. "So, kind of the same thing," she said. Then she gave me a deep, slow kiss, the kind Hollywood actresses are paid millions of dollars to simulate.

We left Thailand the next day, sad to go, knowing we had barely scratched the surface of this complex country. From the language to the culture, so much of it would forever remain a mystery to *falongs* like us. Still, on our flight from Bangkok to India, Traca and I talked about some of the questions we were leaving unanswered. Small things like: Where *did* all those dinner party bugs go? And: Why did our homestay neighbors rent a truck loaded with concert speakers and then *blast* Thai pop music at 4:00 A.M. every day for a week to prepare for a local funeral? More important: What happened to Aum, a fourth-grade girl we all came to know and love at the Nong Kha School?

From very early in our visit, Aum was one of our favorites. She was a bit of a tomboy, with a big smile and a twinkle in her eyes. She also had a great laugh and a sincere sweetness. "Tee-cha. Please," she'd say, guiding me off the road to protect me from a passing car. She only came up to my elbow, yet there she was, ten years old, shielding me from harm. During our first week in Nong Kha, we saw Aum every day. She loved Logan like a big brother and fought with him whenever they were together—soccer games, wrestling matches, she hung on him and laughed and growled like a playful dog. Whenever I looked in her direction, she always caught my eye. All it took was a quick glance and Aum would instantly light up, the beautiful spark within her igniting at the slightest connection.

Then one day everything changed.

Aum didn't come by after school. She stopped talking with Logan, much less climbing on him. She wasn't looking when I looked at her. She simply withdrew her attention.

Many other kids eagerly flowed in to fill the space Aum had once occupied in our lives, but we couldn't help but wonder what had happened. In conservative Thai culture, had she been behaving inappropriately, too intimate with a teenage boy, too bold for a young lady her age? That was our guess, but we never knew for sure. Her downcast eyes didn't tell us anything other than to shield us from the spark we loved so much.

On our last day, Traca and I were teaching one of our final classes. I wrote on the board: "What Do You Like To Do After School?"

"I liiike to play cumputa," one boy called out.

"I liiike play wollyball," another boy insisted.

"Wait," I instructed. "One. At. A. Time."

And so Traca worked her way down the right side of the classroom, asking each child what he or she liked to do after school, while I started down the left side with the same question. That's when Aum stepped into the doorway from outside the room. Her eyes were instantly on mine and they never wavered as I approached. In her hands she held something that she gave to me: a small homemade card with a heart drawn on the cover. This was the first real contact I'd had with her in weeks and I knew it would probably be my last. So I took her hands in mine and said with as much affection as I could: *"Puak row rak kun."* We love you.

Aum spoke softly, her eyes locked on mine: "I love *kun,* too." A huge smile lit her face and her eyes exploded with joy. Then she walked down the hall and out of our lives forever.

There is so much we discovered in Thailand, so much we came to know and love, so much that we will never know; but one thing is certain. More than a family dinner for three dollars, more than extreme natural beauty, it is the people of Thailand that are its greatest treasure. Beyond welcome, beyond kindness, they exude a love and respect that are impossible to miss. It was as clear as the pencil printing on Aum's card, a sentiment that was echoed by so many of our new and unforgettable Nong Kha friends:

Aum love John
Aum love Traza
Aum love Jackson
Aum love Lohkan

Part Five

THE GOOD SHEPHERD AGRICULTURAL MISSION

I have come to realize more and more that the greatest disease and the greatest suffering is to be unwanted, unloved, uncared for, to be shunned by everybody, to be just nobody (to no one).

—MOTHER TERESA

39

THE FARM

When we stepped off the plane in New Delhi and onto the tarmac, it was 108 degrees Fahrenheit at 10:15 in the evening. Thankfully, Clifton was waiting for us—easy to spot, as he was the only white face in the terminal. Clifton was a twenty-five-year-old Tasmanian native and the deputy director of the Good Shepherd Agricultural Mission. The Farm, as it's called, is a Christian orphanage with one hundred kids, and I found it just four days before we landed in India. When I could not procrastinate the planning of our next stop any longer, I typed the words "India" and "orphanage" into Google and there was the Farm, first in line. After a single email, Clifton encouraged us to visit and stay for as long as we wanted. He even offered to pick us up at the airport, which—when you're landing in the late-night insanity of Delhi—was the kind of hospitality volunteers dream about on the road.

The Farm is eight hours due east of Delhi in the town of Banbasa, only six miles from the border with Nepal. On the orphanage website, the kids looked cute and happy and the surrounding jungle looked intriguing. When I wrote and asked Clifton if he ever saw any animals in the wild, his response was both exciting and a little scary. "In the last week," he wrote back, "I have seen a couple elephants, a tiger, and a leopard. Not to mention buffalo, stray dogs, and cows up the wazoo!"

After a quick hello, Clifton guided us out into the heat, past a hundred insistent men all clamoring to give us a taxi ride, and into his waiting car where the air-conditioning was already running. Clifton and his driver, Robert, sat up front while Traca, Jackson, and I took the backseat. Logan got stuck in the far back, and all our packs were roped to the roof. Once we were all settled in, we pulled out into the traffic.

"Traffic" is not really the right word to describe the commotion on the roads of Delhi. In America, "traffic" brings to mind a certain order. It may be jammed and snarled, but there are rules that drivers follow and laws that are enforced. In India, however, such details appear to be optional. First imagine cars, trucks, bicycles, motorcycles, three-wheeled taxis, pedestrians, dogs, and cows all moving in all directions at once. Then imagine no speed limits or lane markers or traffic lights, with everyone honking and passing through clouds of noxious air and intense heat at all hours of the day and night. Into this free-for-all, we headed east. Traca—who drives carefully and patiently at home—was forced to practice a new level of surrender as we weaved and raced our way through the tangle of flesh and metal and darkness. When it was over, she said that it had been the most exhausting trip of her life.

It took a good two hours to get free of Delhi's crush of humanity, but even then the roads were packed with cars, and every car was packed with people. Clifton said they were pilgrims, all heading to Garhmuktesar to participate in a *mela*. This particular *mela* was a mass dip in the Ganges River. Hindus believe you can cleanse your karma by submerging in the brown waters of Mother Ganga—and certainly, many people were eager to participate. Turns out we had arrived in India on the eve of just such a celebration, and as we passed through Garhmuktesar around one in the morning, fires were burning, people were everywhere, and an all-night carnival was growing by the minute.

The largest *mela* ever recorded was the Kumbh Mela of 2013, when more than a hundred million faithful turned up for the ceremonial dipping. By comparison, the *mela* in Garhmuktesar would attract only a paltry one million people, a small event by Indian standards. Still, as we drove through miles of impromptu campsites, countless thousands of people were arriving, claiming a space wherever they could find it. Some were even sleeping on the sides of the Ganga Bridge, a modest four-hundred-foot arch that spanned a narrow point in the mighty river. As we slowly made our way across the bridge, hundreds of souls were already lying down for the night, their bodies packed together, their heads mere inches from our passing tires.

Apparently, people sleeping on the side of the road are not an unusual sight in India. At one point, we pulled off onto the dirt shoulder for Robert to take a quick bathroom break and stopped a car's length away from a human body. "The sad thing," Clifton told us, "is that people can lie like that for days before anyone realizes they're dead." Thankfully, this person moved slightly as we waited for Robert to return, which was more of a relief than it probably should have been considering the fact that she was an old woman lying facedown in the dust.

We stopped for chai (sweet milky tea) every few hours to keep Robert awake, and I was always amazed that these roadside teahouses were open at all. Three o'clock in the morning and people were milling about, selling snacks and hand-woven stools or hand-carved statues or whatever. One guy at a bootleg DVD stand was fast asleep at his counter, but his lights were on and he was physically at his post, just in case some passing traveler desperately required a pirated copy of *Sleepless in Seattle* before sunrise.

As for the road itself, the main route from Delhi to Banbasa may look like a highway on any road map you might check, but it's not. Four lanes become two without warning, then two become one with two-way traffic, and one occasionally turns into a dirt off-ramp that rumbles through a wreck of a town before widening back into four lanes again. Potholes appear to be the only consistent feature.

Logan definitely had the worst seat on this trip, tucked in the back as he was. At one stop, I got out of the car to stretch my legs and found him on his back, legs bent and up in the unflattering "taking a bath in a short tub" pose. He later said he actually managed to sleep a little bit, though how he ever got comfortable in the dead bug position is beyond me.

As the hours and miles ticked by, there was plenty of time to talk, and in the smallest hours of the night, Clifton told us about his life and the orphanage he was helping to run. The Farm had been founded by his grandfather, Maxton Strong, in 1948, the year after Indian independence. Max was originally from the United States, a Presbyterian missionary and a professor of agricultural engineering. His decision to move to India was both practical and spiritual: to create a place where aspiring young farmers could learn valuable skills . . . and

hopefully come to Jesus in the process. When the new Indian government offered him 160 acres of untouched fertile land on permanent
lease, Max and his wife, Shirley, packed up their three kids and hit
the jungle.

In the early years, life on the Farm was harsh. The untamed land
needed to be cleared, wild animals—like tigers and deadly snakes—
roamed the property, and malaria was a constant threat. Tragically,
two of the Strong children died in the jungle, one from fever, one from
a tractor accident. Only Clifton's mother, Maxine, managed to sur-
vive.

Years later, Maxine married a visiting volunteer named Rick Shipway. By then, the Mission had started caring for a few orphaned children who came their way, and soon Rick and Maxine added a few
biological children of their own to the mix, Clifton among them.

Clifton spent some time on the Farm as a young boy and made
friends with many of the orphans. But when his parents had visa problems and were forced to leave India, the Shipway family moved to
Tasmania, the large island off the southern coast of Australia, which
was Rick's home country. Without tropical diseases or lurking predators, life was easy Down Under, and Clifton thrived. By the time he
graduated from high school, he was a happy self-described nerd. He
landed a great job as a computer support officer with the Australian
Education Department, making heaps of money and playing *World of
Warcraft* in his spare time. He was living every computer geek's dream,
but all that changed in 2003 when his grandfather, Maxton, died and
Clifton and his parents reconnected with India.

"What we found was pure evil," Clifton said. The Mission he had
known as a child, where God's love and children's laughter echoed
through the jungle, was gone. In its place, a handful of Maxton's former Indian employees had claimed the property and were running it
as a brutal institution. Children were being beaten, starved, locked in
airless rooms, abused in every way imaginable. Orphans who lived
through this period tell of eating grass to feel full, eating mud, eating
chalk. Resources were being hoarded by the staff, and the kids were
being used as servants. Pedophiles lived on the grounds. Something
had to be done.

On April 7, 2004, at the age of just nineteen, Clifton arrived at the Farm. He brought his muscle-bound cousin Max for backup, and Max brought a baseball bat for the same reason. Together, they walked into the orphanage office and issued a warning. "We are taking over as of now," Clifton said. "If you're with us, fine. If you're not, you have thirty seconds to leave the property." Sensing the sincerity in Clifton's eyes, maybe seeing the grain of Max's bat and the heft of his biceps, most of the staff ran for their lives. Just like that, the evil regime was vanquished! Clifton didn't know how he was going to manage it at the time or exactly what he was in for, but there was no going back. Max flew home, but Clifton and his parents stayed. A hundred Indian children were now counting on them.

At an age when most young hackers were content to plug into their computers and disappear from reality, maybe shoot cartoon Nazis or aliens or whatever popped up on-screen, Clifton dug his feet into the rain-soaked mud of Strong Farm and got to work. In time, he married Priscilla, an Indian woman and former Mission orphan he had known as a child. Now he and Priscilla run the orphanage along with Clifton's ailing mother, Maxine, and his jack-of-all-trades father, Rick. "I plan to spend the rest of my life here," Clifton told us. "You'll see. You won't want to leave."

It was six in the morning—eight hours after arriving in Delhi and a full twenty-four hours since our departure from Bangkok—by the time we pulled onto the Strong Farm property. The Farm consists of a dozen yellow brick buildings around an open courtyard. Set back from the road and surrounded by rice fields, it's a little oasis in the vast Indian chaos. But on the morning we arrived, we had no time to look around; the monsoon was about to begin. Every year, torrential rains cover most of India after months of complete dryness, and as we rolled to a stop, the literal first drops of the rainy season began to fall. We hurried to pull our luggage off the roof of Clifton's car, then scrambled up the steps to our second-story guest quarters just as the sky opened and the parched earth breathed its first sigh of the year—more salvation for this small corner of the world.

I crashed for four hours, completely delirious from lack of sleep, then woke up with no idea where I was. The room in which I found myself was simple; there was a queen-sized bed, a small desk by a window, a spinning fan overhead, and a picture of Jesus looking down from the wall. Traca was still deep asleep beside me. It wasn't until I heard all the children playing and shouting outside that the pieces of our new volunteer project came back together for me in a rush . . . *orphanage, India, one hundred kids.* It actually made me a little nervous.

As exciting as it can be to move from country to country, it can also be nerve-racking. You can read websites and send emails, but you never really know what you're getting into. What will you actually be doing? Will you be of any real use? Will you fit in with the program? The staff? And on a strictly junior high school level: Will these people like you?

I got out of bed and moved to a long red curtain gently fluttering in a warm wind. It was our new front door. Beyond it were our new balcony and a tangle of overlapping voices.

Outside, the rain had stopped. Puddles were everywhere and the humidity was intense, like a sauna. For a few minutes, I watched games of tag, general running around, the usual playground drill. Then I took a deep breath. On our long drive from Delhi, I'd asked Clifton what he wanted us to do at the Farm, and his answer was simple. "Just love the kids," he said.

So that's what I set out to do.

It is perhaps the greatest power we all have. We can't control the results or guarantee the reaction we'll get. But we can show up and we can try. Even if we're nervous. Even if we feel unqualified. With that in mind, I walked down the steps, across the courtyard, and into the swirl of orphanage life.

Just love the kids, I reminded myself as the first children began running toward me.

40

JOB

ACCORDING TO THE MOST RECENT UNICEF FIGURES, THERE ARE somewhere around thirty-one million orphans in India alone. This statistic is an estimate, so who knows how many there actually are. No doubt the real number is higher, but thirty-one million is still a big number, way too big to imagine. Thirty-one million is twice as many people as every man, woman, and child in the six states that make up New England. It's as if the entire states of Texas and Colorado or all of Scandinavia and Costa Rica were inhabited by orphaned children. It's staggering to think of them all at once and easy to picture them as a faceless horde of dirty, helpless, hungry humanity. But as we discovered at the Farm, one by one, one face at a time, these kids are not only individuals, they are downright beautiful.

One of the first children I met was Cynthia. She was three years old. She talked like a cartoon mouse, laughed like a pixie on helium, and entertained visitors with cuter-than-cute improv dancing each evening at dinner. Why her mother threw her away—tossing her into a storm drain shortly after her birth—is a mystery. Luckily, a stubborn branch caught Cynthia on her way downstream, where she was rescued by her grandmother and brought to the Farm.

Not all children arrived in such a biblical manner, plucked like Moses from the river of fate. Most just came out of necessity, like Saloni and her twin sister, Shivani. When we met them, they were three months old and the smallest members of the Strong Farm family. Apparently, they were brought to the Farm by their mother when they were just days old. They were the eleventh and twelfth girls born into a family desperate for a son, and there simply was not room or love for them at home.

"You want them? Yes?" the girl's mother asked when she showed up at the Mission gate one morning. She offered her daughters casually, like two small loaves of excess bread.

At first, Clifton refused. With resources stretched to the limit, he does not and cannot accept every child who is offered to him, and the high-maintenance care required by two painfully small infants was simply too much for the Farm to take on. But a month later, when the twins' mother returned, her daughters now even smaller and appearing to be near death, Clifton relented. From that day on, the girls became part of the family, lucky beyond words, loved and nurtured by hundreds of hands, showered with affection from sunup to sundown.

And then there was Job.

At three days old, Job was dropped at the orphanage. Not an orphan per se, just abandoned like so many children in India. When we met him, he was thirteen and didn't remember any of the dark days at the Farm. He was only seven when Clifton and company stormed the gates, and he was by all accounts a terror in his own right at the time. He killed chickens, stole eggs, and lied; he punched, kicked, and generally bullied the kids around him. Though he was small, Job was the leader of the Small Boys, as they were called (boys from ages nine to fourteen), and he had an intensity that all small leaders share. He also had a quick tongue, a keen mind, and a fire within him that was impossible to ignore.

The first time Job and I were together, I was with Logan and the Small Boys, hiking through the jungle behind the Farm property. The boys all spoke excellent English, having been raised with the language and taught it in school, and they were chatting away about the dangers we might encounter on our walk.

"Elephants, we can see," one boy said with a big grin.

"And snakes and tigers," another boy said, as if promising me a treat.

With this in mind, I was on high alert when we came across two water buffalo standing directly in our path. Water buffalo are notoriously unpredictable; they can be stubborn, they have sharp horns, they often charge. These particular beasts also had long strands of drool that stretched from their mouths nearly to the ground, making them look far from intelligent and somehow more menacing. With small children in my care, I wondered how best to continue. Should we attempt to go around the animals? Should we turn back? But before I could make a move, Job leaped into action. He grabbed a stick off the ground and dashed forward, all seventy-five pounds of him.

"*Ha! Haaa!*" he shouted, waving the stick like a madman, slashing the air.

The water buffalo could easily have trampled him, gored him. But they didn't. They ran as if their tails were on fire. And Job wasn't content just to clear the path, either. He chased them off the trail and across a dry riverbed, shouting all the while, stopping only when they were well out of range, turning to scream triumphantly back at me like a fearless warrior at the end of a battle.

From that moment on, Job acted as my protector and loyal servant, though really it was just his over-the-top way of showing that he liked me. He gave up his seat whenever I entered a room, insisted I sit near a fan if it was hot, scrambled to find me an umbrella in the rain, loved to carry my camera bag, always gave me his mango at lunch, and positively refused any similar treatment from me. Quite honestly, it got to be a little much at times.

I walked down the stairs of our guesthouse one afternoon to find Job waiting for me, holding a long, wide palm branch that he immediately placed over my head. As always, he called me Uncle, the term of respect all Farm kids use for older male visitors.

"Good morning, Uncle," he said. "Please. The sun mustn't touch you." As we walked, he held the palm branch so I was shaded, shuffling along beside me.

"I really don't want you to do that, Job," I said. "You're my friend, not my slave."

"Please, Uncle. The sun is hot. Just keep walking," Job instructed.

I stopped walking and looked down at this earnest little kid who was carefully adjusting the shade between my face and the sun. "Job. I would like you to put that down, please," I said.

Job refused. "Sorry, Uncle. Your safety is my top concern. I cannot place you in any danger." He was joking, of course, but he was playing out this charade with total seriousness and a bodyguard's intensity.

So I asked him: "What can I say to get you to put that down?"

And he said: "If you love me, put it down."

So I said it. "If you love me, put it down." And instantly, Job threw the branch as far away as his small arms could launch it.

"Get away from me!" he shouted in mock disgust at the discarded palm. "I will never touch you again in my life!"

Then Job turned to me, smiled, and hugged me around the waist in a death grip of affection. "Good morning, Uncle," he said.

I watched him sometimes when he was moving around the Mission—barking orders, directing kids like a traffic cop—and I wondered where his intensity would take him. When I asked him one day what he wanted to be when he grew up, he said: a soldier.

"But not just a soldier, Uncle," he went on. "What is the highest job for a soldier in America?"

I said, "I'm not sure. Maybe the Secretary of Defense."

"He is rich, Uncle? This Secretary of the Defenses?"

I said, "Yeah. Probably pretty rich."

"Then this is what I will be. I will be the Secretary of the Defenses in America and when I am, I will have guards that follow me and everyone will stand to see me and I will take my own helicopter and I will fly to your house and I will give you a job that will pay one *lakh* every year. You would like this job, Uncle?"

One lakh is 100,000 rupees, or about $2,250.

"Yes, Job," I said. "I would like that very much."

These were not the orphans I was expecting at all. They weren't the hollowed-out castoffs who needed me to fill them up, not a bunch of statistics on a regrettable and overwhelming page. They were just children—happy children, for the most part, who poured their love into me day after day, filling me up as if I was the one who was empty.

We all gravitated toward certain kids at the beginning. Jackson was fast friends with many of the Older Girls, helping them out with their endless chores during the day, then attending sweaty Bollywood dance parties in their rooms before bed. Logan was an instant hit with the Small Boys, who idolized him as if he were one of the professional wrestlers on the dog-eared trading cards they loved so much. Traca was a constant source of love around the Farm, particularly for the youngest children in the nursery, who never left her open arms empty for long.

And I had Job.

I saw him in the courtyard after the ten o'clock tea break one day. He was wearing his school uniform: yellow shirt, green pants, green tie that was just a strip of plaid cloth on an elastic band. Happy children splashed in puddles all around him, but Job stood perfectly still, like an island, looking directly at me. At that moment, I was surrounded by other children, all wanting to be seen and held. But I excused myself and made my way to Job.

"What's up, buddy?" I said. "How's school going?"

"I am missing you today, Uncle," he said.

Then he wrapped his arms around my waist. It wasn't the dramatic act of a show-off. He didn't move or speak. When I looked down at him, his eyes were closed. His clothes were still drenched from the torrential rains that morning, but he didn't mind, and neither did I. I just stood there in the playground with him, closed my eyes, too, and listened to the children laughing all around us.

41

THE OLDER GIRLS

I don't usually think of myself as old, but I heard that word a lot at the Farm.

One day I was hanging out with the Small Girls, a raucous band of junior divas who loved to climb and tease and spin like tops. On that particular day, I was sitting on the ground talking with a bunch of them, but three of my favorites—Jimika, Anthea, and Khushboo— were standing beside me, looking down at the top of my head.

"Oh. Look at Uncle's hair," Jimika said, as if discovering a fascinating surprise. "So thin."

"You can see his skin," Khushboo said, amazed to find my scalp when she pushed my hair aside.

"So white, his hair is," Anthea said, though I'm sure she meant "distinguished silver."

"Old," Jimika said. "Very old."

I heard the *o* word again a few days later when I was talking to Clifton about the Older Girls.

The Older Girls ranged in age from fourteen to nineteen, and they were perhaps the most isolated group on the Farm. In India, in general, young women are sheltered, hemmed in by a conservative society and bound by codes of modesty and propriety that, by comparison, make your average American teen girl look like a free love hippie tramp. In the pre-Clifton era at the orphanage, girls were beaten for even *looking* at a boy, much less talking to or touching one. Even today, conforming to Indian expectations, boys are not allowed to mingle freely with girls; the Older Boys live on one side of the Farm, the Older Girls on the other. There are a few officially sanctioned coed hours during the week, but even then, no physical contact is permitted.

At only twenty-five years old, even Clifton had to keep a respectable distance from the girls, as did all the young male volunteers who passed through the Farm each year. As a result, the Older Girls were raised almost exclusively by women, from their teachers at school to the housemothers in their dormitory. And since women did all the domestic work in India, they were further segregated into a tight sisterhood of cooking, dishes, laundry, and cleaning, all of them hungry, I assumed—as all daughters are—for a little fatherly affection.

"Some girls fall in love with the first man who gives them a sweetie," one of them told me, which had me concerned right from the start.

When one of the girls playfully called me Daddy, I talked with Clifton about it. I didn't want to step on any cultural toes, but Clifton reminded me who I was. "Don't worry about it," he said. "You're old. Go for it."

Old.

Once the momentary sting to my young-feeling ego was gone, I found my advanced age was a huge asset, freeing me to get to know and interact with these amazing girls in ways they seemed to deeply enjoy.

So I borrowed Clifton's guitar, went into the kitchen while they were making *chapatis,* and sang to them. The bare cement room was hot and smoky, and into this cavernous space I held nothing back, belting out every song they requested, making the songs up if I had to just to hear them laugh. Pop songs, Christian standards, Sunday school ditties I'd learned as a child—I did my best with whatever they wanted to hear.

> *Amazing grace, how sweet the sound,*
> *That saved a wretch like me!*

Some days after lunch, I helped them clean the kitchen floor, though many of the girls found this hard to watch. "Don't do it, Uncle," they cried. "It is so girlie!" But I didn't care. As they laughed and covered their mouths in mock embarrassment, I swept and scrubbed and got down on my knees with a spatula to scrape away dried dough.

"Uncle is one of us," one of the girls said, smiling sweetly at me.

"Uncle is an Auntie," another girl teased, and the room exploded with shock, shrieks, and apologies that had me physically rolling on the floor laughing.

Once we got to know one another, we started meeting most evenings after dinner. While the other children ran around outside, burning off the last energy of the day, the Older Girls and I sat on the sidelines and asked one another questions.

"Tell us about your home, Uncle," they would say, never tiring of the details of ordinary family life. And so I told them how we spent Christmas and what we did for birthdays and what our house looked like and on and on. In return, they told me stories of their lives: boys they fancied, dreams they had, how they came to the Farm, what their early days were like.

"Oh, the Aunties used to beat us so badly," Shirley said with a laugh.

The Aunties were the Indian housemothers who had apparently taken sadistic delight in acting as evil prison guards before Clifton and company vanquished them.

"And not just with a switch," Vanita chimed in. "With a stick. Round as *this*." She made a circle as large as her thumb and index finger would allow.

"For no reason, Uncle," Hope added. Hope was a sweet-faced Older Girl with sparkling eyes and a near-constant smile. "The Aunties would hold me underwater, in a tub, until I will drown and all the while she is beating and beating me." At which point Hope started laughing, seemingly tickled to the tips of her toes at this memory.

"Why are you laughing?" I asked. "That sounds horrible."

More laughter from Hope, with many of the Older Girls joining in. I'm sure there's a psychological reason for this. Or maybe it's like Robert Frost—later quoted by Jimmy Buffett—once wrote: *If we couldn't laugh, we would all go insane*. Whatever the source, the pattern was always the same: horror story followed by lots of laughter. Things like:

"They would shave our heads so we would not be so proud." *Laugh.*

"They would lock us in at night with no fan and no toilet." *Laugh.*

"And we were fed one month only radishes." *Laugh.*

"Radish for lunch and radish greens for supper." *Laugh*.

"My hand was broken five times, Uncle." *Big laugh*.

"And they would land us, anywhere." *Laugh*. (By "land" she meant "hit," as in with a stick.)

"On the head. On the face, they would land us." *Laugh*.

"Especially after church. That was the worst." *More laughter*.

It seems insane, of course. Clearly, love is a better guiding principle for a Christian orphanage, but back in the dark days, the Aunties ruled the Farm with Old Testament wrath, beating the love of God into these sinful little creatures. Church was a particularly dangerous place, regimented with many rules that were easy to break. If a young girl, say, smiled or laughed or—heaven forbid!—glanced at a boy, the Aunties would take note and dole out the punishment after the final Amen.

"They would say this to us," Hope added. "They would say, 'I see the Devil in you. I see Satan in your eyes.' And they would land us." *Laugh*.

As a former Farm girl herself, Clifton's wife, Priscilla, knew all about this. "It did not matter where," she told me. "I once received the stick in my eye and it swelled so badly, I could not see." This happened when Priscilla was ten years old, and she recalled the incident with the typical—if inexplicable—abused orphan smile on her face, a smile that held even as the story got worse. As it happened, visitors were due to arrive shortly after the beating. Naturally, to avoid the appearance of blatant child abuse, the Aunties locked Priscilla in a room, without treatment or even windows, for an entire month. She was not let out for school or play or even church. She was fed three meager meals a day and kept caged like an animal, locked in a sweltering room with her eye swollen shut and only a bucket in the corner in which to relieve herself.

She healed, thank God, and as Clifton's wife, she now lives a life of beauty, meaning, and relative luxury, far beyond what her maltreated ten-year-old mind ever dreamed of, I'm sure. So maybe that's why she can smile when she talks about the past. Maybe when life improves so much, you laugh out of sheer relief.

It wasn't all bad, I guess. When they weren't comparing their childhood bruises, there was friendship and mischief and God to see them through. Still, the constant smiling at the memory of such terrible abuse was a little hard to swallow, so I asked them directly.

"You seem happy now. But *are* you happy?"

"Oh, yes," everyone said in unison. Like happy robots.

I dug deeper. "Really?" I asked. "Not here in front of me or in front of the staff. But when you are alone. When you are in your own room and you are being totally honest with yourself, are you happy?"

"Yes, Uncle," they said. "We are happy."

And I believed them. Most of them.

Among the Older Girls, there was one in particular who seemed to be the most traumatized of them all. I'll call her Beti, which means "daughter" in Hindi. When she was small, starting around the age of ten, Beti's father began prostituting her out for small things he needed from the market: a bag of sugar, a new shovel, a pair of shoes. He once even turned his beautiful daughter over to some disgusting shopkeeper in exchange for a single beer. Clearly, something had to be done.

After enduring the knowledge of her sexual abuse for many years, Beti's village finally got together and, in an amazing act of collective conscience, removed her from her home, threatened her father should he attempt to retrieve her, and brought her, at age fourteen, to the Farm.

By the time we met her, Beti was sixteen: tall, quite pretty, though still deeply damaged. In many ways, she acted like a child. She could not retain the simplest information, so she did not attend school. She rarely spoke and was understandably distrustful of men. Most of the time, she stood in the background of any activity, alone in her own private world, not talking to anyone but herself.

Then one day, as I sat in the shade reading a children's book to a few of the Small Girls, Beti approached. She was wary, like a frightened animal, so I just kept reading, using the silly character voices that the Small Girls liked. It took a while, but soon Beti was sitting with us, not laughing at first, but not leaving, either.

From then on, we read together each day, the same way I used to read to my own children, and I pulled out all my old tricks. I played every part with exaggerated gusto, milked laughs like an eager come-dian, even tickled Beti's chin when necessary to keep the laugh going.

"Again," Beti would say softly when the story ended, and I would start from the beginning.

Soon we were walking together, sometimes arm in arm, some-times hand in hand. In the evenings, when the Older Girls and I had our talking time, Beti started joining us, always sitting beside me with her head on my shoulder. In time, she even started looking me in the eye, briefly at first, but long enough for me to take her face in my hands and tell her—as easily as I told my own daughter—that she was beautiful, that she was special, that she was loved.

"I love you, Papa," Beti said to me one night before bed.

In that moment, I have never been so happy to be so old.

42

SHY BOY AND BIRTHDAY GIRL

FARM LIFE WAS SO ACTIVE, WITH SO MANY SEPARATE DEMANDS FOR OUR individual attention, that my family and I usually split up during the day and focused on the people and activities that most appealed to each of us.

Aside from helping out wherever and whenever she was needed (doing dishes, washing clothes in the laundry, baking bread), Traca's pet project on the Farm was yoga. In the West, yoga is a relatively new phenomenon, a trendy fitness alternative complete with designer clothing labels and recycled earth-friendly mats. But India is yoga's birthplace, with roots that go back five thousand years or more. It was created as a spiritual practice, a way to open the body and still the mind in preparation for meditation and, ultimately, enlightenment. For a long-term practitioner like Traca, a trip to India was nothing short of a pilgrimage, and in her spare time, she scoured the Internet, hoping to find the perfect ashram for an authentic Indian yoga retreat. She also shared her passion with the orphanage, introducing yoga to a pocket of India that found it either comical or, in some cases, blasphemous.

After purchasing some yoga mats in a nearby market, an item so rarely requested that they had to be imported by a local shopkeeper from a contact in Nepal, Traca led a daily beginners' class in the Small Girls' courtyard. Each day before dinner, young children, older staff women, and an assortment of Farm girls came to stretch, laugh, and— well, mostly laugh. All the strange poses were pure comedy for most of those in attendance, and while there wasn't a lot of enlightenment going on that I could see, Traca didn't mind at all.

"I'm just planting seeds," she said. "That's all I can do."

Her efforts did manage to attract the attention of a guest preacher who stopped by the Farm one Sunday morning. The man was in his late twenties, Indian, wearing a carefully pressed shirt, a perfectly cinched tie, and a fresh convert's zeal. Though the impromptu chapel at the back of the dining hall was hot and the preacher was visibly sweating, it didn't stop him from tossing a bit of fire and a dash of brimstone on the seeds Traca had been planting.

"Some people may try to bring yoga to you," he warned, staring directly at me. "But beware! This is the first step toward the Devil!"

I'm sure he feared some kind of nefarious Hindu infiltration, but that was never Traca's intention. She was just trying to share some of the joy yoga had given to her, a joy that positively bubbled out of her at the Farm. I'd often see her walking slowly across the grounds, holding a child's hand in each of hers, with many eager hand-holders following in her wake. At these times, she seemed to be perfectly at home, at peace—and she said she felt it, too. "I could run an orphanage," she confessed to me one night, almost wistfully. "I *get* this."

Unfortunately, not everyone in the family felt so settled at the Farm, at least not at first.

Logan and Jackson led their own lives at the orphanage: making friends, helping out, playing games with the Small Boys and Girls. And though it all might have looked harmonious to a casual observer, I know it wasn't always easy for them.

Logan's biggest hurdle was the Older Girls. Coming from Thailand, where girls his age essentially bowed at his feet, swooned over his every antic, and openly adored him for simply being white and alive (and cute, no doubt), the Farm girls were a tougher crowd. For one thing, they spoke excellent English, so relationships based on mere swooning and fawning were—much to Logan's dismay—no longer necessary or available. The Older Girls were also, in spite of their Farm isolation, more worldly and complex than their Thai sisters. Perhaps as a result of being abandoned, many of them abused, they were no pushovers and initially they teased Logan as he had never been teased before.

"Hi, Shy Boy," they would say. Or "Good morning, Shy Boy." Or, the double whammy, "Why are you so shy, Shy Boy?"

At first, Logan didn't know how to handle them. He'd push back when he was teased, trying too hard to prove them wrong. But acting bold when you're not really feeling it was a posture the Older Girls saw right through.

"Shy Boy. Shy Boy. Shy Boy!" they hounded, driving Logan deeper into his shell.

"Are you enjoying the Shy Boy game?" I asked him one afternoon when I found him hunkered down in his room in the middle of the day.

"Oh, yeah," he said, looking up from a book. "I think it's nice." And by "nice" I could tell that he meant "terrible."

On the opposite side of the shy scale, Jackson struggled through a few obstacles of her own, most of them involving a seventeen-year-old girl named Jeevana. What Jack had done to piss Jeevana off was a mystery.

"Maybe it's the way Jackson rolled out *chapatis*?" one of the Older Girls speculated after Jack helped out in the kitchen one day and Jeevana rudely rejected every flattened ball of dough Jackson offered her.

I didn't think that was it. In fact, the more Jeevana huffed around, ignoring Jackson's repeated requests to talk, the more I thought the cause of the rift was something much deeper, some intangible insult that Jackson represented more than anything she had actually done.

I often wondered what we looked like to the children on the Farm. On one level that was both true and false, we probably looked rich. Though we had taken out a loan to finance our trip, the Farm kids knew and cared nothing about home equity lines of credit or mortgage refinancing. With our stories of other countries, our American roots, our freedom and resources to come and go, we must have appeared to be privileged beyond measure—and I suppose we were. On another level that was probably even more powerful, we were a family—the one thing every orphaned or abandoned child yearns for and by definition does not have. As father, mother, son, and daughter, I wondered if we shimmered like some dream come true as we strolled across the grounds. Maybe we reminded Jeevana of the family she'd lost, the daughter she would never be, the father and mother she would never have.

Or maybe she just liked a bit of drama.

As it is for high school girls the world over, drama was the juice—along with lip gloss and talk about boys—that kept the days on the Farm interesting. As far as Jackson was concerned, the drama meter spiked as her fifteenth birthday approached. Jeevana said she was not going to attend the party, and she repeated this to me every time we met as if I had zero short-term memory. Then, for no apparent reason, another Older Girl, Vari, jumped on the birthday boycott, proclaiming that she, too, was staying in her room on the night of the big bash. I asked the girls about this but they wouldn't answer. Whether they had a legitimate gripe with Jackson or they just enjoyed the power their refusal gave them, I never did find out.

Thankfully, the vast majority of girls were excited about the party and—on their own—got to work: making a Happy B-Day banner, baking a cake, assembling snacks and gifts, and creating what I'm sure will go down as the most memorable birthday celebration of Jackson's young life.

My personal favorite part of the party was the way Traca and I were treated. Rather than relegating Mom and Dad to some place at the back of the room or banishing us entirely from the festivities, as would happen at most American parties, the Older Girls set two extra seats at the head table. Jackson sat beside April (a Farm girl with the same birthday), and Traca and I sat on either side of them like honored guests. Leave it to orphans to know how to treat parents.

Like most birthday parties, this one had singing and presents and plates of food—though there was also end-of-the-world rain falling outside and a bat circling the room looking for insects and a way out. To make things even more interesting, as soon as I took my first bite of cake, the lights went off. This was a fairly typical occurrence. Most days, multiple times per day, the power would simply stop. Sometimes it was off for only a few minutes, sometimes for hours. In the heat of the day, no power made you appreciate the fan that had been spinning above your now-sweating head. In the sweltering night, an outage made sleeping all but impossible. At the party, it plunged us into total darkness. The space filled with the shrieks of the girls, and everyone moved to the exit, where a generator light was still shining.

What followed was the kind of party event that you simply cannot plan.

One by one, the kids ran out into the rain. Water from the roof drain came down like a fire hose and Logan took it on the head, grabbing girls around him and pulling them into the deluge. He looked so happy, so alive. Beside him, Jackson danced in the deafening downpour, splashing in shin-deep puddles. Traca and I were standing off to the side, dry beneath a protective overhang, when Jeevana and Vari walked past us. I wondered if the two of them, the only birthday party holdouts, had come to make some further protest . . . but they hadn't. After a brief stubborn pause, they raced into the rain with the others, hugging their sopping friends, hugging Jackson, all of them laughing directly into the monsoon's face. Whatever magic was in the air, it washed all lingering drama away for good.

Logan won the Older Girls over that night as well, not by being brash and bold, just by being himself. "We've cured him of his shyness," one of his worst tormenters said to me the next day, and perhaps they did help a bit. Either way, Logan definitely made an impression. Three of the Older Girls told me privately that they were in love with him. One even had a dream that she married him and they had twin baby girls. Another, who was only thirteen, worried that she was too young for him.

"Not a problem," I told her. "When Logan's twenty-four and he comes back here, you'll be twenty. That'll be fine."

She laughed, but her smile showed a bit of relief as well.

43

DOWN BY THE RIVERSIDE

"CAN WE PLEASE WALK IN A GROUP?" JOB SHOUTED.

We were making our way between the rice fields behind the Farm. The other Small Boys were up ahead with Logan. We were taking them for a swim in a nearby river but I was moving slowly. I had Job and a boy named Rohit with me. Rohit had a terrible tumor on one side of his face. Even so, he was quick to smile, holding one of my hands while Job held the other.

"It's so sad for Rohit," Job said. "He has cansa. Uncle Rick says he will die and we shouldn't tell him. So sad, it is."

Rohit certainly heard all of this. The path was quiet. The word "cansa" hung in the air like a crow.

"Let's talk about something else," I said, squeezing Rohit's hand. Though his tumor crowded half his mouth, Rohit smiled as best he could. He was probably twelve.

"Okay," Job agreed. "We will talk of George Bush. You like George Bush, Uncle?"

"Not really," I said, which was an understatement as vast as India itself.

"He is a great leader," Job insisted. "And Obama is a baby killer."

"What? Who told you that?"

"Auntie Maxine," Job said as if that settled it. "He kills babies. You like this, Uncle?"

Auntie Maxine was Clifton's mother. She was a frail woman in her late sixties with white hair and a pale complexion. Though she was confined to a wheelchair or bedridden most days, she always made time for any children who needed her, acting as surrogate mother for all the Farm kids. "I'm so unworthy to be called mother," she told me one day with characteristic humility—though she certainly deserved the title. She was the heart at the center of the Farm, offering not only her endless supply of love but her fierce Christian faith and her right-wing conservatism where political matters were concerned. It wasn't my way of thinking—I voted for Obama—but I wasn't the one laying down my life to raise unwanted children.

"Let's change the subject," I said to Job. Arguing was futile.

"Can we please walk in a group!" Job bellowed again. The other Small Boys were getting farther and farther ahead of us. They did not reply. *"Uncle is getting very angry!"*

"No, I'm not!" I shouted.

We walked on, entering a tiny village. There were no more than ten houses, all made of mud. Small children were everywhere, dressed in filthy clothes but smiling and waving at me as if I were their favorite parade float.

"Why do you wear this necklace, Uncle?" Job asked, pointing at me.

"What, this?" It was a small silver Ganesh medallion on a black leather string. Ganesh, the elephant-headed Hindu god, is thought to be the remover of obstacles, but I didn't wear the icon for that reason. I wore it because Traca had given it to me and because I liked it. I said as much.

"It is Hindu, Uncle," Job said with contempt.

"I know. I like Hindu," I said.

"You should take that idol from around your neck, shoot it with a gun, destroy it, and bury it in the ground."

I looked down at Job and he smiled. It was like taking a stroll with Glenn Beck Jr.

It always amazes me to hear young people be so certain, especially where religion is concerned. When I was Job's age, I really struggled with Christianity. Even though I, too, had it spoon-fed to me by an unwavering and faith-filled mother, I was full of questions.

I remember talking privately with my pastor after my last confirmation class. I knew all the official explanations, had grown up with the stories my whole life. But there were some parts of it I simply did not understand.

"How does Jesus dying on the cross save me from my sins?" I

asked, feeling almost guilty for saying it out loud. "And what could I do in my short life that would be so bad anyway? If my soul is eternal, this life is just a blink of an eye, isn't it? So why would God, who loves me so much, send me to hell just for being unsure?"

Beyond all of this, the big question that loomed over me was: Did I accept Jesus as my personal savior? When I was called to the front of the church the following Sunday, before the congregation and God and, most important, my mother, how would I answer? If I had doubts, shouldn't I wait? If I wasn't planning to take it as seriously as it was being proposed, shouldn't I keep looking? God didn't want a yes-man. He wanted a believer. Didn't he?

I honestly can't remember exactly what my pastor's answer was, but what I heard was something like this: "Even if you have a few doubts, John, you might as well go through with it. Just in case, right?"

And so when Sunday rolled around, I stood beside the pulpit in my blue blazer and my braces, and when the big question was posed, while the rest of my confirmation class said "Yes!" in unison, I just made a nondescript sound that would *look* like "Yes!" to my mom sitting in her pew, but which I knew in my heart meant "Not just yet, thanks."

At the river, the boys stripped down to their underwear and dived in. The sun was intense, the humidity was high, and the river was brown and choppy.

The first boy in was Clifford, a polite, gentle twelve-year-old, and he came up shouting. "So hot, it is," he said, visibly uncomfortable. Indeed, when I dipped my toe in, the water felt like a bath, not refreshing at all. Worse, the surface was covered with thousands of small dead fish, a massacre that was never explained. Recent rains also had the water flowing quite fast and deep in some spots, and as the boys fanned out to play, Logan and I kept watch. To take it all in, I climbed up on a high bank and hoped my rescue services would not be needed. Not only am I a terrible swimmer—a champion sinker, in fact—but I was not eager to submerge my body in warm dead-fish murk, either.

It's amazing more things didn't go wrong at the Farm. With a hundred kids to take care of, a certain hands-off attitude was necessary, a solid faith required to get through the day. There were no hovering soccer moms, no antibacterial soap, no mosquito nets, limited medical care—though supplies were on hand if necessary and a hospital was not far away. And unlike American parents who worried about un-likely dangers like H1N1 flu and child abductors, the Farm kids had real dangers to contend with every day.

One afternoon, a large snake found its way into the Older Boys' hostel. It just crawled under the door gap and curled up in the corner, coiled and ready to strike. I was in my room when Ikindar, one of the Small Boys, burst in. "Uncle! Uncle! Get your camera! There is a cobra!"

I ran across the courtyard toward a tight group of boys, ready to snap a few pictures of this legendary Indian menace . . . but I was too late. Ikindar apologized for what I found. "Sorry, Uncle," he said. "We already killed it, but I thought you would like to see." Sure enough, the snake was dead, its head smashed to a bloody pulp.

This was just another day in the life of these kids. There were el-ephants, tigers, and leopards in the jungle, spiders, scorpions, God only knows what else—but all they could do was dive into each day. Sink or swim. No arm floaties for these guys.

"Uncle! Come. We have such an insect," Kamal shouted.

I was standing at my makeshift lifeguard perch. Off to my right, Kamal, Clifford, Job, and Rohit were huddled around some bug big enough to warrant their attention. Sonny, Ikindar, and Gordon were out in front, sitting in the rushing water. Amir was off to my left.

"Can you watch Amir?" I asked Logan. I could tell Logan, like me, was less than eager to take a dip in that hot brown broth of a river.

"I guess so," he said hesitantly, which I knew meant "If I have to."

He had to. Amir was unpredictable.

He was a tall, gangly boy with some kind of learning disability. His hands and arms made jerky palsy motions and his speech was slow, almost like a stammer but more like simple repetition. If I asked him to please stop slapping me on the back, Amir would just smile. "No no no no no no no no no," he'd say before winding up one of his oddly cocked arms and swinging again. He lacked coordination and almost certainly could not swim. Of all the boys, he was the one I was most worried about.

"Uncle! Job is trying to kill this insect!" Clifford yelled.

"I am not killing," Job protested, and I could hear the confrontation level rising.

So I climbed off my perch, scrambled along the bank, and hopped down to see what all the insect commotion was about. Turns out it was a very large grasshopper. I'm not sure if it was a locust, but that's what came to mind. Best of all, it was iridescent green with impressive horns and yellow spots. The group was divided as to its fate.

"Do not let them hurt it," Clifford said, very worried.

"I will splat it with my *chappal*," Job said, raising his rubber sandal more to frighten Clifford than to threaten the locust.

It was just an ordinary moment. Four boys in the sun. One mostly motionless insect. A riverbank.

That's when it happened.

I didn't see any of it. I was looking down at the bug, admiring it, when Amir went under. He must have waded out from shore to where the current was deeper and then lost his footing. Considering he was clumsy even on solid ground, this was not hard to imagine. Logan was looking in my direction when Ikindar screamed to him.

"Brother *bhai-ya*," he said, "Amir is drowning!"

By the time Logan turned, Amir was mostly under. All Logan saw was a flash of Amir's brown smiling face, his flightless arms flapping, and then he was swallowed by the brown current. Gone.

Reacting more than thinking, Logan dived in and swam through the fish, the murk, the potential disaster of that moment. The water was over his head and he had to struggle, but he somehow managed to find Amir, hook him with one arm, and haul him to the surface. Then he swam as hard as he could for shore, kicking, pulling, and finally dragging Amir up and onto the bank.

"I don't think he had any idea what was happening," Logan told me when I'd rejoined him and he'd described the rescue to me. By then, the danger was long past.

"Are you okay?" I asked him, holding him by his wet shoulders, sizing him up.

"Yeah," Logan said, trembling, the reality of what he'd just done finally hitting him.

I looked down at Amir, who was still sitting on the muddy bank. He was drenched, wiping his eyes, a huge smile on his face. Thank God.

Later, we walked back through the jungle, Job and Rohit and now Amir at my side. We passed water buffalo grazing off the path and approached a large puddle that was blocking our way.

"Stop!" Job ordered me. "We will make steps for you. Find stones!" he shouted, and Rohit and Amir began looking immediately.

I didn't want him building me a stepping-stone path, but there was no stopping him. I wasn't in a hurry, either.

"Can we please go?" I asked.

"Just a moment, Uncle. This will be much nicer," Job insisted, back in security guard mode.

As I waited for the rocks to be arranged, I looked up and saw the Small Boys walking with Logan. His clothes were drying in the sun and he was safe. They were all safe. In that moment, I said a humble prayer of thanks to whoever was watching over us.

"God is love," Job told me often, and I have no doubt he is right. He is the love that creates orphanages when the need for them arises. The love that dives in and rescues a boy who does not even realize he needs rescuing. He is the even the love that carefully gathers stones so a friend's feet don't get wet.

"We are falling farther behind," I said, and Job looked up, annoyed.

"Can we please walk in a group!"

44

FAITH

"Uncle John!" Job shouted from below my window. "Cana time, Uncle." *Cana* means "food." It was lunchtime.

"Just a minute," I yelled down. I hadn't quite finished reading in my room.

I'd been thinking a lot about Job—the biblical character, not the boy—and that led to my bedside Bible. I knew Job had his very own chapter in the Old Testament, but I couldn't remember any of his story. He was patient, right? The patience of Job, as the saying goes. But what was he being patient for? I had no idea.

"Uncle John!" Job shouted, sounding impatient to the point of desperation.

"Almost ready!" I called out as I turned the page, speed-reading.

As it's written, the Book of Job is one of those Bible lessons that drive me absolutely crazy. The gist of the story is this:

God is hanging out in Heaven when some angels come before Him. For a reason that's never explained, Satan also shows up. Why these two are spending time together is beyond me. God: the Almighty Creator of Heaven and Earth. Satan: the fallen angel and leader of the underworld. It's like Gandhi and Hitler getting together for a picnic . . . times infinity! Anyway, they're in the same room, talking about work, when God brings up Job.

"Hey, how 'bout that Job?" God brags. "Now, *there* is a faithful man."

Apparently, the world is filled with sinful disappointments and Job shines above all the rest of humanity. He's perfect with his burnt offerings, has the right amount of fear and trembling, just an all-around superstar when it comes to faith.

But Satan, being something of a Debbie Downer, dismisses God's pride with a wave of his pointy tail. "Job is only faithful because his life is easy," he says. "He'd drop you like a hot poker if things got bad."

God knows better. (Of course he does. He's God!) "Job would never desert me," He says with divine certainty . . . and this gives the Devil an idea.

"If you're so sure about Job," Satan says, hissing with sadistic delight, "why don't you let me test his faith?"

This is the part of the story that pisses me off. Accepting for a minute the absurdity of the whole setup, *God actually goes along with this idea!* He's got this one guy down on Earth, Job, who is so special, so devoted, and how does He repay him? He turns him over to the Devil on a casual bet.

"Okay," God says, as if he weren't capable of creating another universe at that moment or turning Satan into a moth for His heavenly butterfly collection. "You can do anything you want to Job. But just don't touch him."

So that's what the Devil does. He zips down to Earth in a cloud of black sulfur and starts destroying everything Job cares about: his five hundred oxen, his five hundred donkeys, his seven thousand sheep, his three thousand camels. Not satisfied with livestock, Satan then murders Job's seven sons and his three daughters. Ten children, dead and gone. All of this happens in the same *day*!

And what does Job do when he hears the news? He rips his robe, shaves his head in grief, and then falls to his knees in praise of God, the same God who sold him out to the Devil in the first place.

If this were the end of the story it would be maddening enough, but it's not.

Some time later, God has Satan over for another little meet and greet and the subject of Job comes up. "What did I say?" God gloats. "Is Job not the man?"

"Not bad," Satan admits, "but it doesn't prove anything." Here I picture the Devil leaning in close to God, his eyes flaming red, his dark heart clearly visible. "Give me his flesh and bones," he hisses, "and we'll see how long he lasts."

Keep in mind, Job has just lost all his wealth and his entire family in a pointless ego duel, but is that enough for the Source of All

Love and Compassion in the Cosmos? No, sir. God thinks this new wager sounds like another good idea. "Okay," He concedes. "Take him. But don't *kill* him." Because, of course, how can someone praise you if they're dead, right?

So once again, the Devil teleports back to Job's side, probably puzzles over his bag of tricks for a minute or two, and then inflicts a plague of painful open sores on every inch of Job's body, from the bottoms of his feet to the top of his head. It's so horrible, in fact, Job takes a piece of broken pottery and tries to scrape his festering skin off. The rest of the chapter is basically Job wishing he had never been born.

"Uncle John!" Job bellowed at the top of his lungs, out of patience, still beneath my window. *"Cana!"*

So I ran down the stairs and went to have lunch.

After the meal, I ended up talking with Catherine, one of the Older Girls. Since it was on my mind, I mentioned Job—the Bible guy, not the Farm kid. It just didn't make sense to me. What kind of god tests his children like that? And not only Old Testament Job, God's faithful servant, but the Farm kids before Clifton arrived, and so many innocent others like them around the world who have not yet been rescued. "Why would He do that?" I asked.

Catherine smiled because the answer was so simple. "It is about faith, Uncle," she said. "Not only faith when things are good. Job reminds us to have faith even when things are very bad."

My rational mind wanted to argue, to point out the absurdity of it. But Catherine just touched my arm softly and looked into my eyes.

"Have faith, Uncle," she said, smiling. "Everything is working out for you. I'm sure of it."

45

SMILING AT THE ANGELS

As if it were a condition of her Indian visa, Traca could often be found holding one of the tiny twins, Saloni or Shivani. Traca has never been fond of the human jungle gym routine older children can often require, but give her a fussy three-month-old girl ready for a nap and she will rock her to sleep and beyond. She even offered to stand in as babysitter whenever needed—which is why we ended up with baby Saloni sleeping in our room one night.

It wasn't a sacrifice, actually. At just three months old, Saloni was a champion sleeper. Even in the heat and noise of regular Farm life, she could just shut down as if her battery were dead. Then she could be passed around, barked at, kissed, or changed and she would not wake up—a valuable skill when you share your life with ninety-nine active and chaotic brothers and sisters.

On the night we had her, it was hotter than usual. The fan in our room circulated the air more like a convection oven than a cooling device, but Saloni didn't seem to notice. She lay on her back on our bed, arms and legs spread wide, dressed only in a cloth diaper, sound asleep. As Traca and I lay on either side of her, watching her perfect face by candlelight, she brought back a flood of memories.

"She looks like Jackson in Paris," Traca whispered.

"Only less sweaty," I said, knowing exactly the moment Traca was referring to. Jack was five years old and sharing a bed with her brother, both of them exhausted after a day of sightseeing. We were on our way to Portugal, cutting across France, when a friend offered us the use of her apartment in the shadow of the Eiffel Tower. Just before I went to bed that night, I poked my head into the kids' room and found Jack fast asleep, on her back, arms and legs spread wide like an X. She was sweating all over, trying to cool off, while Logan slept on the edge of the bed, in danger of falling, accommodating his brash little sister as usual.

"Our kids were good sleepers, just like this little one," Traca said softly, touching a finger to Saloni's tiny hand.

"Remember that party at your parents' house?" I asked, and Traca smiled, nodded. We'd been playing some game that had us screaming at the top of our lungs. Traca's two sisters, her parents, and the two of us, all simultaneously shouting as if we were each competing for the title of Loudest Family Member. When the cacophony reached its hilarious and earsplitting climax, someone pointed to the ceiling and we all remembered: The kids' room was just at the top of the stairs. We all knew that no living creature with reasonable hearing could have slept through the din we'd just created, but when I ran up to check on them, there they were: fast asleep.

"I love this age," Traca said, the nostalgia thick in the room now. "The way Logan used to smile at the angels . . ."

It was code for something Logan used to do. When he was Saloni's age, we liked to bring him into our bed in the morning and lay him on his back between us. He was a happy child, fun to engage . . . but sometimes he'd stare at the ceiling and smile as if something was up there. He'd laugh and kick his feet, his eyes fixed on some wonderful vision above him. Traca liked to think he could see the angels that surrounded us, but whenever I rolled over and looked up, all I ever saw was the ceiling.

We talked this way for a half hour or more, jumping from memory to memory before putting baby Saloni in her bassinet and climbing into bed together. But as we lay there in the shadows with the candle burning down, the conversation stayed with me. There was something so intimate about it: the ability to return together at the slightest prompting to a particular moment in time. It's one of the greatest treasures of a long-term relationship, I think, that kind of shared history. Not simply the big events, the public triumphs or tragedies, the births and deaths . . . but the everyday moments that no one else is paying attention to, common moments that become special ones because they were shared.

At our darkest times, I've tried to imagine starting over with someone else. Wiping the slate clean. What would it be like? I'd meet someone new, someone nice, and I'd sit across from her at a restaurant, and inevitably she'd start the small talk off with something like "So. Where are you from?"

And I would start with the major plot points, the big picture. Because honestly, no matter how into you someone new wants to be, they don't really care about your daughter lying on her back in Paris, or your son smiling up at the angels. If they have kids of their own, they have their own moments that are precious only to those who were there and still care enough to remember. It's like looking at a stranger's wedding pictures. If you're not in the shot or connected to the event in some way, another bridal party in front of another church is about as meaningful as a tuxedo ad.

"Are you sure you don't want to come to the ashram?" Traca asked, whispering into the candlelight. "It looks amazing."

She sounded sleepy, her own battery getting ready to shut down. Through the years, I'd seen it happen many times: She'd ask me a question and before I could finish answering, she'd be fast asleep. I could tell by the tone of her voice that her night was almost over.

After much Internet searching, Traca had enrolled at the Parmarth Niketan Ashram in Rishikesh, a holy city ten hours north of the Farm on the banks of the Ganges. Her plan was to take a ten-day yoga retreat, complete with 4:00 A.M. meditation and chanting, daily yogic breathing classes, endless poses . . . all of which sounded like pure death to our little Jackson. Like an obstinate water buffalo, Jack wasn't ready to leave the Farm just yet, and when I thought about it, neither was I. Though I knew how powerful yoga retreats could be, I felt there was much more for me to learn with the Farm kids than by myself on a mat.

"I really want to stay," I said gently. "Is that okay with you?"

"Of course," Traca said, sounding farther away. "Logan and I will tell you all about it."

Though the Small Boys begged him to stay, Logan had decided to head north as well. I know he loved the Farm as much as I did, but as an acutely sensitive son, he was not going to let his mother leave the family alone, protecting both her feelings and her safety.

He's always been considerate of Traca in this way. When the kids were younger, if we were at a party or out to dinner as a family and we had two cars, Jack always rode home with me. "I'm going with Dad!" she'd blurt, as if the first one who said it was the winner. If Logan also wanted to ride with me, he never made an issue of it. He'd just hug his mom and off they'd go. The same thing happened at the Farm.

With less than six hours until their bus left for Rishikesh, Traca and I lay beside each other in bed, mostly naked, on top of our sheets. And as I watched our ceiling fan futilely chop the air, or the angels that were up there smiling down at us, I had a thought.

"Trace?" I said.

At that moment, I wanted to thank her, not just for being okay with the time apart that we both felt would be a good thing, but for all the years we'd spent together. For being a part of all the tiny moments of my life. Where was I from? Only one person really knew, because she had been there, too.

I wanted to tell her that, but I was too late. When I rolled over to look at her, she was already fast asleep.

46

LEAVING AND STAYING

GETTING FROM ONE PLACE TO ANOTHER IS THE MOST BASIC FUNCTION of travel, and usually there are some simple steps to follow. First, you must decide on a destination. Then, you buy a ticket or arrange some type of transportation to get you there. After that, you simply wait for the designated time to begin your journey, take your seat when the time arrives, and pass the miles between Point A and Point B in whatever way they unfold.

With those steps in mind, you might think that catching a direct bus from Banbasa to Rishikesh would be a straightforward affair—but travel follows a unique set of rules in rural India. As we discovered, there are no clean and tidy bus terminals. No orderly lines. No assigned seats. In fact, without a seasoned Indian traveler to help us navigate the madness that was waiting for us that morning, I seriously doubt there is any way Traca and Logan would have found the bus they needed, much less hopped on it as they ultimately did.

The adventure began at 4:30 A.M. with a simple drive into town; I tagged along to see Traca and Logan off. Our driver was Rick Shipway, Clifton's dad, and even so early in the morning, he was wide awake and raring to go. Rick was nearly sixty years old, mostly bald, with a mustache and a wiry build. He was also constantly in motion, always fixing, building, plowing, or planting something on the grounds. He first visited the Farm (and met his future wife, Maxine) in the late seventies, when he delivered a planeload of high-milk-yielding dairy cows to India. It was to be a humanitarian effort, so naturally the Indian government impounded the cattle and demanded that absurd duties be paid before the cows could be given away. Unable and unwilling to pay, Rick contacted Mother Teresa, who not only persuaded the government officials to back down, but became Rick's lifelong friend in the process. Knowing a little bit about both of them, I can see how they got along. Like the Angel of Calcutta, Rick is a powerhouse of energy, a focused force for good who moves through the world with a sense of purpose and conviction—qualities that also come in handy when attempting to make sense of the confusion that is daily Indian life.

The bus we needed was leaving at 5:00 A.M., and we were cutting it close as we approached the main road. Right away we had a decision to make. If we turned right, we had a ten-minute drive to the city of Khatima, a crowded metropolis of merchants and traffic, with a polluted black river in the middle that looked like stagnant crude oil. If we turned left, we had a one-mile sprint to the town of Banbasa, a dusty, much smaller tangle of shops where a surprising number of vendors sold nothing but small handmade scythes. As we watched a few buses rumble past, heading for the Khatima side of things, Rick wasn't sure which way to go. "We may have missed it already," he said, checking his watch. "They don't always run on time." Then, taking a chance, Rick turned left for the short ride to Banbasa.

Even at five in the morning, Banbasa was bustling. Shopkeepers were opening for the day while their children swept the dirt in front of their stalls. Stray horses loped alone down the center of the street. Cows slept here and there, mostly here. Hundreds of men walked in every direction with cars honking all around them. And a string of run-down old school buses—colorfully painted, with indecipherable Hindi printed on them—lined the road.

Rick pulled alongside each bus and shouted out about Rishikesh. His Australian-accented Hindi made the girls on the Farm laugh, but none of the men in Banbasa laughed. They didn't seem to react much at all. They mumbled . . . pointed . . . chattered on about something that Rick later translated as simply "rubbish." Several times, he jumped from the car and bulled his way through the crowd. If the Rishikesh bus was around, I had no doubt that Rick would find it . . . but we'd just missed it. We had to go to Khatima after all.

"Now let's see about getting across that river," Rick said with a smile as he punched the gas pedal and raced back up the road.

Two years before we arrived, the Farm and the area had experienced the biggest flood in its history; a whopping twenty-eight inches of rain fell in one day! Naturally, the normally dry riverbed swelled beyond capacity and the only bridge that connected the Farm to the Khatima side of the world was washed away. Two years later, the rebuilding effort was still limping forward.

We'd stopped one afternoon to watch the construction process and I was shocked to find cement being delivered by a line of old women. Dressed in colorful saris, these women carried the cement on their heads, one basketload at a time, as they plodded back and forth, granny labor in the midday sun. I asked Rick why they didn't use younger bodies for such a backbreaking task, and he corrected me.

"They're not old," he said. "They're probably around twenty-five or thirty. Just a hard life, is all."

With work on the bridge still in progress, the only way across the river was to drive *through* the river—no problem in the dry season, but a bit dodgy once the monsoon had set in. In typical Rick fashion, he raced to the water's edge, eyed the flowing brown water for a split second, and then gunned it. I've heard it said that a car can be washed away in as little as six inches of running water, but if that's true, it's not always true. A wave of water splashed over the hood, coating the windshield. Tires lunged over the rocky river bottom. For a moment we were more boat than car, but we made it. Back on dry land, Rick honked at no one in particular. "Horn still works," he said. "Can't drive in India without a horn."

There is a wonderfully dispassionate quality to honking in India. In the States, if you honk at someone, even in a friendly way, the one being honked at almost always takes it personally, and responds with the first obscene hand gesture and/or verbal expletive that comes to mind. In India, though, everyone honks, everyone gets honked at, and no one seems to care about either giving or receiving honkage. It's like the way bats travel, sending signals out into the world and receiving feedback from all around. Many trucks even have the words PLEASE HONK or HORN PLEASE painted on their mud flaps or bumpers or tailgates—a sentiment I'll bet no U.S. trucker has ever shared.

Back on the road, Rick was racing the clock, punching the gas pedal, honking at every dog, donkey, and monkey that even thought of getting in our way. The monkeys were the biggest obstacle. Down one particular stretch, a large band of wild macaques swarmed across the roadway.

"They're waiting for an offering," Rick said, blaring his horn, not slowing down.

It was a Hindu thing. Twice a week, believers paid homage to Hanuman, the monkey god, by feeding this troop, turning them into dependent beggars. Rick took us to pay our own respects one afternoon and we were quickly surrounded. Macaques are much bigger than Sweetie and the other spider monkeys back in Costa Rica. They're also capable—I assumed—of taking much bigger bites out of my hide. Thanks be to Hanuman, they were content with the day-old *chapatis* we frisbeed to their greedy little fingers, leaving us in peace and intact.

Racing past mother monkeys with babies, humping adolescents, and lazy males sprawled out on the asphalt, Rick was a rocket, his Bolero quickly approaching eighty miles an hour on the narrow two-lane road. The Bolero is a type of Indian-made jeep with no frills and a stiff suspension. Not made for speed, it whined and rattled as Rick pushed it faster and faster. "If this whole Mission thing doesn't work out," I said, gripping the dash and shouting above the protesting engine, "you can always get a job as a race car driver." Rick just smiled and hit the horn.

Naturally, we missed the bus in Khatima by just a few minutes and Rick made a quick calculation: With a little hustle, Traca and Logan could catch the 5:30 bus to Haridwar, then hop a short Rishikesh transfer from there. "We'll have to hurry, though," he said, as if there was any other way he traveled.

Back toward Banbasa, back to the river—but there was no getting across this time. A truck overloaded with garbage was stuck in the water and no one could get around it. Cars and buses were backed up on both sides of the river, and everyone was forced to pull off the road, making way for a backhoe to rumble through and haul the stalled truck to safety.

While we all waited for the river to be cleared, Rick made an impulsive decision to cut the line, passing two dozen vehicles and earning zero friends in the process. When the backhoe began to back up toward us, pulling the stalled garbage truck behind it, we barely managed to squeeze out of its way, slipping into a small gap between two giant buses. We were stuck there as the oncoming traffic began to flow.

From this point on, it was pure travel insanity.

A motorcycle tried to squeeze past us, only to be pinned to the side of our car by a huge truck going in the opposite direction. His rearview mirror was bent backward, and the rider barely pulled his legs to safety.

"Everybody out," Rick ordered. "We'll have to hop the bus right here."

Packs were tossed down from the roof. Trucks and buses rumbled past in clouds of thick black smoke. *"Other side of the road!"* Rick shouted over the roar of diesel engines. *"He won't stop!"*

How he knew the right bus was coming was a mystery to me, but Rick's tone was clear: There was no time to waste.

On command, Logan scrambled through the line of traffic . . . but Traca hesitated.

"Let's go! Right here!"

A mad dash, like running through an elephant stampede. Traca and I made it to the other side just as the Haridwar bus lurched up the bank. With her huge pack on her back, Traca tried to jump in the moving open door but missed. With Logan already in his seat, the bus started up the hill. As it began to accelerate, our chance to board was almost past. At the last moment, Rick grabbed Traca . . . she jumped, he shoved . . . and she landed inside the bus with a thud. Looking back, her face was a question: *What the hell am I doing?*

"Goodbye!" I shouted. *"I love you!"*

Logan just raised his eyebrows and then was gone, ten hours to Rishikesh ahead of him.

Back on the Farm, all was quiet, and when the 6:45 breakfast bell rang, Job was waiting for me. "You are really staying, Uncle," he said, gripping me as tight as a corset around my waist.

I said, "Yes. We are staying."

"Then my prayers are answered," he said.

47

A SMALL BLUE MARBLE

TIME ON THE FARM IS TIGHTLY SCHEDULED. WITH SO MANY KIDS AND A skeleton staff, order and control are of utmost importance. Vacation time looks a little different, but when school is in session, the daily schedule for all school-age children goes like this:

6:45 A.M.: Breakfast
7:30 A.M.: School begins
10:00 A.M.: Morning tea
10:15 A.M.: More school
1:00 P.M.: Lunch
1:30–4:00 P.M.: Rest and free time
4:00 P.M.: Afternoon tea
4:15–6:00 P.M.: Study and free time
6:00 P.M.: Dinner
6:30–7:30 P.M.: Free time
7:30 P.M.: Kids head to hostels
8:30 P.M.: Bedtime (except for big kids)

One day after lunch, I spent the rest period with the Small Boys in their dormitory. Nine of them shared a cramped space with five bunks and two ceiling fans. The walls were painted a soothing blue with a few posters taped up for decoration. My favorite was a picture of a mansion with a Ferrari parked out front and the caption EVEN IN DARKNESS, LIGHT DAWNS FOR THOSE WHO BELIEVE.

When I entered the room, the boys were playing their favorite card game. They used a deck of collectible World Wrestling cards, each card depicting a different hulky star with various statistics printed along the bottom. Things like height, weight, chest, biceps, rank, and fight—though what "fight" is and how it is determined is one of the great mysteries of the game. To play, one boy deals the cards, then the player to the dealer's left looks at his first card and selects the statistic he thinks will top all others. He might say "Weight: two hundred seventy" or "Fight: one twenty-two." In the game's purest form, all other players draw their first card without looking and see how their wrestler compares in the selected category. In a biceps battle, for example, if your wrestler has the biggest arms, you win all competing cards. It should be simple. The problem is that the boys are consummate cheaters who craftily scan their hands looking for larger chests or higher ranks, toss these ringers into the fray, then fight about them like rabid spider monkeys before moving on to the next hand.

On the day when I joined them in their room, one such cheating argument got so heated that Auntie Violet, the boys' strict den mother, appeared in the doorway. Violet was in her early seventies, a stern Indian woman who did not tolerate commotion. "Stop this nonsense!" she ordered. "And get in your beds this instant!" The boys obeyed without protest, even though it was 2:30 in the afternoon.

I assumed this was my cue to leave, but Job grabbed my arm.

"Don't go, Uncle," he begged. "Rest with us. This bunk is empty."

"Yes. Stay here," Kamal said.

"We will make it so nice for you," Clifford promised.

I looked at Violet and she did not forbid it, so I had a choice to make. To be honest, my first instinct was to decline. I had had a talk with Maxine just the night before and she'd told me about lice: what a constant problem they were, especially for the younger children. With this knowledge fresh in my mind, all I initially saw of the upper bunk being offered was the unwanted infestation it most certainly harbored. But as the Small Boys began scrambling around, now buzzing at the prospect of my joining their nap time, my desire to please them overcame my aversion to itching. Lice or no lice, I climbed up and lay down.

Like a sleepover at the home of the seven dwarfs, the bed I was given was ridiculously short for me, ending at the bend in my knees. To fix this, the boys built a box tower and placed pillows on the top to support my lower legs. Then they removed my sandals and gently placed them on the ground. A boy named Jackie brought me a dirty red silk sleeping mask. (What's a few more lice among friends?) And Ikindar sprinkled powder on my neck.

"To keep you cool, Uncle. So nice, it is. Yes?" he said.

Another pillow was delivered, forced under my head. And something was placed in my shirt pocket.

"From Kamal," Kamal whispered in my ear.

The topper to this pampering was a lullaby Job sang to me. As the boys settled into their beds, screaming at each other to be quiet and not to disturb Uncle, Job sang two lines again and again, his voice soft and high-pitched, tender as if singing to a baby:

> Sweetie Sweetie, go to sleep. Have a lovely sweetie dream.
> Sweetie Sweetie, go to sleep. Have a lovely sweetie dream.

I actually did fall asleep. Even with both ceiling fans swirling overhead, the room was hot and I was tired. For one hour I was just another Small Boy, resting on orders from Auntie Violet, dreaming of that Ferrari in the poster on the wall. . . .

When I woke up, I was sweating, looking through red silk, delirious. I sat up in bed and pulled my mask off, careful not to have my head lopped off by the fan above me. With my legs bent over the edge, they nearly touched the floor, and I looked down. Job was sleeping on the bare concrete beside my bed, curled up like a puppy.

My plan was to just slip out and let the boys sleep, but they all sparked to life at my smallest movement. "Please stay, Uncle," they said. "Tell us a story. Sing us a song." So I grabbed Clifton's guitar from his office and we sang Christmas songs in the baking heat of the late Indian summer. "Hark, the Herald Angels Sing." "Deck the Halls."

"Clap hands!" Job ordered after every song—and everyone clapped.

"You have a song for Logan?" Ikindar asked during one break in the Christmas medley. It was a strange request, but the Small Boys all hushed, eager to hear my answer. They all missed Logan now that he was gone. Some even wrote stories at school in honor of his visit. One such story was titled "The Story of Family" and it began with the line *There was a best friend and his name was Logan and Ikindar.*

Turns out I did have a song for Logan, something I wrote for him when he was small, something I've sung to him hundreds of times to get him to fall asleep. It was about drifting on the ocean, asleep without a care, totally safe as the wind gently carried you home. I sang it for the boys:

> *. . . So goodnight, my Logan*
> *I know where you're going*
> *And I'll have the wind take you there.*
> *Off you go now, my Logan*
> *You're heading for home*
> *And when you awake you'll be there.*

"Clap hands!" Job said, and everyone clapped.

Then it was time for the question.

It took me by surprise, as it always did, though I suppose I should have been used to it by then; I'd been bombarded with the question ever since we'd arrived. I usually avoided giving an answer or changed the subject, but the Farm kids were persistent. It was something they were desperate for me to answer "correctly," so I guess until I did, they needed to keep asking. With sincere conviction, leaving me not an inch of wiggle room, Job sat up straight on the floor in front of me, looked me in the eye, tipped his head slightly to the left, and asked, "You are a Christian, Uncle?"

I shook my head and decided to answer honestly for once. I spoke as gently as I could. "Actually," I said, "I believe in what Jesus taught. And the example he gave us. But I also believe, and I'm not saying I know, but after meeting so many wonderful people from many different religions, I just feel in my heart that there must be more than one way to get to God."

There was silence in the room, all boys looking at me, not one of them buying it for a second.

"Then we cannot listen to you, Uncle," Ikindar said.

"Yes. Auntie Maxine says you are wrong," Kamal added.

They were not angry with me, just telling me the truth. And as I looked from face to face, the simple certainty I found struck me like a slap. It was a supremely humbling moment for me, an "aha moment" (as Oprah would say) when I finally fully realized who I was talking to. Faith for these boys was not something to debate or deny. It was something to hold on to, a lifeline for them when the world had tossed them aside. It was their lullaby. In a very real sense, it was their Father. Who cared what I thought? For me to cast any doubt into their lives, these boys whom I had come to love, filled me with a sense of shame that made me blush and sweat and backpedal with every ounce of sincerity in my body. "Actually," I stammered, "I think that what you believe is . . . one hundred percent correct."

"Yes. It is," Job agreed, and we left it at that.

It was four o'clock: time for tea.

As I walked to the dining room alone, I remembered the gift Kamal had placed in my pocket before my nap. Pulling it out, I found a pink plastic Easter egg with a smaller green plastic egg inside. Inside the green egg was a small blue marble, scratched and chipped from use but still—like a child's faith—clear and brilliant in the afternoon light.

48

CHORES

I LOVED MEALTIME AT THE FARM. ACTUALLY, I LOVED THE TIME JUST before the meal, which was technically the time after the big bell rang (calling everyone to eat) and before the tiny bell rang (quieting everyone for prayer). During this time, for five or ten minutes as everyone was getting settled, I liked to walk from table to table, connecting with as many kids as possible. Jackson started doing this as well, and we took different paths through the dining hall, like dueling politicians working the crowd. To watch Jack crouching with a group of younger children, all of them jabbering for her attention, touching her hands . . . to see her fully engaged, loving them, taking in their love . . . it was the opposite of witnessing her plugged-in cyber life back home. She was awash in a sea of adoring humanity, and I could see on her face how much she enjoyed it.

The trick to this table surfing was not to linger too long in any one place. The room had ten rectangular tables with seats for one hundred. Not everyone ate together; married staff members, including Clifton and Priscilla, usually ate in their homes, an arrangement that was encouraged to provide a bit of private family time in the otherwise communal life that Farm members led. As a result, meals were attended almost exclusively by kids who sat according to age at assigned tables, boys on one side of the room, girls on the other. The only exception to this symmetry was the staff table, reserved for volunteers, usually Rick if he was around, and the Small Boys' den mother, Auntie Violet.

"Do you know my name, Uncle?" a big-eyed girl asked at one of my first table stops as I cruised the room. She was clutching my forearm with both hands, and when she smiled, her face lit up with so much hope, I almost laughed.

"Of course I do," I said casually, stalling. Back home, at work or around the neighborhood, I was notoriously pathetic at remembering names. I could meet clients a dozen times or hang out with fellow fathers at countless sporting events for years and I didn't remember who they were. I always said I was just bad with names, as though it was a genetic defect of some kind, but that wasn't true. I simply wasn't paying attention—not half trying.

At the Farm, however, the stakes felt much higher, and so I started applying the same "sour tea crap" technique I had used in Thailand, assigning memory pictures to each hard-to-remember child in a desperate attempt not to disappoint them.

Like the girl in front of me who was waiting to hear her name. She'd already told it to me at least twice . . . but it was tricky. How did I store it away?

She's wearing glasses. She's just about the only girl here who wears them. She saw something. With her glasses. What did she see? She saw a tree . . .

"Saw-a-tree," I blurted. It didn't sound right, but it got a smile.

"SAH-ba-tree," Sabithri corrected, clearly thrilled at being more or less remembered this time.

"And what is *my* name, Uncle?" another girl teased.

I took this little girl's beyond-beautiful face in my hands and didn't need to stall this time. "Kurena," I said playfully, and she beamed with satisfaction.

"And what about me?" Pinky asked. "You do not know?"

This game was played in spurts, one request triggering another, and I couldn't always remember. When I was honestly stumped, I'd crouch beside the child and say with utter seriousness: "Tell me once more so I will never forget."

"Rashwari," Rashwari would say.

"Rashwari. Rashwari," I'd say. "Got it." Then I'd mentally scramble to cement it into my Swiss cheese of a memory.

Rashwari. This girl is wary of something. Wary of . . . rashes. She is rash wary. Rash-wary. Rash-wary. Don't forget.

It wasn't all name games, my drift through the dining hall. Most of it was just hellos, high fives, fist bumps, or a blast through a complex secret handshake Logan and I introduced to the kids. It had a dozen steps and everyone loved to show that they knew it. Especially the Small Boys.

"Hey, Homey," Job said as I approached his table, doing a bad American street slang accent. Before Logan left, he'd taught Job a new greeting every day for a week and Job loved to recite them in one long line. "Hey, Dude. Hey, Bro. Hey, Dawg. Hey, Boss. Hey, G. Hey, Man. Hey, Homey," he said.

"Good morning, Job," I said, placing my hands on his shoulders. "And how is everyone today?" The other Small Boys smiled.

"Fine, Uncle," Clifford said, beaming. "We are lucky. There is egg today."

"Chicken butts," Job said, cracking himself up. "You like chicken butts, Uncle?"

"Ahh. So rude, you are," Clifford said, disapprovingly.

"What? It's from a chicken's butt," Job said with mock seriousness. "You don't think it's from a chicken's butt?"

"You're just showing off for Uncle," Clifford said softly, his eyes flicking up to me.

"I am not showing off," Job warned, his voice rising like a threat. But there was no heat behind it. As I slipped away, the playful chatter resumed.

I tried not to show it but I did have my favorites, most especially Beti. If she was in the room, I never missed her. The Small Girls at her table made sure of it. "Uncle. Beti is here," one of them called, presenting her. As usual, Beti did not make eye contact easily. Her gaze was downcast as I sat beside her.

"Good morning, Beti," I said, as if talking to a five-year-old child, not a sixteen-year-old who was taller than Traca.

"Good morning, Papa," Beti said, looking at the floor, smiling.

"You look very beautiful today," I said, lightly touching her hair. "You could be a Bollywood actress, you know."

The Small Girls shrieked with laughter. Beti shook her head, her smile fixed.

"I'm serious," I continued. "You and Shah Rukh Khan could make a movie."

That got a huge laugh from the Small Girls, including Beti. Shah Rukh Khan was the king of the Bollywood actors. Everyone was in love with him.

"Sing 'Paisa Paisa,'" Geeta shouted. Geeta had a shrill voice that could cut through steel. I shouldn't have mentioned Bollywood.

"Yes. Sing 'Paisa Paisa,'" a chorus of music lovers chimed in. "Paisa Paisa" was a Hindi song the Farm children had taught me, and they loved to hear me butcher the words, requesting it over and over, following me around the yard if I refused, wanting to hear it again as soon as I gave in and sang it.

"Not now," I pleaded. "Maybe later."

"Please, Uncle. For Beti," one of them said sweetly, batting her eyes, trapping me. But before I could spit out the long musical string of words with corresponding hand gestures, the tiny bell rang. It was time to pray. Alleluia!

Feeding so many people at once was a huge undertaking, and it was all done by the Older Girls. Breakfast began long before sunrise when fires were lit and dough was rolled out. By mealtime, the morning crew of teenagers had dozens of loaves of bread baked and a small wading pool of porridge prepared. Other than the occasional "chicken butt" (eggs were rare), this was pretty much it for breakfast: porridge and toast, tea and milk, butter and cane syrup. Lunch was usually rice and *daal* (lentil soup) or some type of curry and vegetables, along with fresh *chapatis* that were also made by the Older Girls each day. Dinner was more of the same. It wasn't gourmet but it was hot and tasted good, and, most important, it was consistent. Every day at 6:45 A.M., 1:00 P.M., and 6:00 P.M., the Older Girls made the food, served the food, then cleaned everything up by hand: pots, pans, plates, cups, silverware, serving pitchers, dishes, platters . . . three times a day, seven days a week, all for one hundred *diners*.

After that, the girls had other chores to do.

And let's be clear: By "other chores" I don't mean making a few beds or taking out the trash once a week. "Other chores" means things like shoveling the cow patties from the paddock and dumping them into the methane collection bin—a nasty if ingenious contraption that powered the kitchen, recycling cow poop gas into fuel to fire the stoves. It also means the Farm laundry, a task that was both constant and—by push-button American standards—incredibly labor intensive.

I liked helping out in the laundry, mostly because it was fun but also because it was a tiny way to push back against the strict gender stereotypes that still gripped Indian society in general and Farm life in particular. As no self-respecting Indian male, orphaned or otherwise, would be caught dead handling another man's underwear, the Older Girls always mildly protested my involvement, acting embarrassed when I showed up in the laundry and offered to help; but I could tell they liked it. Whether or not it cast aspersions on my American manhood, I cannot say. I just took a spot somewhere on the rinse line, prepared to get soaking wet, and started wringing out whatever garments came before me.

I especially liked to see Jackson rolling up her sleeves and rinsing away, too. At home, the idea of doing a load of laundry was as foreign to her (and Logan) as speaking Hindi. But on the Farm, where nearly two hundred kids and staff and volunteers created a steady tsunami of dirty bedsheets, school uniforms, towels, pants, shorts, shirts, dresses, saris, bras, undies, and diapers, Jackson was more than game to pitch in—a fact that was even more remarkable considering how difficult the job was.

Compared to our upright washer/dryer in Gorham, an appliance that takes exactly one finger and two buttons to operate, laundry on the Farm was an assembly line of manual labor. First, you washed a load in the anemic agitator, then you drained it and rinsed it in three consecutive tubs of water before cramming it in an industrial centrifuge and letting it spin out. It didn't help that most of the laundry's electrical equipment had faulty wiring that would randomly send electric shocks through anyone who happened to be standing in water—which, when you worked in the laundry, was everyone.

As for the Older Boys, they also worked long, intense hours, but their chores were done outside. Under Rick's supervision, they tilled the fields, planted and harvested the crops, maintained the equipment, constructed new buildings, and generally worked to improve the sprawling Farm grounds. While I didn't hang out much with these guys, Jackson did manage to spend one full day with them on a tractor, chugging through the mud and breaking a few stereotypes of her own, much to the boys' delight.

Though the work was hard, with no end in sight, I never heard anyone complain. In the dining hall when meals ended, the Older Girls sang as they cleaned up, splashing one another as they scrubbed the dishes. In the laundry, they cranked Christian rock or Bollywood hits, dancing their way around the puddles. And as they hung the millionth clean shirt out to dry on a spiderweb of clotheslines and prayed for sun, they were simply doing their part. They were loving one another by working together—which is exactly how I felt as well.

49

THE ICE STORM

JACKSON AND I WERE EXHAUSTED. IT WAS ANOTHER HOT NIGHT NEAR the end of our stay, and after a day of working and hard-core playing, it was time for sleep. We were ready. All we had to do was walk across the courtyard, climb the stairs to our guest quarters, and crawl into bed. The only trouble was that the power was out, we didn't have our headlamps, and the night was as black as the back of every cobra that was lurking out there in the grass.

"Daddy, I'm kind of freaking out," Jackson said like the little girl she once was. She took my arm and together we walked on blind faith alone, hoping not to encounter anything that slithered away when we stepped on it.

Eventually, with much nervous laughter, we made our way back to our room, only to find our lights didn't work, either. Our building usually had a backup battery that kept our fans spinning even when the rest of the Farm was fanless, but for some reason our system was dead. With the temperature still in the high eighties, we had two options: try to sleep in the oppressive heat, or wait for a bit and hope that the power came back on.

We opted for hope.

Pulling a couple of chairs out onto the balcony, where it was a little cooler, we sat together beneath a black Indian sky. The Farm was asleep; other than a few huge bats flapping in the mango trees, nothing moved. As we sat there, we talked about joining Traca and Logan up in Rishikesh. We were leaving the Farm in a few days.

"I wish we could just stay here," Jackson said, and I agreed. Though I was eager to get the family back together again, I felt at home on the Farm, useful and alive. It was everything I'd hoped to find on the trip.

"Who's your favorite Small Boy?" I asked, for no real reason.

"Ikindar," Jack said. "He's such a cutie." She called him Sparkle. They were buddies. "How 'bout you? Probably Job?"

"I don't know," I said. "He stood outside my window this afternoon singing to me. And, no kidding, he actually sang these words . . ." I broke into song: *"Amazing grace, how sweet the sound, that saved a wretch like Uncle John."*

Jackson laughed hard at this and so did I. Then we talked about something else.

In spite of the heat, the night reminded me of an ice storm we had back in Maine many years ago. It was one of those times when the temperature was just right for the rain to freeze on everything it touched, coating the world with a half inch of ice or more. While this was a hazard and an inconvenience for most of us, it was a nightmare for the utility companies as tree branches snapped under the ice's weight and tore down miles of electric lines. When the storm ended, huge sections of the state were without power, and in some places, it stayed off for more than a week.

Before service was restored, I ran into my friend Hannah, who lived in one of the areas that was hardest hit. Hannah was a single mom with two teenage daughters. Under the best of circumstances, her girls were a handful, and I asked how it was going for the three of them.

"At first it was hell," Hannah said honestly. "The girls didn't know what to do with themselves. No TV. No computers. Nothing worked." Then a small, satisfied smile spread across Hannah's lips. "But it's funny," she said. "In a few days, things began to change. We've started cooking dinner together. We play games by candlelight. We sing songs. And we talk the way we used to when they were little. About anything."

"It's not easy," she confessed. "We huddle around the woodstove to keep warm. But you know . . . there's a part of me that never wants the power to come back on. I have my girls back. And I hate the thought of losing them again."

The Farm was my ice storm. I don't want to embarrass Jackson (or have these pages burned before they hit the printer), but she changed in India. At home, like most teen girls, Jack was primarily focused on herself. Not a tyrant or a diva, but not overly aware of others, either.

She'd leave her clothes in the middle of the bathroom and expect someone else to pick them up. She'd enter a room, announce her desire to get a ride somewhere "right now," and be shocked if you couldn't drop everything and run to the car. In short, she was the sun (the Jack-sun) and everyone else was a planet.

But at the Farm, where girls her age worked tirelessly and happily from morning to night, she was beginning the beautiful process of focusing away from her immediate needs and noticing, with a compassionate heart, what was going on around her.

One simple story that Jackson hates involves an umbrella. On the morning after we had baby Saloni for a sleepover, back when Traca and Logan were still around, we woke up to find it pouring rain outside. Not the April showers kind of spring rain that seeds in their dark dens enjoy bathing in. This was one of the build-an-ark, run-for-high-ground downpours that India is so famous for. Ordinarily, the rain wouldn't have presented a problem. We'd just dash to the dining hall, get soaked a bit, then dry off as the day went along. But this particular morning, with a tiny baby in our care, we stood in our doorway holding her, considering our options.

"I can just run her over," I suggested. "She won't melt."

Jackson simply was not going to allow this.

"Wait here," she insisted and then ran out into the rain. Across the grounds she went, splashing through growing puddles, totally drenched by the time she came back. "Here you go, little lady," she said to Saloni, opening an umbrella to protect her small head and handing it to Traca. "And here, Dad," she said, handing me a second umbrella. "I'll see you down at breakfast." Then she ran back out into the storm and was gone.

When I told Jack I was going to write this story, she was outraged. "No!" she said. "That makes me sound terrible. Like getting an umbrella was such a big deal."

But that's just it. From my point of view, it was. From the daughter lying on her bed back home, texting and lifeless and ignoring me as I watched her, to the daughter with the umbrella who actually saw me standing there in the doorway—it was a change that felt as big as my love for her, which is big.

Our time at the Farm was winding down and our time on the road would be over before we knew it. True to form, I didn't have the rest of our trip planned. Maybe Africa. Maybe Portugal.

But all that could wait.

For now, the power was still out, the night air was cool enough, I had my beautiful daughter back again, laughing, chatting in the chair beside me, and I was not going anywhere.

50

THE BEAUTY AND
THE REWARD

AFTER FIVE MONTHS OF REPEATED PACKING UP AND MOVING ON, THE Farm was by far the hardest goodbye of them all. "You will cry, Uncle," many of the Older Girls said before our departure date, and I expected they were right. Jackson and I had been at the Farm only four weeks, but I knew these kids would not be letting go of our hands or our hearts easily.

To wrap things up, Jackson and I threw a couple of parties. For the Small Boys we decided on a *Lord of the Rings* movie night. (The boys chose the film.) I really wanted to take them all to an actual theater; they'd never been, and that nearly qualifies as child cruelty in my book. Ironically, they'd seen movie theaters only in videos, so they didn't really grasp the scope of the experience.

"Picture a forty-foot screen," I said as we sat in the courtyard one day after an impromptu soccer match. "As large as that tree. With speakers all around. And the action so big and loud you feel like you're really there."

The Small Boys were spellbound by this description. "So nice, it sounds," Clifford said. But it was not to be. The closest proper theater that did not feature X-rated films was more than three hours away, so their cramped TV room would have to do.

As far as viewing experiences go, it was not ideal. The ceiling fans drowned out most of the softer audio, the room was hot, we had to ration popcorn and soda when many of the Older Boys turned up, but none of that mattered. The Small Boys loved the movie night like Christmas morning and talked about it for days. Amazing what five dollars of snacks and a few hours can be worth.

For the girls, we went back and forth. Initially, Jackson wanted to take them for an overnight in the jungle. She even offered to use most of her birthday money to cater the adventure. "They work hard every day," she said. "They deserve a night off." But when the monsoon turned the jungle trail to mud and made the river all but impassable, a field trip and picnic was not going to work. We needed a Plan B.

One evening, I was out talking with the Older Girls when I found three wrapped candies in my pocket. The kids called them "sweeties"— not to be confused with the man-nibbling monkey in Costa Rica with the same name. A bag of one hundred sweeties sold for one dollar in Khatima, so I bought a bag when I was in town. After that, I started carrying a few of these penny toffees around with me each day, discreetly passing them out to unsuspecting Farm kids, creating small moments of pure delight that I never got tired of. It was a great reminder to me of just how inexpensive happiness can be. Anyway, I was sitting with the Older Girls, found the candies, pulled them out, and held them up.

"Anybody want a sweetie?" I asked. Everyone did.

"Let's have a contest," one of the girls suggested. "The best song wins."

Banbasa Idol. I loved it!

There were no amazing performances that day. April, a heavyset girl, sang two gruff lines of a Hindi song, then said "Now give me the sweetie!" and tried to wrest one from my clenched hand. Shirley, a typically reserved girl, stood up and proclaimed that she would be singing "in anger," then proceeded to belt out some Bollywood tune as if she were shouting it at her worst enemy. The girls laughed hysterically at all of this, cheering when a winner was selected, enjoying even the worst, most embarrassed attempts. In fact, they were so alive, so eager to play, it gave Jackson and me the idea we were looking for.

We decided to hold the first-ever Strong Farm Talent Show, and the girls were instantly on board. A sign-up sheet was posted the next day, and in no time, eighteen acts stepped forward, all singers or dancers, all girls. I was hoping to get the boys involved, but the strict gender separation rules would not allow it. Besides, "Boys will just tease and make fun," one of the participants said. "Only girls is better. Plus Uncle."

As for talent show prizes, Jackson and I and Kim (a sweet twenty-four-year-old volunteer who'd just arrived from New Zealand) walked into Banbasa one afternoon armed with twenty dollars. Jackson was in charge of this operation, and like a Kardashian in training, she grabbed rings and bracelets, earrings, hair bands, nail polish, makeup, and any other girlie trifles that caught her eye.

"Oh, these are so pretty," Jack said at one point. "Can I have one for myself?" I said that she could. At forty-seven cents, the flashy silver anklet in question seemed like a bargain even to my budget-conscious mind.

When all the prizes were purchased, we then loaded up on drinks and popcorn and cookies for the big night. Our goal was not to skimp. We wanted the girls to pig out if they felt like it. Not a handful of popcorn each. We wanted bucketloads and leftovers. Perhaps it was my abundant American mind-set, but I thought that to the Farm kids, the gift of "too much" might feel as wonderful as the gift itself. Plus I think the food all cost around ten bucks.

The day of the talent show, I was asked one question over and over again. "What are you going to sing, Uncle?" When I signed up to do a song, I just wrote "Surprise" as the song title, mostly because I couldn't decide. I wanted something that spoke to these girls, something that said a little bit about what I felt for them. By noon of the big day, I still didn't know.

As showtime approached, I was amazed at how much work the girls had done. They created a talent show banner to hang behind the stage, they rigged up a curtain to frame the action, they organized the musical accompaniment and pulled together the equipment to play cassettes and CDs and whatever else was needed. Food was ready. Programs were printed. Jackson, Kim (the Kiwi volunteer), and Priscilla (Clifton's wife) were the judges. I was the host. Every girl on the Farm—from the youngest to the oldest, Jeevana and Vari included—was in attendance and eager for the show to start.

What can I tell you? It was a smash. Amanda risked impropriety and did a moderately provocative dance to "Sexy Lady on the Dance Floor" and everybody cheered. Then Hope and Usha did an ultraconservative and simple pom-pom dance and everybody cheered just as loud. Geeta screeched a mercifully brief a cappella tune that didn't win a prize but did manage to scare away all the stray dogs for ten kilometers. (And everybody cheered.) Then Inis dressed up like a man and rocked out a hilarious dance number that had Jackson and all the girls buckled over with laughter.

When my turn in the program came up, I strapped on Clifton's guitar and played a new song called "I Want to Thank You." I'd made it up fast that afternoon and it is without a doubt the most unapologetically sentimental song I have ever written. No subtlety here, no hidden meanings. I just wrote how I felt and trusted the girls not to cringe. They didn't.

> *. . . I want to thank you for holding my hand*
> *All of your laughing, smiling eyes make me a happy man.*
> *And I want to thank you for all that you do.*
> *Just like my daughters across the water*
> *That's how I'll think of you . . .*

The song went on, verse after simple verse, and the girls absolutely loved it, especially the part where I sang to each one of them, thanking all fifty-two Farm girls by name in a long musical list. Jackson held my papers, I tried not to stumble over the complex Rina-Meena-Sabrina-Kurena-Seema tongue twister, and when the final name was sung and the chorus kicked in again, the explosion of applause that filled the room was a sound that I (and probably the surrounding villages) will never forget. It was beautiful.

The next day, as Jack and I prepared to leave, everyone turned up to say goodbye, giving us a send-off that was nothing short of overwhelming. The kids made stacks of cards for us, the Older Girls sang "Our Golden Days Are at an End," many of them openly weeping throughout the song. I was holding up pretty well, just floating along on a river of love and good wishes . . . until I saw Job.

He didn't say anything. He just walked through the crowd and handed me a card. "You okay?" I asked and knelt down to his level. He didn't answer. Without even looking at me, he wrapped his small arms around my neck and hugged me with all the tenderness in his young body. I could feel him sobbing against me and I started crying right along with him.

I'm including Job's note here not for what it says about me or him but for what it says about the power we all have to affect the lives of others, just by reaching out, by trying, by showing up. We don't have to save the world or even have much of a plan. We just have to place ourselves in the same room where there is need and see what happens. What we will be asked to do and how we will be used are things that will unfold. It doesn't have to cost a lot of money or take much time. All it takes is a little faith and a willingness to give. It's almost selfish, really. For if I touched Job's life, he most certainly touched mine, and that is both the beauty and the reward that all giving holds.

> *Dear Uncle John*
> *May God bleass you. I will miss you very much. Pleas come*
> *back. Thank you for everything you have gived us. Thank you*
> *very very much for coming hear. I will awals rember you. God*
> *sent a gift for me and you are the gift. Thank you. Love from Job*

Part Six

THE SIDDHARTHA SCHOOL

*Our prime purpose in this life is to
help others, and if you can't help
them, at least don't hurt them.*

—THE 14TH DALAI LAMA

51

THE CLOCK STARTS TICKING

THE DIFFERENCE BETWEEN A SHORT VACATION AND A LONG JOURNEY IS not so much the length of the trip as your relationship with time. On a seven-day vacation, for example, no matter how restful or distracting it is, there is still a ticking clock in the background relentlessly counting down. "Only four more days!" becomes "Only three more days!" and there is a low-level sense that it's all wrapping up too fast—because in fact it is. On the road, we discovered that weeks rush by, but months amble. Six months positively plods. Back in Costa Rica, there was no real reason to focus on the end of the journey; it was so far away, it felt more like an abstract concept than an actual deadline. With less than a month to go, however, our countdown clock officially started, and it unleashed a flood of pent-up emotions and repressed desires. Jackson, always the most connected to our world at home, heard the clock most acutely and, like a horse heading for the barn, was ready to pack it in.

"Can't we just go home?" she asked one night after leaving the Farm. "I want my friends. I want my room. I want my bed. I want new clothes. I want a hot shower. I am *done.*"

"Almost" was the best I could offer.

We technically had one more stop. Two, if I could pull another one together. In a few days, we were heading north for a week in a tiny village high in the Himalayas. After that, I didn't know. I was hoping to spend some time in Africa but it just wasn't panning out. I'd contacted lots of intriguing African volunteer possibilities, like teaching kids to surf at Jeffreys Bay in South Africa, or working at a hospital at the base of Mount Kilimanjaro in Kenya, or living with elephants on a ten-thousand-acre game preserve in Botswana. But all these opportunities ultimately fell into two camps: Either they were wildly expensive and not willing to bargain ($2,000 per week *per person* to chill with the pachyderms!) or they were not big on answering emails. Plus, plane tickets to all these places were brutally expensive. The only organization that unconditionally welcomed us was a small community development project in Uganda offering basic food and shelter in exchange for our assistance.

"But I must warn you," the acceptance email said, "malaria is very bad here. There is every chance you will contract it. Most probably."

"Yeah, that sounds really promising," Logan said sarcastically when he read the note. "Write back and see if they can guarantee leprosy, too."

As no one seemed eager to bring a deadly disease home as a souvenir, I cast my volunteer bait into another half-dozen African service pools. When I didn't get a single nibble, I decided to start fishing outside the Dark Continent.

To do this, I contacted our travel agent to see what the least expensive stopover countries would be. We had to fly back to the United States anyway, so where could we stop on the long flight from Delhi for the least amount of money? Her answers were: Egypt and Turkey.

Refocused, I dived into researching these two ancient civilizations with my complex method of inquiry: I googled the words "Volunteer Egypt" and "Volunteer Turkey" and started clicking around. I had a vision of volunteering at the Pyramids, riding to work on a camel, or pitching in on an archeological dig somewhere, but the best I could unearth was one organization outside Istanbul looking for volunteers to help them study soil erosion. Blah. Call me crazy, but after monkeys, WWOOFing, Thai students, and Indian orphans, soil erosion felt like the blandest of bland desserts.

I was still scrambling to nail something down by the time we headed to Rishikesh; Traca and Logan were wrapping up their yoga intensive, and Jackson and I would be joining them at the ashram.

From the Farm, our trip north was a grueling bus ride that set a new standard for uncomfortable travel. When we first boarded the bus, Jack and I grabbed the front-most seat, thinking it might have a bit more leg room, but it ended up being where a mound of extra luggage was piled. Cramped, hot, and trapped, we were at the mercy of a bipolar bus driver. He was a short, balding Indian man with a bad comb-over who was constantly adjusting his strategy behind the wheel. When we were in heavy traffic, he drove recklessly, his hand pounding the horn. Then, when we passed through the open country-side, he turned into an old lady, creeping along the empty roads. Above the driver's head, a plastic plug-in Shiva statue was lit for good luck, but all night long, the light flickered on and off as if our luck was constantly changing. Somewhere around three in the morning, as I tried to get comfortable on a musty duffel bag, having given up on falling asleep, I heard Jackson mutter something behind me into the hot, stale air.

"Kill me now," she said weakly, not so much to me as to the universe in general.

After ten hours, two hundred miles, and zero sleep, Jack and I crawled from the bus, took a three-wheeled rickshaw to the Ram Jula Bridge, then staggered across the misty morning Ganges. It was 5:45 A.M. and we were beyond wiped out. My backpack felt as if it was going to tear my arms from my body and I was prepared to let the arms go if it would lighten my load. Jackson was equally spent as she struggled beneath the weight of her pack, looking less like a hiker than like a pack animal being ridden into the bustle of the Rishikesh morning. Though it was early in the day, the alley leading to the ashram was already crowded, packed with holy men in orange robes, and mango vendors, and big blasé monkeys (who scared the crap out of me), and small girls dressed as bridesmaids, and old women in colorful saris, and lecherous men who ogled Jackson's every step, and honking motorcycles, and massive obstinate cows chewing plastic bags, and cow poop everywhere, all of it clouded by flies that made rural Thai cooking look like sterile surgery.

In spite of all the chaos, the Parmarth Niketan Ashram was easy to find. It's big and pink, the largest ashram in a city of ashrams. Eager to get away from the buzz and smell of the alleyway, Jack and I climbed the wide marble staircase that led to Parmarth's front gate, then entered a courtyard filled with Hindu statues. It was the usual cast of characters: blue Krishna, Ganesh with his elephant head, Hanuman the monkey god. But there were also many gods I'd never seen or heard of before: a tiger-headed god, placidly ripping his chest open to expose his bloody heart for some reason; a horse-headed god in a half-lidded, almost flirtatious pose. The variety of the collection seemed to be endless.

Compared with the simple arithmetic of the Trinity, the Father + Son + Holy Spirit addition that makes up the one God in the Christian faith, Hinduism is nothing short of advanced calculus. By one account (and I doubt these are actually listed anywhere), there are three hundred thirty million gods in the pantheon of Hindu deities, a lineup so extensive that if you recited a deity's name every *second,* day and night, for ten years, you'd still have another fifteen million deities to go.

But I wasn't thinking about any of that when Jack and I first arrived. We just continued our zombie hike . . . past the statues . . . to the office . . . learned that Traca and Logan were already in yoga class at the other end of the compound . . . happily accepted the simple dorm room that we were led to . . . dropped our gear to the floor as if abandoning it forever . . . and crashed in bed until one in the afternoon. Somewhere in that deepest sleep of my life, I had a vivid dream.

The world was white, like an overexposed vision of heaven, and a cow walked slowly toward me, clouds surrounding its hooves. Unlike the dirty street cows I'd seen in the alley outside Parmarth, this cow was clean and resplendent, decorated with ornate cloth and sparkling jewels. On its back, a woman was riding sidesaddle. She was dressed in a gauzy white gown, her face hidden in a blaze of light. As I watched her approach, I was immensely attracted to her, hoping she was coming for me. Then, to my great delight, the cow stopped directly beside me and the woman's beautiful face became visible.

"Are you ready?" Traca asked, like an angel preparing to lead me into the afterlife.

I woke moments later in my small, sterile ashram room. I was sweating and thirsty. Jackson was still asleep in her bed. Closing my eyes, I tried to return to the dream, but Traca and the cow were gone. *What had she been asking?* I wondered, not fully awake. *Was I ready? And, if so, for what?*

52

MORE FLIES

AROUND LUNCHTIME, JACKSON AND I FOUND TRACA AND LOGAN IN THE cafeteria. It felt so good to have everyone back together again. Traca was clearly in her element at the ashram, already close with most of the staff, sitting easily on the marble cafeteria floor as if chairs were silly inventions. She looked extremely happy. From my own yoga retreat experience, I recognized the bliss on her face, and I felt a bit of it myself. The Farm kids had grounded me, centered me, opened my heart in the same way yoga did for Traca. We were both energized, relaxed, and we swapped stories about orphans and swamis like best friends catching up.

Logan seemed good, too—though he did admit there were moments when he wished he'd stayed at the Farm. Missing the adoration of the Small Boys, picturing himself at the *Lord of The Rings* party we told him about . . . it made the daily regimen of ashram life feel a bit hollow by comparison. It didn't help that he was the youngest yogi in the class by a good fifteen years, but he made the most of it. He explored Rishikesh with his mom, stretched and meditated during the program hours, then launched into hard-core training mode in his free time. With his final high school cross-country season fast approaching, Logan was determined to finish strong, so he hit the Rishikesh alleys, dodged the crowds and the cows and the crap, and even ran laps on the ashram roof when heavy rains turned the neighborhood streets into cow poop soup.

As for the actual yoga program itself, Logan said it was . . . okay. "You should come to a class," he suggested. "See for yourself."

Jack and I had been considering volunteering at the ashram so we could stay for free; you can cook, clean, and wash floors in exchange for your room and board. But since it costs only $7.50 per person per day to eat and live at Parmarth, we decided to just chill out and pay the bill for a change. As residents, we were free to take part in all ashram activities, so on our first full day, we decided to take Logan up on his offer. Putting on our stretchiest clothes over our unstretchy limbs, we set out for the main yoga hall, walking down a tree-lined path that Logan had nicknamed Monkey Row.

Monkeys are everywhere in Rishikesh. Not the wiry spider monkeys of the Osa—these are rhesus macaques, a monkey often used in medical experiments. They are brown, bold, and scrappy, looking like pitiless thugs as they squat on the tops of walls or on tree branches. For the most part, they seemed satisfied to occupy the higher perches around the ashram, but they were occasionally found on the ground looking for food. "Do not feed the monkeys," one Parmarth staff member told me with a smile. "They can become very aggressive and can inflict dangerous bite wound." I thanked him for the warning but assured him he was definitely preaching to the choir.

Logan told me about walking to class one day down Monkey Row when he and some other ashram guests were confronted by a gang of macaques. The monkeys were sitting in the path and they looked both pissed off and not in a hurry, the way all bullies who know they have the upper hand look. Having been trained in *maaawn-kay* etiquette, Logan was eager to avoid a confrontation, but a man next to him was not so compliant or wise in the ways of the troop. This man, let's call him Dead Meat, grabbed a thin stick off the ground and began shouting and slashing the air, a provocation that drew loud, clearly hostile barks from the slowly advancing monkeys. Not one to back down or take a hint, Dead Meat shouted louder, slamming his feeble weapon against the concrete. The monkeys inched closer, eyes like lasers. Dead Meat was not backing down. *"Go on! Go!"* he ordered. And then—

Logan has no idea what happened after that. He took off running in the opposite direction, as if Sweetie were nipping at his heels, and found his way to class by another, less hostile route.

Luckily, the coast was clear for Jackson and me.

At the yoga hall, we chose spots at the back of the class and spread out our thin borrowed mats. The hall was impressive, with high white ceilings and a white marble floor. Large arched windows were open, letting in the heat, and fans swirled impotently overhead. Traca and Logan were already there along with a dozen other students, mostly white Europeans. A sedate Indian woman sat up front, ready to lead the posture flow. The class lasted for an hour and a half.

My favorite part of yoga is the end. Not the get-up-and-leave end, but the final pose, which is called *savasana*, or corpse pose. After all the postures are done, *savasana* is a time of integration, a brief moment of stillness before getting back to your life. To do the pose properly requires zero effort; you lie on your back, feet hip-width apart, arms at your sides, palms up, eyes closed, totally still until you are told to return to movement. Many times in this pose, I become so relaxed that I open my eyes to find that everyone is gone, that I've been asleep for fifteen minutes or more beyond the end of the class. I'm told this is a good thing: If you need to sleep and you put yourself in a place of complete rest, you will sleep even if your intention is to stay awake. But it can be disorienting. You set out determined to remain present. You end up feeling slightly drugged but refreshed, all alone on the floor in an empty room.

With this as my track record and still feeling a little sleep-deprived, I anticipated crashing like a child on the ride home from Disney World . . . but that was not what happened. In fact, as *savasana* rolled around and I assumed the position, I quickly realized there was no possible way I was going to accidentally nod off to sleep this time.

The true joy of yoga in general and *savasana* in particular is to get out of your head. Yoga postures can be intense and challenging, requiring you to drop all the mental chatter and focus on the twisting of your spine or the trembling of your legs. As a champion compulsive thinker, I find it virtually impossible to worry about work or replay some argument I had two weeks ago when I am upside down trying to maintain my headstand and not topple like the first domino into the head standers beside me. But on the marble floor at Parmarth, as I lay on my back, fully prepared for either mental stillness or unexpected sleep, I was not prepared for the fly that landed on my face.

The general rule in *savasana*—and it's not a strict catechism edict—is not to move. If you have an itch, leave it alone. A desire to simply shift around . . . don't. Be still. Let the sensations arise, observe them, and then watch them dissolve.

But ignoring flies on your skin requires a whole new level of self-control that I clearly lack. As I suddenly focused my entire being on the creepy little insect tango being tapped out on my cheek, my mind went into overdrive, freaking out, remembering . . .

Back at the Farm, Clifton had a dog, a boxer named Petey. Petey was a big coiled spring of energy who loved to chase balls into the monsoon rain and dive for them face-first into deep muddy puddles. The kids loved him and Petey was patient in return, even when they pulled him or teased him or squeezed him too tight, which was often. One day Petey got a cut on his leg and Clifton cleaned it up. A few days later, Clifton went back to see how the wound was healing and found it crawling, absolutely alive and wriggling, with a happy little nest of maggots. This is another thing flies do. When they're not licking the rim of your glass, they're looking for tiny holes in your skin-deep armor to lay their insidious eggs, not to mention what they track around on their nasty little feet, all of which played like a health warning newsreel in my mind as I lay there at the end of yoga class trying not to think. Visions of cow poop and Petey's leg and the sensations of the fly on my face wiping its feet on my cheek, scuttling down past my nose, maybe headed for a drink at the corner of my mouth—

Before I screamed, my hand shot up and brushed the fly away, but it was pointless. No sooner did I settle back into *savasana,* palms up, arms at my sides, than another fly landed on my forehead and another on my nose. Then a third began exploring my right leg.

At the front of the class, the teacher provided some calming instructions, attempting to lead our awareness away from habitual thought and into the sensations of the here and now. "Feel your shoulders," she said in a heavy monotone. "Feel your elbows. Feel your hands. Feel your fingers . . ."

But I couldn't. All I felt were the flies, little pinpoints of attention crawling on my skin. It was all I could do not to swat myself like a man on fire and run screaming from the room, down Monkey Row, and into the holy, and fly-free, Ganges.

"How do you stand it?" I asked Logan after class, still itching all over.

"I bring a sarong to cover me," he said, a practical solution I hadn't thought of. "But not Mom," he added, clearly amazed. "She doesn't move. Even if they're on her *lips*."

It's hard to imagine the level of discipline or the depth of transcendence required to allow flies access to your mouth, but hearing this fact about Traca made me suddenly convinced of two things. One: She was clearly operating on a different, more tolerant plane from me. And two: The fact that we had not done a lot of kissing since our reunion was—if only on a very basic hygiene level—maybe not such a bad thing.

When I mentioned this to Traca later that night in our dorm room, she laughed, then wiped her mouth with the back of her hand and kissed me. It wasn't a lover's kiss, just a peck, but it matched the playful mood in the room. There was a lightness between us that felt new, a clear, settled feeling that our time apart had given each of us.

We talked for a long time that night, leaving the lights off and enjoying the darkness. Outside, a heavy, steady rain was falling and the air felt almost cool. Traca sat cross-legged on her bed while I sat beside her in a chair. The kids were in the next room watching a movie.

"I've done a lot of work," Traca said at one point. "Peeling away layers. And I can see how I created my part of this relationship. My fear of not being loved the right way. My judgments. My inability to speak up and say what I want." Then she paused and looked at me, a mix of love, surrender, and sadness on her face. "We haven't been good together for a long time," she admitted.

"I know," I conceded. "Maybe we're just better out here. On the road."

Traca smiled. "I could keep going," she said, her eyes shining at the possibility. "Stay longer in each place. Go deep as a lifestyle."

At that moment, the rain outside seemed to double in intensity, and Traca looked to the window, listening to the torrential noise. "Just keep going," she said, barely audible over the downpour. "I could do that."

We both listened to the deluge for a while, and as I watched Traca sitting there, I realized something that felt fundamentally true for me. *I didn't want to keep going.* In fact, when I thought about it . . . I was excited to go home, to add some money to our dwindling bank account and start thinking about the kids' college and my career and a dozen other practical things that occurred to me all at once. I loved the trip and wasn't eager for it to end, but when it was over, I'd be ready.

I didn't mention any of this to Traca for fear of killing the mood in the room, but I knew what I wanted. I had peeled my own layers, I suppose. Maybe that's what makes long-term relationships so difficult. Everyone sheds their old skin, evolving at different speeds into something new over time. You never promise your partner you won't change. How could you? But can the relationship change with you, becoming less of a stagnant vow and more of a dynamic promise that recommits to each new stage of life?

Before long, the heavy rain stopped as suddenly as it began and Traca turned, refocusing on me. "I can't believe it's almost over," she said.

"Tell that to the Himalayas," I said with a smile, and Traca clapped her hands, ready to go.

53

HUNNYGOES

THREE DAYS LATER, I HAD A MASSIVE HEADACHE. IT WAS A DULL PAIN that made my brain feel like a drying sponge, and it was pinching my eyes shut. There was pressure inside my head. Or maybe it was coming from the outside. Either way, I felt woozy, and I knew exactly why.

We were standing on a small runway that looked like a landing strip on the moon. All around us there was dry rock and nothing else, leading to the base of towering mountains capped with a cloudless blue sky. After a quick one-hour flight from Delhi, we were now 12,500 feet above sea level—which put us *way* over the recommended daily allowance for elevation. Above 7,000 feet, or so the hiking code says, humans are advised not to gain more than 1,000 feet per day, assuming you are not already acclimated to the higher altitudes, which we were not. Biologically, the higher you go, the less air pressure there is to drive oxygen into your red blood cells. If you fly directly into an airport at such a high elevation, as we did, you need to take it slow. If you exert yourself too quickly, even with simple walking around, you can develop a severe condition known as Acute Mountain Sickness (AMS), leading to swelling of the brain, a loss of consciousness, and—if you don't get to a lower elevation quickly—death.

The best way to avoid this swelling and dying scenario is by resting, meaning complete inactivity, for twenty-four to thirty-six hours—so that's what we planned to do. A man named Angdu would soon be picking us up and driving us to the tiny village of Stok, about ten miles east of the airport. After that, we'd sit in our hotel rooms, watch birds play in the apricot trees outside our windows, gulp water like landlocked fish, and concentrate on growing more red blood cells.

Welcome to Ladakh.

Unless you are passionate about Tibetan Buddhism or an extreme mountain climber, you probably don't know much about Ladakh. I know I didn't. Ladakh (pronounced la-DOCK and meaning "the land of high passes") is a region of India in the northern state of Jammu and Kashmir, not far from the Pakistani and Chinese borders. Like a trough between two mighty waves, Ladakh lies between two of the largest mountain ranges on earth, the Himalayas and the Karakoram, which cut this region off from Tibet in the north and from the Indian subcontinent in the south. For years, Ladakh was completely isolated, like a cultural time capsule; it opened to tourism only in the late 1970s. Even now, it's not easy to get to. From Rishikesh, visitors can take a bus, but the road is notoriously long (like four days long), un-comfortable (like hell), and dangerous (like buses fall off cliffs and everybody dies). Though flying is a much more expensive option, it's also quicker and safer, and the view is spectacular. To cruise the top of the world, to approach a tiny airstrip with your wingtips seem-ing to tag the mountains on either side, to be left breathless (and woozy) in the official middle of nowhere . . . it felt more like a journey to another time or another planet than just another stop on the volun-teer road.

Leaving the runway, we walked toward the plain one-story build-ing that functioned as the terminal. Along with a few locals, there were a dozen other Westerners who made the trip with us. Some of our fellow passengers were clearly hikers; the gear on their backs and their Patagonia–North Face style gave them away. Others were prob-ably Buddhists if the white silk scarves around their necks or mala beads they were wearing were any indicators. Either way, they were pilgrims, come to pay their respects to either the highest mountains or the oldest traditions on earth. I suppose we were pilgrims, too, though not just for the trekking or the Buddha. We came to pay our own re-spects to one man with a very long name. A Buddhist monk named Khen Rinpoche Geshe Kachen Lobzang Tsetan.

I first met Khen Rinpoche—pronounced RIN-po-shay, an honor-ific title for a religious teacher—on a winter night in Portland, Maine. He was giving a lecture at the Maine College of Art. Traca had seen him the night before and raved about him. "Just to be in his presence is enough," she said, still beaming as if remembering a blissful massage.

She couldn't make the next lecture—she had a class to teach—but she encouraged me to go, and I did. I bundled up, braced against the icy wind that whipped up Congress Street, and found my way to a large classroom where I joined thirty people who were waiting for the discourse to begin.

On a purely superficial level, Khen Rinpoche looks a little like the Dalai Lama. He's in his mid-seventies, bald, dressed in a deep red robe with a slash of gold showing on the right shoulder. Beyond this, his most striking feature is his smile. He doesn't just curl the corners of his mouth like most people. He curls his entire face, his entire being, revealing a chorus line of perfectly white teeth that see more airtime in an hour than most people's see in a month. It's his expression of choice—not a forced grimace, but a natural and easy smile that makes the world smile back at him. You can't help it. Sit with him for any length of time and you will come to understand that Khen Rinpoche is one of those rare human beings who is grounded to the earth like an oak tree, a man for whom "inner peace" is not some far-distant goal but the reality of his daily life. Though he is getting on in years, the man bubbles with an internal well of youthful glee that makes him appear much younger. He likes to joke, to tease, to laugh from his toes. And Traca was right: I liked him immediately.

The only problem was that I couldn't always understand him. Khen Rinpoche's first language is Ladakhi, and he speaks English with a halting, guttural accent that requires a certain tuning of the ear to decipher. His voice is low; he drags out vowels, emphasizes odd syllables. For example, when he talks about the way all people want to live, he might say, "You want to have enjoyment. You want to have compassion. You want to have love." But what it sounds like is "You *waaan* hiv in*joy*min. You *waaan* hiv cum*pish*in. You *waaan* hiv *laaav*."

Most of the time, his meaning is clear enough, but every now and then he tosses a word in that sends my brain scrambling for a translation. Like the word "hunnygoes." The first time I heard him talk, he said it over and over again as part of his lecture. I was sitting near the front of the crowd trying to makes sense of the word when Khen Rinpoche looked directly at me with his delightfully twinkling eyes and flashed his patented billion-watt smile.

"Hunnygoes," he said. "You unda*stan*?"

I almost laughed out loud because I could not for the life of me figure out what he was trying to say. Honeycombs? Here we go? Horny goat? Hug my clothes? It could have been almost anything. It was only later that someone explained he was saying "hungry ghost," a Buddhist term for someone who is driven by cravings, searching for satisfaction where it can never be found: in the past . . . in the future . . . away from the present moment.

Diction aside (and let's be fair—his English is, and forever shall be, worlds better than my Ladakhi), I could not help but love this man. He just exuded lovability. So at the end of his talk, I approached some of his supporters to learn a little more about him. What was a perfectly good monk with bare arms and a bald head doing in ice-cold New England anyway? The answer—I was surprised to learn—was fund-raising.

More than a decade before we met, without two rupees to rub together, in one of the most remote parts of the world, Khen Rinpoche decided to build a school. From where he stood, he might as well have proclaimed his desire to build a rocket ship to Venus out of rice and *daal,* but there it was. He wanted not only to give the Ladakhi children the quality education that was so lacking in the region, but also to expose them to Tibetan language and art. Ladakh's culture is very similar to Tibet's—it's known as "Little Tibet," in fact—and with the Chinese government systematically eradicating the Tibetan way of life from the face of the earth, Ladakh now stands as one of the last remaining places to preserve this rich heritage. The Siddhartha School, as it was to be called, would help in that preservation.

It was a long shot, but Khen Rinpoche was never one to back down from a challenge. At seven, when most boys his age were entering the second grade, dreaming of being soccer stars or astronauts, he began his monastic training, committing to a life of celibacy, prayer, and Buddhist scripture. At the time, nearly a quarter of all Tibetan males were monks, and Khen Rinpoche—with his parents' blessing—

felt called to join the order. At fifteen, he was accepted at the fabled Tashi Lhunpo Monastery in Shigatse, Tibet. Tashi Lhunpo was the center of Tibetan Buddhist teachings, founded in 1422 by the first Dalai Lama and presided over at the time by the tenth Panchen Lama. There was only one catch: The school was eight hundred miles from his home village of Stok, and to get there, Khen Rinpoche would have to walk.

Under the best of circumstances, that would be a long journey. Chicago is eight hundred miles from San Antonio; Paris is eight hundred miles from Naples. But for Khen Rinpoche, the distance was only part of the challenge. To get to school, he had to hike through the Karakoram, a range that boasts the world's highest concentration of peaks over twenty-six thousand feet. Food and shelter were provided by kind strangers along the way. There was no hiking gear, no Nalgene water bottles. In fact, once his homemade shoes were worn to rags by the jagged scree he was climbing over, he completed most of the two-month trek in his bare feet.

Clearly this was one determined individual.

"I need some water," Jackson said. "My head hurts."

We were standing outside the terminal, resting in the shade. Altitude affects people differently, but everyone seemed a bit sluggish, as if nursing a mild hangover. While we waited for our ride, I just stared up at the towering Karakoram peaks.

"Do you think you could walk over those mountains?" I asked Jackson. She was fifteen, the same age Khen Rinpoche had been when he'd made his epic walk to school.

Jackson just closed her eyes and put her head on my shoulder. "I don't think I can walk to the car," she said.

54

STOK VILLAGE

THE DRIVE FROM THE AIRPORT TO THE VILLAGE OF STOK TOOK ABOUT forty minutes. The road was straight and dusty, two simple paved lanes, with majestic snowcapped peaks on both sides. Along the way, we passed permanent Tibetan resettlement camps and a huge Indian military base with armed sentries keeping an eye on their Chinese neighbors to the north. As in all of India, everyone drove as if they were being timed, including our driver, Angdu. He was a childhood friend of Khen Rinpoche's and a staunch supporter of the Siddhartha School. Despite Angdu's old-world Tibetan features, he had a Western feel about him. His English was excellent, he wore a baseball cap and a sportfishing vest, and he was constantly on his cell phone. I couldn't tell if he was making deals or just checking on his farm—he spoke Ladakhi on the phone—but he was definitely a player in this part of the world. He was an elected member of the Autonomous Hill Council (the local Ladakhi government), and he seemed to know everyone we passed. He also owned the hotel where we were staying.

"We'll have some breakfast and some rest, sir. Okay?" he said. He spoke softly, with great humility . . . even as he raced past a slow-moving truck and narrowly avoided a head-on collision with an approaching taxi.

Out the car windows, the mountains surrounded us, towering another twelve thousand feet or more into the air. Many Hindus and Buddhists believe the great Himalayan peaks are where the gods live, and it was easy to see why.

"Do you ever get used to seeing these mountains?" I asked Angdu, breathless on several levels.

"No, sir," he said. "I never do."

We crossed the Indus, India's second most holy river after the

Ganges, passing over a bridge that was absolutely smothered with prayer flags, thousands of them, like the pelt of some multicolored beast, and began our ascent into Stok.

It was like a trip back in time.

Unlike the hectic capital city of Leh we'd passed through back near the airport, and light-years from an urban colossus like Delhi, Stok felt like Plimoth Plantation, a tourist place in Plymouth, Massachusetts, that re-creates seventeenth-century life at the time of the Pilgrims. Only in Stok, it was real, a time capsule of the way rural Tibetan life was centuries ago. There were no gift shops. No I'M STOKED TO BE IN STOK bumper stickers for sale. Life just . . . went on.

Angdu told us most people were farmers; they tended animals, grew crops, made their own clothes, used donkeys to carry heavy loads, bathed outside, cooked over a fire. Farm families worked together as a community. They shared a primitive watering system of surface irrigation ditches fed from glacial melt at the top of the town. Twice a day, a simple metal gate was lifted, releasing ice-cold water that flowed through every Stok farm on its way to the Indus below. This was an honor system, requiring farmers to self-police, blocking up their share of the flow with rags and rocks when their crops were sufficiently watered. As a result, Stok was much more lush than I expected. While most of Ladakh was a barren lunar landscape, Stok was alive with waving barley fields, groves of poplar trees bowing in unison, and gardens in full bloom.

Even the homes were more beautiful than I expected in a poor village. All of them were trimmed with ornate wooden moldings, carefully painted with deep red and yellow accents, with hand-carved doors flanked by welcome committees of sunflowers. Some people clearly had more than others—at least it looked that way to me at first; some of the houses were huge! But Angdu said this was more a function of time than of wealth. The larger homes tended to be the older ones, with one generation adding a small room and the next doing the same.

It was a slow, ancient way of life, but it was still working. Everyone we met seemed to be content. There were not huge disparities of income or crushing poverty. In fact, from the moment we arrived, my family and I were greeted with kindness and generosity at every turn from people who had nothing by Western standards. So what was the secret? I wanted to know.

I talked about this with an old villager one afternoon. He was a farmer, dressed in plain, handmade clothes, and his face was deeply lined from years spent toiling in the intense high-altitude sun. He also spoke English. "What makes your village work so well?" I asked him.

The farmer thought about this for a long moment, looking off at the mountains. "We work together," he said—and I thought that was it. Then he smiled, his face wrinkling like an apple left in the sun. "It is simple," he said. "If you are rich, you are a failure."

"Why would you say that?" I wondered.

"Because," the man said, his smile widening, his wrinkles deepening, "that means you have not learned to share with other people."

55

GAZING INTO INFINITY

AFTER A FULL DAY OF REST AND PLENTY OF WATER AT THE HOTEL HIGHland, we set out to find Khen Rinpoche at the Siddhartha School. Since we weren't fully acclimated to the altitude yet, we took it slow. The air was crisp and the sky was cloudless, with a view of the Karakoram range that took our shallow breath away. Downhill from the hotel, the school was an easy walk, a slow fifteen minutes past a long *mani* wall that was a monument to devotion. *Mani* walls are roadside structures made of sun-baked bricks and topped with hundreds—sometimes thousands upon thousands—of hand-carved stones. Some stones are big, some are small, but all are carved with the same intricate Tibetan mantra: *Om mani padme hum.* This mantra roughly translates to "Hail to the jewel in the Lotus," and apparently the locals can't get enough of it. In Stok, the *mani* wall we passed was eight feet high, eight feet thick, and a quarter of a mile long, every inch of it stacked with stones. In the one place I checked, the stones were piled ten deep.

When we reached the school and entered the dusty courtyard, our plan was to pitch in wherever we were needed. But after finding Khen Rinpoche, meeting most of his staff, and drinking a glass of milky tea, we could already see one thing clearly: They didn't really need us at the Siddhartha School. Teachers handled the classes just fine. There was no manual labor to be done. And owing to their supernatural humility and genuine sweet nature, the staff was far more interested in having us rest or eat something than contribute in any meaningful way. Before arriving in Ladakh, I repeatedly wrote to Khen Rinpoche—he's on Facebook, of course—to ask if he had a specific task for us: a wall that needed building, a ditch to dig, a local family that could use a hand (or eight) in the field. But he never replied to these notes.

Volunteering is never a sure thing. Some NGOs may desperately need your help. Others may just need your money. Some will be well staffed and have experience putting volunteers to work. Others will require you to be more self-motivated. At the Siddhartha School, we were pretty much left to fend for ourselves, and once our tea glasses were empty, we just started looking around for ways to be useful.

While Traca and Logan worked their way into a classroom, I decided to take a portrait of every student at the school. The Siddhartha School costs around $100,000 to run each year—which seems like a modest budget to me, considering that that figure includes all teaching salaries, supplies, materials, gasoline and maintenance for four buses, building repairs and maintenance, and lunch each day for over three hundred students and staff. To help cover this cost, the school developed a sponsorship program, taking a page out of the "Feed the Children" playbook. For just $1 a day ($360 for an annual sponsorship), donors can cover one child's share of the total school operating budget for the year. Since sponsors are primarily linked to their chosen child through a photograph, I thought an updated picture might come in handy. It certainly felt like a more useful contribution than drinking another glass of tea or eating another dumpling.

Armed with a camera and Jackson, I began my portrait taking in the kindergarten; I took the pictures, Jack managed the crowd. The only real challenge was getting the names right. Names are tricky in Ladakh. No one uses family names like Smith and Jones. At birth, baby names consist of two auspicious words that refer to either enlightened beings or positive spiritual qualities. (No Britneys or Justins or other trendy pop star names are ever selected.) Many times, names are chosen by Tibetan holy men known as lamas—or by the Dalai Lama himself, which is considered a great honor—and I suspect that this third-party naming tradition is the reason for all the repetition we found. Many children were named Tenzin, which is the Dalai Lama's birth name, while in one class, we found three students referred to as Stanzin Dolma A, Stanzin Dolma B, and Stanzin Dolma C.

Working with homeroom teachers and following a printed student list from the office, we began calling kids up. Those children with name tags I photographed right away. Those without—and that was most of the younger ones—got handwritten name tags from Jackson. For my part, I worked to inspire a smile or at least a spark of animation to the painfully shy or borderline terrified faces that appeared in front of me.

Khen Rinpoche says it's a cultural thing, this shyness. When asked a question, many Ladakhi children just flash an embarrassed smile and look at the ground. Or they speak so softly that a whisper would be an improvement. Still, there is a purity about them, an unguarded, unjaded quality that is hard to resist. In picture after picture, when they relaxed enough to look into the lens, their faces appeared totally unaffected. There was no goofy mugging for the camera, no self-aware posing, no forced smiling or awkwardness. These were children who had not yet seen beautiful teen actors on TV or been made to feel wanting by the perfectly airbrushed faces in magazines. They were just kids, pure and simple, staring at my camera as if gazing into infinity. And as I looked into their eyes through my viewfinder, I felt I was doing the same thing.

Throughout the day, as we worked our way from class to class, I took hundreds of pictures. In the upper grades, Logan stepped in, writing names and student ID numbers as fast as he could, then passing them to me as he called the children up. But at one point, the slips stopped. I looked over. Logan had lost his place somehow.

"Let's go, boy," I said. "Who's next? Chop-chop."

"Hold on. This is almost like work," he said with a smile. Then he located the next child on the list and called out the name. "Padma Dolker," he said. "Padma Dolker?"

I had seen it many times on our trip and I saw it again here: a flash of the adult that Logan was becoming. In his Thai classes; returning from the jungle with Pincho in Costa Rica; on the Farm leading a group of starstruck boys to the river—he was no longer a rudderless teen. There was a confidence about him, a presence that was rising to the surface, peeking out from time to time in the tone of his voice or the look in his eye. And as another cute child stepped in front of my camera, looking at the ground, I knew that Logan would not be my assistant much longer.

56

TIBETAN SUPERHEROES

Back in Thailand, I had checked the Dalai Lama's website to see whether he might be in India at the same time that we were planning to be there. Traca and I both consider His Holiness to be one of the most inspiring leaders in the world today, and to see him in person was a dream we both shared. As fate or the Buddha would have it, not only was he scheduled to be in the country, he was going to be speaking just four hours north of Stok in the tiny town of Diskit in the Nubra Valley. The Nubra Valley has been an important corridor for centuries to the people of northern Ladakh. Once part of the old Silk Road between South and Central Asia, it is now a strategic military buffer between the Pakistani and Chinese borders. Eager to visit this remote part of the world and attend the Dalai Lama's three-day event, I checked in with Khen Rinpoche on Facebook to see if he was planning to go. This time, I got a reply.

"YES, I am planning to attend to HH Dalai Lama teaching," he wrote back. "Would you like to go with me?"

While this was by far the easiest invitation we've ever had the honor of accepting, there were still a few details to work out. Because of its sensitive location, the entire Nubra Valley is a restricted area, requiring special visitor permits. Once we figured out how to obtain these, we needed to find a way to get there. (There wasn't room for the four of us in the car Khen Rinpoche was taking.) Under ordinary circumstances, cars and drivers are easy to arrange, but the Dalai Lama's visit was no ordinary circumstance. Not surprisingly, everyone and his mother—residents and visitors alike—were planning to go to Nubra for the big event, and every car for miles around was already spoken for. Not having anticipated this obvious pitfall, we were left with a one-word solution upon which to pin all our Nubra Valley hopes: Angdu.

It took a few trips to Leh and a few favors called in, but Angdu pulled it all together. We had our paperwork, a private driver named Dorjay, and the promise of door-to-door service. "No problem, sir," Angdu said with an embarrassed smile as we thanked him profusely and headed out of town.

Still, getting to the Nubra Valley is no easy task. There's only one road between Stok and Diskit, and it requires six hours of white-knuckle, bone-jarring, high-altitude driving from anyone looking to make the trip . Narrow and winding, the road is mostly one lane with occasional pullouts to allow huge diesel trucks to squeeze past. No guardrails, just sheer cliffs promising certain death below and rising into jagged, snowcapped mountains above. The morning we left Stok, we drove back toward Leh, took a right before entering the city, and just started climbing. Logan and Jackson seemed to enjoy the ride, marveling at the spectacular scenery and taking the perils all around us in stride. It was Traca who had the hardest time, reciting a safety mantra in the backseat for much of the trip—which probably wasn't a bad idea. As we made our way higher, we spotted the burned-out shells of many rented cars just like ours lying forgotten on the rocks below. Massive potholes waited at the highest altitudes. Rock slides were a constant threat. Of all the poorly maintained, potentially life-threatening roads I've ever endured, this was by far the worst. But then, as the sign at the summit proclaimed, this was no ordinary road:

THE KHARDUNG LA PASS

THE HIGHEST MOTORABLE ROAD IN THE WORLD

18,380 FEET

As I stepped from the car for the obligatory pictures at the top of the world, I felt winded and delirious. In three hours of driving, we'd gained another six thousand feet of altitude. My head was pounding. My lungs and eyes hurt. I felt like lying down in the snow and going to sleep, *forever*. Thankfully, Traca was there to help me back to the car, and soon we erased the altitude gain, rolling *down* eight thousand or so feet into the spectacular Nubra Valley.

We inched the last few miles, down a switchback road that was like a train of cars, stopping for checkpoint guards who inspected our paperwork while lines of walking pilgrims made far better time than we did. When we finally pulled in to Diskit, we found ourselves in the middle of what I can only describe as a Buddhist carnival. The streets were packed with people dressed in traditional Tibetan garb. Monks and nuns in red robes were everywhere, along with local men wearing black felt hats with steep swooping sides like ski jumps. Old men wrapped in heavy cotton robes spun prayer wheels on every corner, while old women in colorful capes showed off their jewelry, their necks adorned with massive strings of red coral and blue turquoise. Some women even sported huge ceremonial headpieces that must have been sweltering, stacked with turquoise and flanked like blinders by two huge black wings made of yak wool. On all sides, we were barraged by an impromptu bazaar of vendors offering Tibetan artifacts, jewelry, mala beads, and prayer bowls as well as more utilitarian items like clothing, sneakers, umbrellas, food, you name it. I would not have been surprised to find a Buddha Moon Bounce for the kiddies.

What we did not find, however, was a room for the night.

Even with his considerable connections and influence, Angdu could not locate a single room within the Diskit city limits for us. Many people we met were resorting to communal army tents. Some were camping in the countryside. So pressed, in fact, was the entire Nubra Valley to accommodate the thousands who were arriving from all across the area that even Khen Rinpoche had to settle for a tiny back-alley second-floor room. Of course, this arrangement lasted only until the local monks caught wind of it, tracked him down, and installed him—with much bowing and reverence—in a small but ornate monastery on a hill: the region's official residence built specifically for the Dalai Lama. To be hosted in such a way was an immense display of respect, and it made us fully realize just what a Buddhist rock star we were traveling with.

It was as if he had a secret identity. On his own, around us, Khen

Rinpoche was just a mild-mannered, unassuming monk, quick to smile, working hard for his school. He loved our kids and had an easy rapport with them, teasing them like a playful grandfather, making time for them in his busy schedule. But around other monks, as in the Nubra Valley, it became obvious that he was one of the most honored figures in attendance. All monks bowed in his presence, careful to keep their heads lower than his as a show of respect. How a simple monk rises from lowly Stok village to the very top of a major Buddhist sect is certainly a story of unlikely transformation. It's also a story that begins with—of all things—the kidnapping of a six-year-old boy by the Chinese government.

In Tibetan Buddhism, the Dalai Lama is the most revered and the best-known lama, but he's not the only one. In fact, there is a long lineup of lamas most non-Buddhists have never heard of, the second most celebrated of whom is the Panchen Lama. While both are considered spiritual leaders, the Dalai Lama is also the political leader of Tibet, while the Panchen Lama traditionally acts as abbot of the Tashi Lhunpo Monastery, the same Tibetan monastery Khen Rinpoche walked barefoot to study in—though it now has a smaller, less fabled campus-in-exile in southern India. As the two highest-ranking lamas on the team, so to speak, their lives have been intertwined for more than three hundred fifty years, as each has been responsible for finding the next reincarnation of the other. As in: Dalai finds reincarnated Panchen. Panchen finds reincarnated Dalai. Not always, but usually. This process began in 1662.

Which is why, on May 14, 1995, after interpreting signs, consulting astrologers, and conducting multiple in-person interviews with potential candidates, the current Dalai Lama determined that a young boy, six-year-old Gedhun Choekyi Nyima, was in fact the eleventh reincarnation of the Panchen Lama. This announcement, while celebrated by the Tibetan faithful, was greeted with less enthusiasm by the People's Republic of China. In a move that was obviously political, the Chinese government took young Gedhun and his parents and put them in prison, where they have not been seen or heard from since. Then, Beijing put forth their own little boy, a seven-year-old named Gyancain Norbu, declaring *him* to be the real Panchen Lama.

Poor kid. If he'd been made of felt and fitted on Chinese President Jiang Zemin's hand, he could not have looked more like the puppet he was chosen to be.

Indignation, criminality, and bald political motivations aside, this turn of events left Tibetan Buddhism in general, and the Tashi Lhunpo Monastery in particular, with a problem: no Panchen Lama, no abbot. Which is when His Holiness called on—of all possible Buddhist monks on the planet—Khen Rinpoche.

Why was he chosen? Only His Holiness knows for sure. Whatever his reasoning, it was a huge honor. It would be like the president of the United States asking you to be the chief justice of the Supreme Court. Actually, it's bigger than that. It's like Jesus asking you to be the pope. When the call came, however, in an act of characteristic humility, Khen Rinpoche initially—respectfully—declined the offer. What he really wanted to do was build a school. He was planning to go to America to raise money. It really wasn't a good time to become abbot. While this was probably not the answer the Dalai Lama was expecting, I'm sure he could see the commitment and sincerity in Khen Rinpoche's eyes. So he did what any true spiritual teacher would do. He wished him well, cut him a check for 10,000 rupees, and became the first investor in the Siddhartha School.

Ten years later, when the school was established and thriving, the Dalai Lama offered the abbot position to Khen Rinpoche once again, and this time he was honored to accept. As a result, at the age of seventy-five, he is now on a twofold mission: (1) secure the Siddhartha School, both in the long term and from year to year, and (2) raise two million dollars, at the Dalai Lama's request, to build a new assembly hall at Tashi Lhunpo, helping to preserve the most famous institution in Tibetan Buddhist history.

You know, odd jobs like that.

So while our own personal Buddhist superhero settled into the most lavish accommodations in town, we'd already left Diskit, in search of a place to sleep. Turns out our driver, Dorjay, lived in the next village up the road, and after knocking on a few doors, he found a neighbor with a room to rent. It wasn't much, just a cramped dank space scarcely larger than the king-sized bed it contained and carpeted with musty, peeling Astroturf. Not the Dalai Lama's official residence, but not a communal army tent, either. Logan offered to sleep on the floor ("I can sleep anywhere now," he said casually), while Jackson grudgingly agreed to sleep in the bed with her parents, something she had not done since she was two years old. It wasn't ideal, but it wouldn't be for long. Needless to say, we didn't linger indoors.

Before sunset, we all headed out for a walk. Even late in the day, the sun was still hot, but the shade was cold, a high-altitude phenomenon that made it hard to know how to dress. Down a dirt path, past cows coming home from a day of grazing, across a gentle stream that turned much of the arid valley green, we eventually stepped out into what looked like a wide riverbed of stones. This expanse stretched as far as we could see in both directions and maybe a mile or more across—though it was hard to judge distance between mountains that were so tall. So many mountains, on both sides of us . . . some ablaze in the late afternoon sun, others backlit and featureless, silhouettes in the fading light, stacked out to the horizon. There was a timeless quality to this spot; it was silent and utterly still. As the kids spread out to explore, Traca and I sat down in the middle of it all. For a while we just looked at each other, smiling like the happy specks in an enormous universe that we were.

"So what happens next?" I asked generically, knowing it was a question that applied to virtually every aspect of our lives.

Traca answered with the smallest shrug. "We can talk about it," she said softly, then handed me a heart-shaped rock. It was fat and beautiful, granite, heavy. Then, in the silence, Traca simply closed her eyes, slipping off to a place that was deeply peaceful, if the expression on her face was any indicator.

Diskit Monastery shone on a hilltop in the distance. It was built in the fourteenth century and had been keeping watch over the Nubra Valley for six hundred years. On a neighboring peak, a brand-new one-hundred-fifty-foot golden Buddha statue sat looking my way as well, glinting in the sunset. Mountains stood guard, silent Buddhas in their own right. Just like Traca, the whole world seemed to be at peace.

Into this space, I wondered: Was it gone? The distance between Traca and me? The hungry ghost we had created together and carried between us? On the road, it was helpless to assert itself, but was it just biding its time, waiting for us to land back in Maine, eager to drive a wedge between us again? I watched Traca's meditating face, the most familiar sight in the world to me: the shape of her nose, the lines around her eyes that our life together had slowly drawn. Were we reconnected? Were we healed?

I hoped so. As the sun dipped lower, I closed my eyes. In my hand, the granite heart was still warm from the sun, and I held it tight.

57

FRONT ROW TICKET SYNDROME

THE FIRST CEREMONY BEGAN AT 8:30 THE NEXT MORNING. THE DALAI Lama was scheduled to bless the new Buddha statue I had seen from down in the valley the day before, so that's where we were going. Our driver, Dorjay, took back roads to avoid the crowds, but the closer we got to Diskit Monastery, the more packed the streets became. Armed soldiers stood guard as streams of the Buddhist faithful, from the very ancient to the very young, walked toward the festivities. After passing thousands of pilgrims on our drive to the assembly grounds, we were dropped off right on time at the base of the access road that spiraled to the golden Buddha above.

"We're with Khen Rinpoche Lobzang Tsetan," I said to the guard, but even as I said it, I knew it wouldn't work. I needed a badge or a letter or something. Without it, I was just another groupie trying to sweet-talk the backstage bouncer.

Totally ignoring my feeble attempt at gate-crashing, the guard directed us along with every other visitor to an open area where the Dalai Lama's public appearance would take place in a few hours. It was a large roped-off space, two hundred yards long by one hundred yards wide with a few army tents off to the side, a wide ornate podium up front for the dignitaries, and a colorful web of prayer flags strung in the air. Other than several rows of folding chairs near the stage, there was only the hard-packed dirt to sit on.

"Where do we go?" Logan asked.

"I'm not sitting back *here*," Jackson said, referring to the very back of the viewing space, where many spectators were already getting comfortable.

Is it strictly a Western, entitled way of thinking that says you should always want the best seat? Front Row Ticket Syndrome? It certainly didn't appear to be a goal for any of the locals as we entered the grounds. Though there was still plenty of room down front, families were spreading out blankets seventy-five yards from the podium and then other families were sitting behind them in an orderly fashion. They had absolutely no view of the stage. Though there were loudspeakers strung up on poles around the grounds, there were no Jumbotrons to watch. After traveling for days, many having walked into the Nubra Valley, these devotees would likely never get a good look at their beloved leader.

This is a mentality that Traca understands; she has no desire to jockey for position. But I can't deny that I was hugely relieved when a smiling usher pointed toward a central aisle and encouraged us to go to the very front of the stage.

"Now *this* is more like it," Jackson said, her mood improving by the step as we walked past thousands of men, women, and children who seemed perfectly content to let us cut the line. We ended up sitting in the folding chair section, a space reserved specifically for foreigners, thirty feet from the podium.

This kind of preferential treatment was not uncommon for us in India. In fact, in our experience, Western visitors were often treated far better than the average Indian citizen. One good example of this happened back in Leh when I went to negotiate a plane ticket change for our return flight to Delhi.

Before we came to Ladakh, our plan had been to take a bus from Leh to Srinagar at the end of our stay, then fly to Delhi from there. Srinagar has been called the "Venice of the East" and is famous for its lush gardens and its houseboat tours of Dal Lake—but that's not why we decided to go there. Plane tickets from Srinagar were extremely cheap, and at the time, that was really all we needed to hear; money was getting tight and we were looking to conserve. Even though it would be a brutal eighteen-hour bus ride to make our connecting flight (Srinagar is 258 miles from Leh), we bought the tickets and figured we'd deal with that leg of the journey when the time came. Of course, that was before tensions between Muslim rebels and the Indian police began to rise once again . . . before street fighting broke out in pockets around the city . . . before tear gas and bullets were fired . . . before sixty civilians were killed.

The conflict had begun in 1947. At the time, both Pakistan and India claimed the area around Srinagar that was really made up of hundreds of princely states. But after a bloody war that solved nothing, the two countries established an arbitrary and unpopular border known as the Line of Control. In some cases, this line divided villages—even homes—in half, with one half belonging to Pakistan and the other half belonging to India. In Srinagar, the large Muslim majority suddenly found themselves Indian citizens against their will, and decades later, they're still not happy about it.

There's no real rebellion going on anymore, but armed resistance does flare up from time to time. As we had no interest in driving into a war zone, even a small one, our new plan was simple: switch the tickets, fly directly out of Leh, and pay as little as possible for the change. I brought Jackson along with me just to sit there and look vulnerable as we met with Mr. Menon, the Kingfisher Airlines representative.

"This is a nonrefundable ticket, sir," Mr. Menon said politely. He was in his mid-forties like me, wore a thick mustache, and was working on the oldest computer still functioning on the planet. "Srinagar is very cheap. Flights from Leh are five hundred U.S. dollars apiece."

But I was persistent. "Do you have a daughter?" I asked, knowing that he did because I saw the picture on his desk.

"Yes, I do, sir," he said proudly, looking at Jackson.

"Would you take her to Srinagar just now if you were me?" I asked.

Mr. Menon smiled and punched a few numbers on his ancient keyboard, then got up and left the room.

"What are we doing?" Jackson whispered. "He's already said no like ten times."

"Let's just wait," I whispered back. "Look pathetic." Then Mr. Menon returned, still smiling.

"All right. We will do it," he announced happily. "Four tickets. Four hundred dollars total. It is fair?"

I said it was more than fair.

Mr. Menon tipped his head to the side, the matter settled. Then his smile completely disappeared and he became suddenly stern for the first time since we arrived. "But I can tell you this," he said, leaning closer, his eyes flashing. "Had you been an Indian man, I would have thrown you out right from the start!"

Western favoritism or not, I was grateful. I felt the same way as we strolled to the front of the Dalai Lama's stage and took our seats, a courtesy that was extended to us every day that His Holiness spoke.

On Day Two, we arrived late, but we knew the drill. We used the center aisle to bypass the thronging thousands—only to find the foreigners' section already full. With no place to sit and the crowd already packed to the very back of the viewing area, we did something so bold, it still surprises me when I think of it.

We climbed onto the stage.

There was an empty space off to the left against the side wall, and we took it. As the only Westerners on the platform, I fully expected us to be kicked off at any moment . . . but we weren't. As the seconds ticked by, we hunkered down, trying to act casual, a growing sense of glee blooming among the four of us. The kids were thrilled. Even Traca raised a sneaky eyebrow at me. We felt lucky, even more so when other foreigners tried to follow our lead and were turned back.

"What about them?" an Australian fellow said, pointing at us.

The guard stood firm. "They are allowed," he said emphatically. "You, sir, are not."

It blows my mind, actually. I just can't imagine an Indian family attending, say, a presidential speech in the United States and being ushered to seats of honor reserved at the front simply because they were visiting from a foreign country, or being allowed to share the raised platform with the dignitaries and sit twenty feet from the most beloved figure in the country.

But then, there was a lot about that day that I still find surprising.

Like the way they offered tea to everyone in attendance with relay teams of novice monks running up the aisles to fill thousands upon thousands of glasses; or how beautiful the sea of multicolored sun umbrellas looked spread out before the stage like a rippling rainbow; or how cool it was to see Khen Rinpoche sitting just a few feet from the Dalai Lama's throne, smiling at us with a child's delight when we caught his eye; or how much I loved to listen to Logan strike up a conversation with a stranger next to him, talking about volunteering, asking questions, sounding so happy.

As for the Dalai Lama himself, it was a thrill to see him. It reminded me of the time Traca and I saw Maya Angelou speak in New York City. When she stepped onto the stage, such a wave of emotion swept through the crowd that it felt like a physical thing, like a huge blanket of respect and love that we all wove on the spot and passed around. The same was true of His Holiness. To see him appear amid the horns and drums and pomp, to see his little-boy smile up close and in person, to see the reverence on the faces of those around us, it was a sincere honor to be there. We all felt it . . . at least for a while.

Actually, to be completely honest (and I hope this doesn't sound disrespectful or shallow), three days of the Dalai Lama speaking in the Nubra Valley wasn't the nonstop blissfest I thought it was going to be. At ten thousand feet or so, the sun felt much closer than usual, blazing down from a cloudless sky as if it was trying to cook us in the paper-thin air. And His Holiness, while revered and inspiring, spoke only in the local dialect, with no translator that we could hear. After an hour, then two, then three, then another day of the same, it was like watching a really long foreign language documentary with no subtitles and only one camera angle. Logan and Jackson earned their Non-Complaining scout badges by the second day—but they begged not to go back for the third. Feeling more than sated myself, I stayed with them back at the guesthouse while Traca hit the viewing area for one more incomprehensible three-hour lecture.

"How can you stand it when you don't know what he's saying?" Jackson asked when we were all back in the car, heading out of Nubra for the long, winding ride to Leh.

Jack wasn't looking for an answer and Traca didn't give one. She just watched the snowcapped mountains out the window. But I knew why she went back for Day Three. As she had said about Khen Rinpoche the first time she met him in Portland: Just being in his presence was enough.

58

THE ILLUSION
OF THE WORLD

AFTER ANOTHER PERILOUS JOURNEY UP AND OVER THE HIGHEST Motorable Road in the World (an experience that does not get easier with repetition, we discovered), we arrived back in Leh, said goodbye to Dorjay, then stepped out into the bustling streets of the capital city for some last-minute shopping. For a town that's been open for business only since the late seventies, Leh hasn't wasted any time dropping the sleepy-little-time-capsule image that Stok has so far retained. Down every narrow street, we found hundreds of vendors selling pashmina scarves, yak wool clothing, Tibetan artifacts, Ladakh T-shirts, and trekking experiences. Butcher shops sold cuts of meat that were completely hidden under blankets of flies. Goat heads were for sale, too, displayed in buckets with their horns, teeth, and startled eyes still intact. Pharmacies sold drugs the way farmers markets sold tomatoes. When I wanted something for a headache, the man at the counter shouted: "How many?"

I said, "Two."

"Five rupees," he said, handing me two pills, roughly six cents apiece.

Old women lined the streets, sitting on the sidewalks with displays of fresh vegetables in baskets or on blankets. One woman sold only cabbages. Another specialized in carrots. Behind them, alleyways were packed with spontaneous bazaars: sunglasses, necklaces, turquoise by the gram. And all around there were restaurants and Internet cafés and bookshops and crowds and cows and beggars, with more of the same on the next street and the next.

Compared to a hive of humanity like Delhi, where beggars are a common sight, Leh has—at least for the moment—relatively few.

Even so, I was approached often as we walked around, especially by kids. Maybe they could tell I was a sucker, or maybe they could sense that I liked them. Whatever the truth, I found them hard to resist as they held out their empty hands or offered inexpensive items for sale, smiled, and acted cute. I was told by the locals not to give them money. *It will only encourage them,* they said. But I couldn't help it. In fact, I usually carried around a roll of five- and ten-rupee notes in my left pocket, my own personal encouragement fund. It wasn't a lot of money, but passing out these colorful slips of paper always made me feel abundantly rich—which, in comparison to the children I handed them to, I certainly was. No matter that I was essentially handing quarters and half quarters to kids who desperately needed far more than pocket change. Whether it was right or wrong, helping or hurting, that's what I did. If I was asked for money by a boy in the street, I usually talked with him for a bit, found out his name, took his picture and showed him his smiling face on my playback screen, then slipped him a bill as discreetly as possible. When all the bills were gone, I had done my giving for the day.

As we made our way around Leh, I didn't have my usual wad of small-denomination notes, just big bills that I really didn't want to give away. The road is filled with absurd choices like this: Buy souvenirs or hand a hungry child a $25 bill. With a few last-minute gifts to buy, I just apologized when asked for money and kept moving. But one particular girl, maybe ten years old, dogged me in the market. "Sir. Sir. Ten rupees. Ten necklaces," she repeated.

She had a sweet face and a smile that was lightning-quick, transforming whatever darker thoughts might occupy her most of the time into sunshine the instant I looked at her. Her hair was pulled back and looked as dirty as her colorful dress, which was adorned with sequins but muted with grime. Her left arm was loaded with hundreds of simple necklaces, long strands of tiny colorful beads, and her offer was a good one: basically two and a half cents per necklace. But necklaces weren't what I was looking for.

"No, thanks, honey," I said as gently as I could. "I'm all set."

"I'm gonna run in here for a second," Jackson said as she opened a shop door.

We were outside a Tibetan store filled with statues and carvings, textiles and masks, jewelry and religious artifacts—the same basic collection we'd seen up in Diskit. I was just happy to get off the street as I followed Jackson inside.

It may not be a universal truth, but in our experience Tibetans don't like to bargain. They set a fair price, and they might come down slightly to be polite, but that's it. Maybe it's pride or cultural upbringing, but they never appear desperate for a sale and will let you walk away—unlike their Kashmiri counterparts we encountered all over town.

In the Kashmiri shops, transactions often go like this: You see something you like and you say so. The shopkeeper praises your good taste and the item's superior quality. He'll ask: How much are you willing to pay? You'll look at the tag and offer 10 percent of the asking price. Hearing this, the shopkeeper will act insulted beyond belief. "Can you not see the unique item you have found?" he'll shout. You'll say there are five hundred other stalls all selling exactly the same thing. Fifteen percent "and that's my final offer," you'll insist, which will prompt more outrage. "You have insulted me for the last time!" the shopkeeper will bellow, neck veins bulging. "I would never part with this valuable item at such a price." So you must leave, walk out into the street . . . and wait for the merchant to stop you before you arrive at a competing shop. "Okay, okay. Let's discuss this, then," he'll say. And you'll buy it for 20 percent of the original price. Win–win. Everybody's happy.

Jackson was the family master of this kind of negotiating. Traca would happily pay *more* than the asking price, eager to help the nice shopkeeper and avoid conflict. And Logan wasn't big on buying much of anything. But Jackson was a shark in the marketplace, even with the hard-line Tibetans. If the item she was after wasn't marked, she'd ask how much, hear the offer, then say, "Oh, no, no, no," and suggest a much lower price, delivered in her sweetest, most innocent voice. The merchants were always kind, respectful, but Jackson was firm. Maybe it was because she was so young and cute, but she usually got what she was after. Or close to it. I suspect this will be true throughout her life.

After buying prayer flags and simple earrings for friends back home, Jack and I stepped out of the shop, only to find the street girl with the necklaces still there, targeting me with laserlike focus. "Sir. Sir. Ten rupees. Ten necklaces. Please."

It can be tiring to spend your day refusing people, saying no, and it is tempting to tune them out. It doesn't make you a bad person; sometimes you just get overwhelmed. I once watched a German tourist as he was approached by an Indian woman. She was clearly desperate, dressed in rags, holding a naked baby. Both mother and child looked as if they were starving, and the woman stood beside the tourist with her hand out, pointing to her baby's mouth and then to her own mouth. She was like a zombie, her face devoid of emotion, her eyes devoid of light. The tourist was looking at a display of colorful scarves as the mother and her hungry baby silently implored him. But the man did not look at her, not once. He even removed his wallet full of cash directly in front of the desperate woman's face, leafed through it, pulled out a handful of bills, bought a beautiful red scarf, and walked away.

"Sir. Sir. Please. Ten rupees." The girl was behind me, and like the tourist buying the scarf, I didn't want to turn around.

"No, thanks," I said, without looking back. Sometimes walking away is all you can do. Focus on your shopping, your own kids, your own problems. You can't help everyone.

"Sir. Please!" the girl said louder. "Sir!"

So much need. That's the thing about the world. India. Even in Leh. Everywhere. It never ends. It's so full of—

"My dear! I am here!"

I stopped dead in my tracks. I had goose bumps on my arms. Turning around, I saw the street girl standing there, smiling, eyes bright, head cocked to one side, arm of necklaces extended. "Please," she said sweetly.

I walked to her.

"What's your name?" I asked the girl.

"My name is Maya," she said. In Hinduism, Maya is the illusion of the world.

"Well, Maya. I don't need ten necklaces," I said, "but I would like one. Okay?"

"Okay," she said.

"Ten rupees for *one* necklace. That's the deal. But you have to choose it for me. Which one should I have?"

Maya did not peel off the first necklace her fingers touched. She looked up at me and then down at her collection. She touched a dozen strands of beads, considered the colors in each one, then looked back at me with a smile.

As she did this, I thought of my own daughter: strong, beautiful, a sharp negotiator. A survivor. Just like Maya.

"This is the one," Maya said, handing me her choice. "It suits you."

"It's perfect," I agreed.

59

PRECIOUS JEWELS

BACK AT THE SIDDHARTHA SCHOOL, OUR WORK WAS PRETTY MUCH done. We listened to the children sing traditional Ladakhi songs and drank more tea, feeling more like honored guests than volunteers. Without any real assignments, we just tried to interact. Logan and Jackson played keep-away with a baseball cap while tiny herds of first graders nipped at their heels, shrieking with joy. And Traca and I sat and talked with the older students to help them with their conversational English—which was surprisingly good.

When Khen Rinpoche first opened the Siddhartha School in a rented one-room house back in 1995 (the year Jackson was born), all the students were illiterate and none could pass the government proficiency exam. Today, every Siddhartha School student is taught in four languages: Tibetan, Ladakhi, Hindi (the national language of India), and English, with the graduating seniors now receiving some of the highest marks in the region.

As we talked with some of these soon-to-be graduates, we weren't testing them, just wondering: What did they want to be when they grew up? Some said pilot, doctor, nurse. Most of the girls said "teecha," which was probably the only profession other than farmer that they'd ever been exposed to. Beyond that, we talked about their homes, their families, their hopes and dreams. Then, for no real reason, I asked one of the oldest girls with the best English what she was most grateful for, and she answered without hesitation.

"I am most grateful for my beloved parents," she said. "They provide me with all that I have and they are like the precious jewels I have been given but do not deserve."

Her answer was so sincere, so articulate, so immediate, it really struck me: Why don't all children answer in this way? Parents are the two people in a child's life who—when they do it right—give and give and give some more: time, money, energy, concern, carrying their helpless infants to maturity and beyond, sacrificing on a dozen levels to ensure their safety, happiness, and development. But in exchange for all of this, how are we treated? "Unappreciatively" is the mildest term that comes to mind.

I remember attending Logan's graduation from middle school, an overdone affair that was held in the school gymnasium. While I watched my son and his friends posing as adults for possibly the first time in their young lives, the principal took the podium and made a short speech. I don't remember anything of his standard-issue congratulatory spiel until he addressed me directly.

"And to you parents," he said, snapping me out of my blank stare, "remember: Your child is *going* to push you away, if they haven't already. This is normal. It's their job."

This was meant to be comforting, but it didn't comfort me at all. In fact, it seemed to me like the worst possible message to give to our kids as they sat there preparing for their next big step in life. It's the same message they hear all day long from nearly every movie, TV show, and music video they see. Push your parents away. Kids have all the answers. Parents are idiots. Haven't you heard? They certainly are not precious jewels to be grateful for.

For all its simplicity and old-world customs, there's a lot we can learn from the village of Stok: the sense of community, the humility, the respect. Still, I wonder what the culture will look like in ten years, or in twenty. If the glaciers all melt and their water supply disappears, the town is doomed and will simply cease to be. But more immediate dangers have already arrived. A single power line has snaked its way into town. Propane tanks fire gas stoves in some homes; satellite dishes capture TV signals in others. Many students I spoke with want the progress they see in the rest of the world, not realizing that it can be destructive, too: undermining traditions, eroding families and self-esteem, creating pollution, urban sprawl, unemployment, poverty, slums.

For the moment, though, Stok has none of that. Even the street kids have the whole game backward.

I took a walk by myself one night before dinner, the last of the sun still holding off the creeping purple of night. As I walked, I passed Stok villagers, like extras in a period piece about Tibet, everyone saying *julley* (pronounced jew-lay, meaning "hello") while raising one hand to their nose in a quick friendly wave. A few shaggy yak–cattle hybrids known as *dzos* ambled past, uninterested in me. All was quiet as the Karakoram reflected the last orange light of day.

I saw the three boys just as they spotted me. Instantly, they started to run in my direction, shouting, "Sir, please. Sir!" As they approached, I stopped and reached into my left pocket, finding the familiar roll of small rupee notes. I knew this drill and I was ready to pay up this time.

"Please, sir," the oldest boy said as he stopped in front of me, arriving just ahead of his two friends. His face and clothes were dirty, his teeth bright white in a broad smile. He was reaching into his pocket just like me. Then he held out his hand.

"Apricot," he said.

The apricot was filthy, like the hand that held it, but the message was perfectly clear. "Oh, thank you," I said. "That's . . . nice." I tried not to receive the apricot as if it were a used Band-Aid. I just took it and held it in my hand.

Seeing this, the second boy's face lit up. "Please, sir," he said, "Please." At which point he offered another apricot from his own dirty pocket. I didn't think it was possible to find a dirtier fruit than the one I was already holding, but there it was. I took it with as much reverence as I could muster.

"Thank you," I said. "These are great." Without expecting anything, I looked at the third boy, and his face flashed concern. His eyes darted to his two friends and back to me. It was an expression of almost comic panic. "It's all right," I said. "I'm good." But the third boy was already reaching into his pocket. With extreme reluctance, ever so slowly, he raised his arm and extended his hand. As I watched him, trying not to laugh at the exaggerated hopefulness on his face, he spread his own dirty fingers and revealed a mostly eaten apple, the only thing he had.

I took it, and as I looked down at the least desirable snack I have ever held, I thanked him. When I did, the third boy's smile exploded onto his face before he ran off with his friends, sprinting toward the setting sun.

60

THE LAST PRAYER

ON OUR LAST NIGHT IN STOK, KHEN RINPOCHE INVITED US TO HIS home for dinner. We gathered in his prayer room, sitting on small raised platforms cushioned with thick Tibetan rugs. A large photo of the Dalai Lama hung on the wall along with several colorful *thangka* paintings depicting Buddhist deities. Jackson and Logan sat next to our host, answering his questions about home and school and how they were feeling. Their conversation was so easy and playful, Traca and I just watched, more than content to be spectators.

Of the many wonderful qualities Khen Rinpoche possesses, his love of young people is perhaps his most effortless. When he is with them, on the playground, in the classroom, or in his private study for a goodbye dinner, he is fully present, playful, quick to laugh, to encourage, to affirm. I've seen children he has never met before take his hand and walk off with him, chatting like old friends. I'm sure they sense his complete trustworthiness, his sincere love for them that shines like a safety beacon. And as our food was brought into the room (Tibetan dumplings called *momos*, rice, vegetables, hot tea), I felt a profound sense of gratitude that my own children got to spend so much time with this remarkable man. Especially Jackson.

Khen Rinpoche is not the type to pick favorites, but he had a special relationship with Jack. He teased her constantly, hugged her, made puppy-dog eyes and pouted his lower lip if he wanted her attention. Even during the craziness in Diskit, when I'm sure there were more pressing demands on his time, he visited us at our guesthouse every day, walked with us through the countryside, taught Jackson to whistle (or at least tried to), sang songs with her, strolled arm in arm with her while Jack's head rested on his shoulder. I can't say for sure, but I believe he knew she needed extra love at the end of our trip, a mix of homesickness and road weariness fraying her last nerves. And as we savored our final Ladakhi meal, I watched Jackson soaking up his attention, his laughter, his jokes, the simple affection he poured into her like honey into a pot.

"You *tryyy* soup?" Khen Rinpoche asked, pushing a bowl toward Jackson.

"No, thanks, I'm full," Jackson said.

Khen Rinpoche looked deeply hurt. "You don't *liiike* me?" he said, as if about to cry. Then he laughed his big belly laugh, and Jackson laughed, too.

"Okay," she relented, reaching for the bowl as Khen Rinpoche reached to pass it. Their heads nearly conked.

"*Waaatch* head," he warned. "Or you rec*eeeeve biiig* blessing from *maank.*" Another big infectious laugh. Then: "Ohh, I will miss my friend," Khen Rinpoche sighed, touching his forehead lightly to Jackson's.

When all the plates were cleared and the evening was winding down, there came a moment I will never forget. It was one of those times when, even while it was happening, I knew it was special. It was a gift for Jackson, a seed being planted in her soul. We all received it—but it was given to her.

It started with a discussion of *Om mani padme hum,* the Tibetan mantra carved on all the *mani* stones. "Hail to the jewel in the Lotus!" These are the words all the old men recite as they spin their prayer wheels back and forth. They are a call to the divine nature within each of us, a reminder to shine like the jewels that we are. After a brief explanation of what the mantra means, Khen Rinpoche told Jackson what would happen for her if she repeated this prayer. The room was quiet and he was leaning back, relaxed but focused, looking directly at her.

"When you repeat," he said, speaking softly, no need for his usual odd-syllable emphasis, "the Buddha will hear you. And he will say"— and here he spoke in a playfully high pitch, an unexpected change that was both funny and sweet—"Jackson. My beautiful daughter. Hello. How can I help you?"

Jackson smiled, the way a flower smiles up at the sun.

"And then, the Dharma, all the knowledge, will fly from books like bees and circle you and say"—again with the beautiful high voice—"Jackson. Hello. We love you, Jackson."

The room was completely still and Jackson was at the center of that stillness. All the masks she usually wore—tough, sassy, bored, goofball—were gone, replaced with a simple, open expression, like that of the child she used to be, listening to a bedtime story.

"Then, the community, all the Bodhisattvas at the Buddha's feet, all the great teachers and people will smile at you and say"—one more time, the sweet high voice from the jewel in his lotus to the jewel in hers—"Jackson. You are now princess of the world. Real princess. Not artificial princess."

He was talking about repeating a mantra, but it felt like much more than that to me. In fact, it struck me as the perfect wish for Jackson, for Logan, for Traca and me as a couple, as the end of our trip approached: that we become the people we truly are, not the artificial roles we play for the world or the patterns we repeat, whether we're in high school or in a marriage, whatever that looks like, wherever that leads us.

When the evening ended and we were on the way back to our hotel, Jackson put her arm around me and we walked together. Such closeness would be rare in years to come, and I knew it. So I savored it, didn't push it, just walked. Beside me, Traca and Logan were savoring their own moment, arm in arm, in no hurry, either. Logan had grown in the past six months and was now a full head taller than his mother. It was a subtle shift, but he was no longer holding on to her arm. She was holding on to his, and he was leading the way. Above us, the heavens were crowded with more stars than I have ever seen, packed across the arched dome of the sky. It was like being in church—a sacred space—just the mountains and the heavens and our little family.

In the morning, we were headed to Portugal, a stopover vacation before flying home. None of my last-ditch volunteer requests had come through, which was fine with everyone. Now, virtually ten years to the month since Traca and I had run away to Portugal and spent a year with our then seven- and five-year-old children in tow, we were going back for one week. It was a chance to process where we'd been and to prepare for where we were going. What real and lasting changes we were taking with us from the trip would be revealed later. But as we left Khen Rinpoche's house that night, with my daughter on my arm, with my wife and my son beside me, the future felt as far away as the stars.

I did catch Traca's eye just for a moment on that walk, and even in the moonlight, I could see a look of overwhelming gratitude on her face. In that instant, as happened in the Bahamas, I *saw* her, really saw her, again. Not as my traveling friend or my children's mother, but as the beautiful woman I was making a life with. It wasn't perfect or easy, but after twenty years, we were still side by side, still moving forward, still finding our way in the dark together.

No one talked as we climbed the gradual rise to our hotel. We walked slowly past the long *mani* wall where the countless carved stones were stacked. As we passed them, I imagined the stones were calling to each of us, one single prayer again and again:

Do not forget, they said. *Do not forget.*

Thousands of voices, like bees.

Part Seven

AFTER THE TRIP

We should come home from adventures, and perils,
and discoveries every day with new experience
and character.
—HENRY DAVID THOREAU

61

SUMSING GROUNDED
AND REAL

IF YOU DRIVE ALONG THE SOUTHERN COAST OF PORTUGAL, THE FABLED
Algarve region, just before you reach land's end at the westernmost tip
of continental Europe, you'll pass the small town of Salema. Salema is
a seaside village with around two hundred fifty local residents, many
of them fishermen and their families. Life here is slow and unhurried,
intimately connected with the sea and the past. Men still launch colorful wooden boats off the beach and hunt octopus in the morning.
Women still beat their laundry in the bathtub and hang it out to dry
beside a stretched moray eel carcass or two. The only road through
town is called Rua Pescadores (Fishermen's Street), and it is crowded
with simple homes joined at the edges, wasting no space, lined up
along a sloping hillside like barnacles clinging to a rock. Walk along
the cobblestones of this street and you'll find that all the alleyways
dead-end at the boundless Atlantic while the surf provides a heartbeat, an easy rhythm, to your steps.

We first discovered Salema in 2000, after the death of Traca's father and the murder of my best friend. Back then we were looking for
healing, and we could not have chosen a better spot. *Salema* means
"peace" in Arabic, and that's exactly what we found.

Ten years later, it was summer—August—as we drifted back into
town, and we knew exactly what to do. We walked familiar hillsides,
through fields of rosemary and wild fennel, past ripening fig and al-
mond trees, eventually ending up at our favorite private coves. These
small slips of beach were surrounded by jagged cliffs and could be ac-
cessed only by steep paths that required a mountain goat's agility. But
once on the sand, we were treated to complete seclusion, with nothing

on the agenda but swimming, lounging, and soaking up the boundless Algarve sun.

There was no volunteering in Portugal. That part of the trip was done. We were just four more tourists on vacation. We even started spending some time apart, which I know our kids were ready for.

As a bonus, Logan and Jackson reconnected with their childhood friend Yolanda, who still lived in the village. Yolanda was the first friend Logan made at Salema's tiny public school back when he was seven.

The Escola Primária is a one-room schoolhouse that sits on a cliff overlooking the Atlantic. It houses grades one through six and had eighteen students back when Logan attended. I walked him to school for his first day and we got there a little early; the door was locked and there was no teacher in sight. On the playground, which was really just a dusty expanse around the school building, not a single word of English was being spoken. While Logan clutched my hand with his sweaty little fingers, the other kids were going crazy, chasing each other, shouting as if they were all furious. It was typical Portuguese kid behavior.

There are very few rules for kids in Portugal; parents seem happy to let them run wild in most every social situation. I remember going out to dinner with Traca one night back then, and some local children were screaming in the restaurant's dining room, racing between the tables playing hide-and-seek. (I think the Portuguese call it hide-and-shriek . . . or maybe that's just what they do.) As we ate, surrounded by escalating noise and occasional sprinting, no parents spoke up and tried to calm the game down. I even had one child choose the space under my chair as his hiding spot. When I checked, I found him glancing up at me conspiratorially with his finger to his lips.

But that first morning as I stood with Logan outside his new school, watching the dervish of intense kid play swirl around us, one small imp of a Portuguese girl came up to Logan, casually looked him up and down, and then did just the right thing:

"Hello," she said in perfect English before running off.

Logan exhaled as if he'd been holding his breath, then looked up at me with a huge smile and a *Can you believe* that? look on his face. And everything worked out fine.

She's all grown up now, a tall and beautiful (but still impy) young woman, and she met Logan and Jackson at the beach most days, then took them into town at night. It was surprisingly fun to watch. For the first time in their young lives, our kids were actually going out, leaving the condo at 10:30 P.M. and hitting the local clubs. The drinking age in Portugal is eighteen, but it's really nonexistent. I swear there were two twelve-year-old boys standing next to me at a bar one night, buying beers like old-timers. While our kids weren't drinking like Portuguese seventh graders just yet, they did admit to ordering their first drinks, and they were clearly loving their newfound freedom after so much intense family time.

So with the kids off boozing and partying and tanning the days away, Traca and I were free to simply be. We'd grab some snacks—native clementines, local cheese, fresh bread—and walk off into the countryside alone. We laughed a lot. We talked for hours. We kissed on our beach blankets. We tried to tread water while holding each other close. Life was easy.

One afternoon, after having my fill of sun, I kissed Traca and retreated toward a rock ledge for a little reading in the shade. Stepping back, I found a mosaic heart that someone had created out of shells and left in the sand. Mosaic always reminds me of Salema. Traca learned the art of mosaic tiling from an eccentric German woman named Brigitte on our first visit, and many whimsical bathroom walls and colorful kitchen backsplashes attest to this fact back in Maine. But the heart I found on the sand was more than just a reminder of Traca's penchant for smashing perfectly good square tiles and fastening the broken pieces to flat surfaces. In fact, it looked to me like the ideal symbol for our relationship at that moment. One half was white, one half was deep blue, like the yin and yang symbol in which two opposites come together to form a whole. It was all fragments, dead bits from the past, from two completely different species. White clam shells, dark blue mussel shells, working together to create—however temporarily—something beautiful, something fragile, some approximation of true love.

On our last night in Salema, we all went into town together for what promised to be a party: The International Festival of the Accordion had come to Salema! On the boardwalk behind Fishermen's Street, the whole village had turned up, strings of lights were lit, food stalls were open, dancing was encouraged, all in celebration of that magical squeeze box with keys *and* buttons that the polka had made famous. We started the evening off with a family dinner that I hoped would be some kind of wrap-up meal, a chance to look back on our trip . . . but the kids weren't into it.

"Didn't we already kind of do this the other night?" Jackson asked, annoyed. "Can we just *go*?"

Logan wanted to split as well, and they wolfed their food down as soon as it arrived, disappearing five minutes later into the accordion-filled night.

Despite the failed stroll down memory lane, the evening was actually pretty fun. After dinner, Traca and I made our way into the party and found familiar faces all around. Yolanda's mother, Amanda, our onetime language coach . . . Phil and Sue, expats from Britain, still living in town . . . even Brigitte, the German artist who had taught Traca to do mosaic, was there. Brigitte used to be a big-time artist in Germany back in the day, but she got tired of that scene. So she moved to Salema, got a place in the country, and does mosaic for hire around town. Now in her fifties, she seemed a bit weary behind her thin, regal demeanor, and she was philosophical about love. Relationships had never worked out for her; she'd had a string of disappointments, so she was content to live alone with her dog. But for Traca and me . . . she was hopeful.

"Okay. No couples ah pafict, and blah blah blah," she told me in her German accent that always makes me smile. "But if you get sumsing grounded and real . . . man, you need to hold on to ziss. *Ja?*"

I said *ja*. We both looked at Traca, who was laughing out on the dance floor, lit by party lights and surrounded by accordion music. She looked beautiful, and Brigitte approved.

"Men cannot handle zee woman unbounded, *ja?*" She looked

me in the eye to be sure I understood. "But if you stand wiss her and all zat shit. Wow! Ziss is really sumsing." Then she smiled and nodded. "Don't give up," she encouraged.

"We're working on it," I said.

It was time to go home.

62

OUR HOME'S EVIL TWIN

THE ONLY PROBLEM WAS, AFTER WE LANDED BACK IN MAINE, WE DIDN'T exactly have a home of our own to return to. Not yet, anyway. Our deadbeat renter's lease ran through the end of August and we couldn't just kick her out. Even though she hadn't paid rent for three months and had been avoiding Traca's mom (our rent collector) the way a vampire avoids light, there were procedures to follow, renter's rights that protected her.

I was eager to get over and see the place, but I was worried about what we'd find. One friend, who drove by before our arrival and gave us an email update, said she was "shocked and a bit frightened by the state of things." While I suspected we would not be greeted by fresh-cut flowers on the table and the smell of furniture polish in the air, I never considered the possibility that Joyce, our renter, would have trashed the place with all the gusto of a soccer hooligan.

Jackson and I went to check out the house together. (Logan was off with his friends, and Traca wasn't ready to deal with the mess just yet.) I barely recognized the property. Traca's vegetable garden was a tangle of tall weeds. Our beautiful lawn was a hay field, dry and brittle. Garbage was strewn across the driveway. A front window was shattered like a broken tooth. Other windows were open without screens, curtains flapping in the breeze like waving ghosts. There was an air of neglect bordering on abandonment, and I was glad we had brought a Gorham police officer with us—a precaution I had taken just in case there were bodies waiting to be discovered.

Inside the front door, I found a pile of black garbage bags—seven full extra-large trash bags, open and stinking in the August heat. A cloud of flies took flight as I entered, buzzing past my face and settling back into the stink as soon as I closed the door. Behind the bags, there were two overflowing litter boxes and a party punch bowl of cat food, mounded high enough to feed a small cat army. Connecting the bags and the cat food mountain was a long black stain on the wood floor. Possibly pee. Possibly garbage juice. Either way, undesirable.

Beyond the entryway, the kitchen was in chaos. The dining room table was pushed against the wall as if shoved there in a fight, and it was loaded with boxes, junk, and more garbage bags, all piled high. Clearly no one was eating here, no family meals were being prepared. Broken glass sparkled on the floor. A box half full of dishes sat on the counter, many of our dishes mixed in and ready to be hauled away.

"Oh, my *gosh*!" Jackson said as she opened the refrigerator and a blast of stink hit her in the face. Beneath the salad crisper we found two inches of gray juice that smelled like liquefied fish. The power was off in the house, so the odor practically pounced from the fridge like an uncaged animal. I closed the door and looked up. The drywall above the stove was water-damaged, the result, I feared, of something leaking from the bathroom directly above.

There were no signs of life. Plants hung limp and exhausted. Dirty dishes were piled high in the sink, old tomato sauce dried and all but eaten away by bacteria on pans and plates. Then a cat poked its head through the open basement door and spooked at the sight of us, scampering back down the stairs.

I followed and found a junkyard dungeon, more boxes, more trash, mold growing on the cement floor. The basement door had been left open, acting as an oversized cat entrance. Thankfully there were no meth labs and no corpses, but it was otherwise a deplorable mess, as if a Hollywood set designer had been asked to create a scene of total squalor. The whole house was like this.

On the second floor, Logan's bedroom had been curiously redecorated. His mattress was no longer on its bunk frame, but had been placed on top of his desk and piled—in Joyce's now-familiar decorative style—with a random assortment of dross: more boxes, a mop, coats, shoes, more garbage, fast food bags, dirty clothes. The bathroom was filthy, with a cracked tub that made me wonder: How do you crack a tub? Only Jackson's room was reasonably clean and undamaged, the bed mostly made, the walls decorated with blue note cards, each with an affirmation to help Joyce's teenage daughter get through each day: DON'T GIVE UP and BE BRAVE and LIVE BIG and OPEN YOUR HEART.

The master bedroom was probably the worst. The carpet, a white semi-shag that we had inherited, was now a hopscotch board of cat pee circles. But the bed was the true disaster piece. The cats had been using it as their personal playground, so it was covered with hair, and the comforter had been transformed into a minefield of cat turds, some reasonably fresh, others white and brittle. I counted twenty in all and wondered when was the last time Joyce or anyone human had slept in our room.

The final straw came in the downstairs half bath. Jack opened it, screamed, and slammed the door. "That's disgusting!" she said, eyes watering, blinking the sight away.

I had to look and was strangely relieved to find it was not a severed human head, just a month-or-more-old decomposing mound of human feces in a waterless toilet, another cloud of happy flies buzzing around it, eager to be left alone.

I won't describe the process of evicting a tenant. If you are a landlord, you probably already know. If not, I honestly hope you never need to learn what 14-Day Quit Notices or Writs of Resignation are. I hope you never need to post a 24-Hour Intent to Enter announcement on your own front door. Suffice it to say, we took all the legal steps to begin the eviction process right away, with only one teeny problem: We could not find our tenant anywhere.

When a county sheriff tried to serve Joyce with a small claims notice at our home, a task he attempted seven separate times on seven separate days at seven separate *times* of day, it was his professional opinion that our house had been abandoned. We agreed and moved back in, twenty days after our first walk-through.

To start the cleaning process, I drove two packed vanloads of garbage to the town dump while Traca ripped up our bedroom carpets. Then all four of us mopped, patched, mowed, raked, flushed, swept, repainted, reclaimed, and generally loved our little home back to health. As a final cleansing, we held a yard sale, unloading the many possessions Joyce's family had left behind, with all proceeds going to the Farm and our friends back in India. It was a drizzling day with fall approaching, and we were ready to make deals. With every item we sold and every dollar we raised, we pictured something good coming from our bad luck.

I do wonder, though, what happened to Joyce and her kids. Why would a struggling single mother of two teenage children leave all her cleaning supplies, her new comforter covers, a dozen pairs of sneakers, holiday decorations, *five* new staple guns, a Wii game console, dishes, clothes, her Bible, her credit card, her life? I don't get it. But I did get rid of it.

Still, as the eager bargain shoppers pulled up and started picking through what looked like a moving sale, I did hold a few items back.

In a box, like orphans, were framed family portraits: Joyce's daughter at age five, her son at age four, cute and smiling for the camera, full of hope and promise. Another picture showed the kids a little older: still smiling, scrubbed clean, unaware that they were heading for a life on the run.

I doubt I'll ever see her again, but for what it's worth: Joyce, if you're out there, I still have those pictures. If you want them, you know where to find me.

63

REENTRY

BEYOND DISCOVERING THAT YOUR RENTER IS ACTUALLY THE STAR OF THE upcoming TV reality series *House Trashers,* reentry into "regular" life after an extended world trip can be tough: the expectations, the expenses, the demands. Some people return to find that their lives don't fit quite so well anymore, or that *they* don't fit quite so well into their lives. Even the very basic logistics of finding work, or ramping back up to the fast pace of your previous routines, can be daunting. Luckily for us, once we removed the last bit of Joyce from our home, most of our other reentry challenges, at least on the surface, went smoothly.

The kids passed to their next grade level and started school with their classmates in September. They just had to hustle a bit to make up assignments from the previous semester. Traca contacted clients and yoga centers and started teaching again. And I got rehired by my old boss, Doug, who offered me a deal so sweet, it should earn him a place of honor in the Bosses' Hall of Fame: "Why don't you write down everything you used to do in your old job," he suggested, "then cross off everything you didn't like to do? Whatever's left, let's find a way for that to be your new position."

So I wrote it all down, the fun stuff and the boring stuff, and I crossed off things like "paperwork" and "scheduling" and "managing people" and "budgeting," leaving a purely creative job with virtual autonomy within the company. To my great surprise and relief, Doug enthusiastically endorsed this new position . . . and not a moment too soon.

Three weeks after I started working again, on a Wednesday night with my first paycheck in seven months due to be directly deposited into our account early Friday morning, I checked our online banking statement and found we had exactly nothing—zero dollars in the bank—which was just about perfect. Except for the six thousand dollars we were forced to borrow on a credit card to cover our loss of rental income and other Joyce-related expenses, we ran out of cash exactly one day early.

After we settled back into our lives and started talking with friends about our trip, the big question we got asked all the time was "How have you all changed?" At first, it was hard to answer this with any degree of certainty. But now, as I write, three full years have passed since we returned, and I think it's fair to assume that all remaining changes are permanent. Here's how things shook down:

Logan made it back to school in time for his senior year and ran his young heart out in the cross-country championships. After training with Bob the Kiwi track coach in New Zealand, sprinting past packs of stray dogs in the rice fields of Thailand, running on rooftops in Rishikesh, and jogging through the paper-thin air of the Himalayas in Ladakh, he finished third in the state and was voted Senior Runner of the Year in one online Maine poll. Far from the shy, uncertain teen who had left Gorham, Logan returned home much more confident and excited to engage the world. Upon graduation, he enrolled at Tulane University in New Orleans with an eye to studying international development. To give you an idea of how deeply the trip affected him, I'm including a college essay he submitted. The question he was answering was "In what ways are you unique and colorful?" This is what he wrote:

> I was hanging out with my friends one night, talking about the future. Michael, Nate, Willie, and I are all good students, all going to college. But our goals are a little different. Willie wants to be a rich engineer. Nate's going to be a rich entrepreneur, and Michael has absolutely no idea what he wants to do. "But I want to make a ton of money and live in a wicked huge house," he said. Then it was my turn. How to put this?
>
> I'd just returned from a trip around the world with my family and it completely changed my priorities. Before I left on the trip, I was just like my friends. I wanted money and lots of it, preferably doing a job that took the least amount of time.

But after living with orphans, in rural villages, with people who were happy with nothing and far more generous than most of the wealthy people I knew here in America, I had a new outlook on the world and my place in it. So I tried to explain this to the guys. "Umm, I want to go into International Development," I said hesitantly. "I'm interested in doing some meaningful work helping people, especially children in poverty-stricken countries."

Silence.

My friends just stared at me. It was like I'd just announced I had a contagious disease. Or like I was speaking in a foreign language. Then Michael looked at me, his face twisted in something resembling disgust, and said, "Dude. That is the *last* thing I would *ever* want to do. That sounds *horrible*." Willie just looked at me blankly and asked, "Why?" as Nate cynically pointed out, "We live here so we don't *have* to work in a third world country, idiot."

I don't know if this makes me unique or colorful to you, but it certainly does to my friends. I'm not saying I'm some sort of saint, not by a long shot. I still watch *Family Guy* religiously, love potty humor, and play video games every now and then. But at a deeper level, with a conviction I hope will grow during my college career, I feel that with one life, one very short life, my time here on earth is best served serving others.

Even if that doesn't earn me any bro points for now.

After completing his freshman year at Tulane with honors, Logan spent a year and a half in Central and South America, learning Spanish, volunteering, and surfing as much as possible.

Jackson also returned home refreshed and expanded by the world, but she was also more than eager to get back to her Gorham circle once again. Excited to reconnect with her friends and their lives, she returned to her plugged-in lifestyle like . . . how should I put this? I was going to say: like an alcoholic doing an openmouthed belly flop into a swimming pool of whiskey, but it actually wasn't that bad. She *did* request a new cell phone as quick as she could get one, and her social antennae *did* quiver happily as she entered the texting race once more. All things considered, she was ready for her sophomore year and eager to embrace it all—but not everything was so eager to be embraced. In typical fifteen-year-old fashion, some of her best friends were a little distant at first, which was hard for Jack to understand. After six months of Skype sessions and emails, in which her Gorham gang basically said: "We miss you *sooooooooo* much," she returned home to a bit of the cold shoulder, a reaction that was probably necessary in some weird teenage balance-of-power way. At least that's what I was told.

I ran into a woman on the beach one afternoon, just a stray conversation with a stranger on a gorgeous late-summer day in Maine, and somehow we started talking about this very thing: Jackson's cold reception from her closest friends. After living through the same experience herself as a teen girl and having the benefit of forty years to look back on it, the woman had a theory. "My family took me on a yearlong trip to Europe when I was sixteen," she said, "and when I got home, it took my friends a while to welcome me back. It was almost like: You abandoned us, so we have to abandon you. Then we'll be even."

I'm not sure if this is what was going on for Jack, but she weathered the storm and was soon LOLing with her BFFs as if the trip had never happened.

She's not the same person, though.

Around the first anniversary of the start of our trip, on a snowy night in February, the four of us were eating dinner as a family at an Indian restaurant in Portland and I asked Jack if there was any way she thought she had changed permanently as a result of our adventure. She said: three ways.

"One: I'm not sucked into drama with my friends so much," she began. "I don't like it when someone is mean, and I don't like gossip. When you live with kids who have nothing, it's hard to freak out about little problems. Two: I'm more patient with things that come up. Annoying stuff. If I can ride ten hours on a bus to hell, I can sit through a boring class. And three: I don't take crap. I'm more confident. I've done stuff. So don't mess with me."

The world she inhabits—American high school—isn't easy. It's a complex caste system ruled by Twitter and Facebook and status updates and an intricate web of likes and tags and chats and pokes. It's a world where the pressure to look and act a certain way, to consume and obsess on what the herd approves of, has a predictably soul-crushing effect on a young girl's spirit. Add to this the volatile mix of teenage emotions to process every day, the regimen of extracurricular activities to complete, the legion of horned-up boys to fend off, not to mention those pesky classes to plod through, and you have the perfect recipe for pressure, drama, and the occasional black fireworks around the house. I guess the hardest part for me is watching Jackson have to go through it all and knowing I can no longer drop to the floor, prance and snort a bit, then carry her on my back to safety. Before the trip, I was nostalgic for that role, desperate to unplug her so she would look up long enough to see the world and, hopefully, see me standing in her doorway thinking her name. But after six months together on the road, I feel not only lucky to have spent so much time with her, but also eager to let her stand on her own two feet. She's ready. I've seen her kindness, her hard work, her patience, her strength. I've seen her look beyond herself at an age when every bit of culture and conditioning commands her to be the focal point of everything. Most of all, I've seen the seeds of compassion planted in her heart.

They're growing, and they are calling to the real princess that she is.

Not the artificial princess.

After graduating from high school, Jackson began her college career in Florida, where she is currently studying medicine. Her plan is to become a traveling doctor, working in developing countries where medical care is critically needed. To gain experience, she plans to apply for an internship at a hospital in Tanzania.

64

THE WHITE SHELL

As for Traca . . .

She had the hardest time returning. In a very real way, she felt completely at home on the road. Volunteer work suits her. It's tangible. "Good work," as she describes it. She's really not much of a marketer or a businesswoman, so her yoga classes typically remain small, unknown, though loved passionately by the select few who manage to find her. Volunteering, on the other hand, is something she understands. She knows what to do with orphans, with monkeys, with compost piles. She'd have made a great cowgirl or pioneer—any calling where the work is never-ending and necessary.

But Gorham housewife with grown children? Not so much. After our home was resurrected and our routines reestablished, her *fernweh* began to call her once again, her ache for the distance. As I started working, as Logan and Jackson dived into their busy schedules, as the weather turned cold, as we didn't go back to India for Christmas as we had (irrationally) discussed, Traca decided to go to Kripalu, a yoga center in western Massachusetts, for New Year's Eve . . . and I stayed home with the kids.

You could almost hear the ice start to form, at first just a few clicking crystals at the edges of our relationship. The renewed connection we had enjoyed on the road, a heady mix of distraction and natural beauty and freedom and family and love . . . it pains me to say it, but it just didn't last.

While I watched the ball drop on TV, waiting up for Logan and Jackson to get home, I pictured Traca dancing at Kripalu, her eyes shining, her hair whipping, garments flowing, smile radiating as she poured herself, her soul, her passion, all her desires into that midnight countdown. I knew she loved me. She certainly loved our kids.

But while our trip reminded me of all that I treasured about our life at home, it seemed to have the opposite effect on Traca. She was ready to expand, to grow, to go deeper into her practice and see where it could take her—all of which made me a little anxious about what the upcoming year had in store for us.

More than anything, I wanted this to be a love story. I wanted Elizabeth Gilbert's ending in *Eat, Pray, Love,* in which her relationship troubles early on evolve into a fairy-tale romance with a handsome Brazilian guy in Bali—except substitute Traca for the Brazilian guy, in my case. I wanted that for us: the simple, happy, beautiful ending. I wanted Traca and me to be deeply in love, bonded by the trip and cemented together forever. But it wasn't happening. Less than five months after returning home, we were back in Limbo Land, waiting.

It took another five months of drifting and stalling before I realized I had waited long enough. I'm not sure what triggered it for me, but one day, I woke up with the conviction that I needed to move forward. It was like a delayed answer to the dream I'd had back in Rishikesh, the one in which Traca was riding a beautiful white cow. "Are you ready?" she'd asked me at the end of the dream.

I guess I was finally ready.

That night, I took Traca for a walk on the beach. Though it was still technically spring—early June—the air was warm and we were alone beneath a starry sky. The ocean was calm, gentle waves rolling in and out, and dry shells crunched beneath our feet. As we walked, we did not talk or touch, and I could feel a coldness traveling with us again, our hungry ghost blowing its stale breath on our hearts.

One thing about volunteering your way around the world: It will change you. It might help you appreciate all that you have: your safety, your wealth (no matter how modest), your home, your freedom, your hot shower. Or it might raise a host of questions about your priorities and changes that you need to make and what the hell are you doing with your life? Because you will not come back from such a trip the same person. Your heart will be bigger. Your view will be more expansive. If you were living a small, superficial life before takeoff, you may return ready to live deeper. If you were bound by limiting, long-standing patterns, you may not be able to act out those patterns any longer. Boldness creates boldness. Action leads to more action. At least that's the way it worked with us.

So we walked along the sand, side by side, having circled the whole world only to come back to where we'd first met. The beach. I stopped.

"Can I ask you something?" I said. "And I want your honest answer."

Traca said sure.

I drew a large circle on the sand with a piece of driftwood and picked up four shells, two black ones and two white ones. I handed Traca one of each.

"Sit in here with me," I said.

We both sat.

"I don't want to leave this circle until we've made a decision. Okay?"

Traca said okay.

So I asked her.

Was she interested and willing to commit to our relationship, dropping the past and working to grow together for the rest of our lives?

I suppose it was a marriage proposal, certainly a recommitment request, and maybe it wasn't fair. I knew Traca wasn't interested in the idea of "forever" at that moment. "People change," she was fond of saying, and she was right. We certainly weren't the same two kids who had promised to cherish each other back on our wedding day. But even so, I wanted an answer. I needed one. That's what the trip had given to me.

Long-term relationships are really just another kind of trip, after all. Money or challenges will not stop you if you are committed. In fact, the single greatest requirement for taking a trip of any kind is not the cost or the time or the logistics, it's your decision to go. Not a *desire* to go or a *dream* of one day going, but your ironclad, set-in-stone, for-better-or-for-worse commitment to get your feet out the door. Once you fully commit—to anything—the rest is just details.

"This is really simple," I said. "If your answer is yes, toss your white shell into our circle. If your answer is no, toss your black shell. I'll go first."

I tossed my white shell onto the sand and waited.

I have no idea how long we sat there. Time is measured differently on a beach late at night, cut into waves instead of minutes. While Traca worked through whatever calculations she was wrestling with, I watched the moonlight sparkling on the ocean's surface, the same ocean we had first talked beside twenty-four years before.

As I sat, I silently thanked Traca for the adventure we'd been on, for helping me raise our two fantastic kids, for growing up with me, for infusing my life with her spontaneity and faith. I do not know how marriage shifts from love into something else or from something else back into love. Marriage *is* like a boat—though not in the first-dance, wedding-song way I once thought. Every couple just does the best they can on their own journey, either bailing out at some point or hanging in there another day. I had always assumed that forever was the only option for us, but it wasn't. It was the long shot. I know that now. For those who last a lifetime, I'm sure almost all—with very few true-love exceptions—ride out their own storms: bouts of intense boredom and isolation and doubt and threats from one passenger or another to abandon ship and swim for shore. Some couples sink out of neglect. Other couples, like Traca and me, don't even realize their boat has split in two until they are miles apart.

In the end, the trip didn't magically heal us, but it didn't hurt, either. In fact, it gave us back some precious things we had lost, or at least forgotten, through the years. Things like a sense of adventure, the courage to take risks, faith in the unknown, and a sense of family that we may recapture only rarely in years to come.

David Elliot Cohen, in the epilogue to his book *One Year Off,* answered the question "How do you get along with your spouse twenty-four hours a day, seven days a week?" by writing: "Frankly, it isn't always easy, and a trip like this simply won't work if you're not on very good terms with your spouse. It would be truly suicidal to think a trip would solve any marital problems."

This may be true for some couples but it wasn't true for us. We weren't suicidal. We didn't have a death wish—all monkey bites to the contrary. We had a life wish. A desire not to limp and collapse onto the statistical heap of marital history but to dive into the fire together and see what sparks we could stir up.

There on the beach, as the ocean rocked back and forth, no matter which shell Traca ultimately selected, I realized: The whole thing is a gamble. Traveling, getting married, raising kids, growing up, getting old—it's all a risk.

All just one big, painful, beautiful, unpredictable adventure.

65

WIDE-OPEN WORLD

"Memoir" comes from the Latin word *memoria*, meaning "memory or reminiscence," which makes it extremely subjective. The memoirist views the world through his or her own particular set of filters, chooses to include some details, leaves others out—and that becomes the narrative. But it's all just a memory in the end.

I originally planned to end this story before Traca picked a shell, back when everything was still possible between us. But when many early readers demanded to know what her decision was, I realized I was not alone on this journey. So here's what happened:

Traca didn't decide that night on the beach. Though I insisted we stay in the circle until we had a clear commitment one way or the other, she eventually stood up, unable to choose, and we walked to the car together.

It wasn't until a month later that she finally made her choice. I remember the day clearly because it was the Fourth of July. It was also the day I finished the first draft of this book, a huge milestone for me. Feeling a mixture of elation and relief, I called Traca from my office to tell her the good news. "Let's celebrate," I said. "Are you hungry?"

We met at a local restaurant.

Unfortunately, the dinner was far from a celebration. As I talked about the book, the joy of completion, my hopes for the future . . . Traca just sat there. She seemed sad, not sharing my moment of triumph at all.

"What's the matter?" I asked. "You seem miserable."

Traca smiled weakly and met my eyes. "I think I need to choose the black shell," she said.

We filed for divorce shortly after that.

It bears mentioning that Traca has no recollection of this scene.

She remembers being at the restaurant but she does not remember those words, the black shell, any of it. Though I wrote it in my journal later that night and can clearly picture her saying it, Traca doesn't remember it that way. No doubt her memoir of our trip and our life together would be completely different from the one I've written here.

However it really happened, we are no longer together. It wasn't the choice I hoped she'd make, but it is the path we have chosen. She bought a small house a few miles from mine and still lives in Gorham. We remain connected through, and committed to, our kids and are probably better friends than we've been in years. If there is ever a contest for America's Most Amicable Divorce, Traca and I may enter. I sincerely hope she finds what she's looking for.

When Jackson headed off to college and Logan hit the road for his backpacking trip across South America, my nest was officially empty. Alone in a house far too big for one, I put it on the market and sold it to a happy couple with two young children. Then, when a new owner bought the company I was working for and unexpectedly laid me off, I had a blank slate and a question to answer:

What next?

With this in mind, I looked out a nearby window and watched late-summer maple trees swaying gently in the wind. *Should I move somewhere warm?* I wondered. *Where would I be happy? What memories do I want to make?* Which is when three words popped into my head as if for the first time:

Year of Service.

I laughed at the universe's persistence and didn't think much of it. But later that night, I logged on to my computer and searched the words "volunteer" and "elephants."

Thailand, Namibia, Sri Lanka, Cambodia, India.

So many choices and a wide-open world in front of me.

EPILOGUE

The moment one definitely commits oneself, then providence moves, too. All sorts of things occur to help one that would never otherwise have happened. A whole stream of events issues from the decision, raising in one's favor all manner of unforeseen incidents and meetings and material assistance which no man could have dreamed would have come his way. Whatever you can do or dream you can, begin it. Boldness has genius, power, and magic in it. Begin it now.

—GOETHE

As promised, here is a quick summary of how we prepared for our trip in less than two months, as well as a few lessons we learned along the way. It's not intended to be a definitive guide to extended world travel; it's just what *we* did. If you're the type of person who needs not only your Big Logistical Ducks in a row but also your medium, small, and baby ducks lined up, too, consider this just a rough starting place.

Before we get into specifics, I want to preface all of it by saying: If my family and I can pull off a trip like this, so can you. We were not rich and bored. We were not traveling for work. Our trip was not bankrolled by a book deal before we left home. We did not have any special privileges or connections where international travel is concerned. All we had was our decision to make it happen, which, as I've already mentioned, is your magic ticket out the door. Because it will never be the perfect time to volunteer your way around the world. Most people won't ever have enough money lying around. Employers will never encourage you to take a big block of time off. The potential for danger will always exist out there in whatever form your fears want to fixate on. Your bills, your worried parents, your boring neighbors will all tell you to stay. Your kids will always seem too old or too young. The world will simply never stop spinning long enough for you to launch. Only your decision to go will get you out the door. So make it.

I know an extended trip like this is not for everyone, but I'm not talking to everyone anymore. I'm talking now to the people who can feel this idea fluttering in their chest like a baby bird. I'm talking to the people who are standing at the doorway between staying and going and are desperate to jump through into the unknown. If you feel stuck and bored and hungry to suck the marrow out of life, as Thoreau said, then this is for you.

Once you've made up your mind, you will need some money. Not a king's ransom but probably more than the "Travel for Free" websites would have you believe, especially if you're traveling with kids. Of course, there are as many ways to travel as there are income levels, so just be creative, maybe a little conservative, and come up with a budget that works for you. Ours looked like this:

To pay for our trip, we refinanced our home, rolling a $40,000 home equity loan into our existing principal, and due to a phenomenally low interest rate, our monthly payment actually went *down*! When this deal came through and we had the cash in hand, we used around $10,000 to pay off outstanding bills, which left only our mortgage and Traca's car payment to cover while we were gone. Other than that, we were debt-free—with roughly $30,000 to spend for six months of world travel for four. Not a first-class budget, but still a nice chunk of change.

Once we were armed with an actual dollar amount, we learned the first great lesson of our journey: Getting there is not only half the fun, it's also most of the expense. For flights, I allocated $4,000 per person, a number that really wasn't based on much more than a general feeling that $16,000 seemed like a hell of a lot for our family to pay for airfare. At first I spent some time looking for the fabled Round-the-World tickets—a concept that allows you to fly one way around the planet either for a predetermined amount of time or a predetermined number of stops, all at a substantial discount—but these never panned out. Maybe there are great deals like this out there, but I couldn't find them. I ended up hiring a local travel agent—Tricia at the appropriately named Around the World Travel in Gorham—to shop for deals one stop at a time.

Obviously prices can vary wildly from month to month and from year to year, but just to give you a sense of what we're talking about, this is how the flights ended up. We got to Miami on frequent flyer miles, then Tricia took it from there:

Miami, FL > San José, Costa Rica:	$1,117.16	$278.29 each
San José, Costa Rica > Los Angeles, CA:	$984.52	$246.13 each
Los Angeles, CA > Auckland, NZ:	$2,811.40	$702.85 each
Auckland, NZ > Bangkok, Thailand:	$1,980.80	$495.20 each
Bangkok, Thailand > New Delhi, India:	$1,098.48	$274.62 each
Delhi, India > Leh, Ladakh > Delhi:	$1,400.00	$350.00 each
Delhi, India > Lisbon, Portugal:	$3,028.00	$757.00 each
Lisbon, Portugal > Boston, MA:	$2,149.36	$537.34 each

To save you the math, the grand total ended up being $14,569.72, or $1,430.28 under budget. Way to go, Tricia!

Once we decided what we were willing pay for airfare, that left us $14,000 for six months of living expenses, with the next largest line item being room and board.

You'd think volunteering would be free, but it isn't. Sometimes it is, but not usually. Fact is, accepting volunteers is the way many NGOs (nongovernmental organizations) make the bulk of their money. Yes, volunteers do some work, but they also require staff to manage them and resources to support them, so a fee is justified. Considering the deeply rewarding experience many volunteers enjoy, an additional premium fee also seems reasonable to me. NGOs are helping provide certain vital services, from education to animal welfare, rural development to medical treatment—and volunteers with a passion in these areas give their money and their time to help make a difference. Everybody wins. The challenge for us was to find organizations we could partner with on our measly and somewhat arbitrary budget. My goal was to keep our room and board fees to $1,000 a month for all four of us.

To put this in perspective, $1,000 a month is roughly $32 a day. Divide this by four people and you come up with $8 per person per day—not quite enough to see a Friday night movie. For this price, we were hoping for a place to sleep and three meals each day in six different exotic locations. The beautiful thing is . . . it can be done. But you have to dig a little.

Let's pick a country—say, Costa Rica, which was our first stop. Then type "Volunteer Costa Rica" into your search bar. When your 2.05 million results come back in 1.8 seconds, click the first option just to get an idea what's out there. As I type and click now, I get an organization called GVI, Global Vision International. GVI is one of many volunteer brokers who—for a fee of their own—will hook you up with community and conservation projects all over the world. The good thing about using one of these brokers is that they do all the planning for you and they tend to look after you. Their programs are structured and well attended with lots of past reviews to reassure you before you go. Many times in-country, volunteer brokers will organize tours and extras as part of your experience. They might even offer transfers to and from the airport. On the GVI website as I check now, they are offering five Costa Rica projects including "Jaguar Conservation," which sounds fun to me.

The bad thing about brokers is that they can be expensive. The Jaguar Conservation project, for example, bills out at $1,395 per person for two weeks. (This does not include airfare!) If you want to spend a month, as we did, you can double that figure. If you want four people to go, get ready to spend over $11,000 . . . for one month . . . or most of our six-month budget in the first thirty days.

After a little Web surfing and a lot of sticker shock, I started contacting NGOs directly whenever possible. These were usually smaller organizations that had their own websites, and I almost always ended up dealing directly with either the people in charge or the founders themselves. I liked this for a couple of reasons. First: By dealing directly with NGOs, I was cutting out the middlemen and -women, ensuring that 100 percent of our money, which was really a donation, went directly to help projects on the ground and did not go to cover broker fees. Second: People who start and/or run international service organizations are not doing it for the money. Yes, they *need* money, often working in extremely difficult, underfunded, and understaffed conditions—but they are doing it because they care. If you also care and can express this caring to them, they are much more likely to negotiate a reduced fee (when absolutely necessary) than, say, a GVI staffer might be. On the flip side, if an NGO is simply out of your price range and not willing to budge, wish them well and search elsewhere. I promise you, there is no honor in beating down an orphanage on their weekly volunteer rate.

In terms of where to go, just pick countries that interest you. There are volunteer opportunities everywhere. I just searched the words "Volunteer Antarctica" and came up with this post: *Wanted: travelers who enjoy salt air, seals, icebergs—and lending a helping hand. Knowledge of Russian helpful.* Truly, the world is waiting for you.

Once we secured a few of our $1,000/month partners (the rest we found on the road), that left another $8,000, or $11 per day per person, for things like sightseeing, exploring, shopping, snacking, you name it. This was also our fund from which to finance any delays, unexpected bumps in the road, impulsive desires, and medical emergencies.

Which brings us to Lesson Number Two: When volunteering your way around the world, it is the in-between times that are the most expensive. If you're looking to save, get from one NGO to the next as quickly and efficiently as possible. We did this when traveling from Thailand to India. Clifton picked us up at the airport, whisked us to his waiting car, and sped us directly to the Farm, where we started work later that day. Total cost in transition: a few cups of *chai*. In contrast, the five days we spent in Melbourne, Australia, waiting for the Red Shirt rebels to clear Democracy Square in Bangkok cost us nearly a thousand dollars. Two hotel rooms; breakfast, lunch, and dinner for four; tickets to the zoo; taxis; trains; Internet: It all adds up. No matter how frugal you are, no one wants to visit a fabulous new city and just sit in the hotel room the whole time sharing a baguette. But being tourists costs money, so be prepared.

This may sound insane, but traveling medical insurance was not in our budget. Some NGOs require it. The ones we visited never asked. I'd get it if I were you. I'm not against it, but we simply couldn't afford it. After checking around the Web, it just seemed like too much money for a family that was virtually never sick and was operating on such a shoestring. Sure, we'd have wanted it if a tiger had carried me into a tree or Jack had had to be airlifted from the Osa for snakebite treatment. But we were stupid. Bottom line: We left home without it. The fact that we never had cause to regret that decision is something for which I am deeply grateful.

Did we take any precautions at all? Depending on where you want to go in the world, the Centers for Disease Control and Prevention suggests a laundry list of vaccinations. In India alone, the CDC warns of and recommends shots for Hepatitis A, Hepatitis B, typhoid, polio, Japanese encephalitis, and rabies. They also warn of malaria and dengue fever (no shots available for these) as well as more obscure diseases such as filariasis (from worms), visceral leishmaniasis (from parasites), and avian influenza (from birds), among others. The list of potential dangers goes on and on, with each developing country offering its own blend of foodborne, airborne, waterborne, and insectborne plagues to keep you on your toes. Some people may feel more comfortable getting every shot in the book, but we chose not to.

When Logan was born, we really struggled with this issue. Though not the kind of fanatics who would keep a seriously ill child home and wait for Jesus to heal him, we do believe the body's immune system is the best way to fight off most diseases and we try, whenever possible, not to get in the way. So when a close friend's perfectly healthy two-year-old son went virtually brain-dead following a routine MMR shot around the time Logan was born, we made the decision—fraught with uncertainty but grounded in love—not to vaccinate our little guy. The same with Jackson: no shots at all.

Now facing the wider world, where deadly diseases were as plentiful as ice cream flavors at Baskin-Robbins, where sanitation was terrible and clean water hard to find, we struggled with this decision all over again. Did we believe vaccinations worked or not? Could we live with ourselves if the kids got sick in a way that might have been preventable? It was, and still is, a gray area for us, but in the end, we made a compromise. Each of us received a single HepA shot, and that was that. Obviously, you will make up your own mind on this. Get all the shots you feel are necessary.

As for schools, one thing we didn't want was for our kids to spend all their time doing homework on the trip. We wanted them engaged in the world around them, not filling out online work sheets. When we ran our trip idea past the Gorham High principal, Chris Record, we were thrilled when he wholeheartedly endorsed it. He recognized the incredible educational opportunity we were offering our kids—his students—and he pledged his support to help make it work. Some teachers were not as enthusiastic, but what can you do? Logan missed half of eleventh grade; Jackson missed half of ninth. Some teachers passed them with an independent study assignment (such as keeping a Spanish journal while in Spanish-speaking countries), while others simply said they'd have to make up the work after they got back—which they did. It is beyond obvious to us that world travel beats classroom anything, so this was a no-brainer.

What else? Passports. Obviously, you need them. Many countries require that your passport be valid for six months beyond your arrival date. Other countries, including India and Brazil, require you to get visas before you leave home. So there's a little homework to do here.

Packing? Pack as little as possible. Bring clothes for warm and cold weather. Bring a rain jacket. Bring comfortable sandals. The usual suspects. Additionally, we each brought journals, iPods, cameras, mosquito nets, bug spray, sunscreen, a Swiss Army knife for scorpion killing, snorkels and masks, and a few random bags of drugstore items like Band-Aids, antibacterial cream, Tylenol, and tampons. We actually got some expert advice in this area from two of our closest friends, Heidi and Liv Naesheim. They're sisters, roommates, blond, Norwegian, gorgeous—and their apartment served as our home base for a brief stopover in Los Angeles between Costa Rica and New Zealand.

Heidi and Liv are the best kind of friends: the kind you pick right up with after years apart without a single awkward moment, the kind who make you feel ten times funnier than you actually are because they laugh so easily and with so much enthusiasm, the kind who borrow as many stuffed monkey toys as they can find to decorate their home in honor of your monkey-bitten arrival. You know . . . *that* kind of friends.

They are also a wealth of information. Ten years ago, they took their own, even more epic world trip: seventeen countries in twelve months. Along the way, in addition to fending off the advances of every third-world suitor in their path, they became experts at traveling smart and light. Acting as our personal travel fashion police, Liv went through each of our bags, item by item, setting aside anything she deemed unnecessary, redundant, too revealing, made of the wrong material, and so on. When she was finished, we had two full boxes of clothes ready to mail back home, and our traveling party was twenty-two pounds lighter. If you want the full Naesheim experience, Liv's extensive "What to Pack" list can be found on my website: www.john marshall.com.

One splurge that deserves mentioning is the Katadyn Pocket Water Microfilter. We bought ours on sale for around $250 and it paid for itself many times over. If this constitutes an ad for the product, so be it. This little marvel is compact, uses a ceramic cylinder to collect all microorganisms larger than 0.2 microns (which is everything), and can pump clear drinkable water out of the gutter. It not only saved us money as we sweated and hydrated our way from country to country; it also helped us avoid contributing to the world's glut of plastic bottles, which is critical. No matter where you go on the planet, plastic is ubiquitous. Virtually all travelers buy water for safety reasons, but recycling is simply not a reality in many parts of the world. So bring your own pump, pump your own water into the reusable water bottle of your choice, and leave not a single plastic bottle behind, if possible. The world will thank you.

Finally: work. We quit our jobs, but there are other ways to go about it. Though I didn't need to implement any of their excellent advice, I did read *Six Months Off* by Dlugozima, Scott, and Sharp, which walks you through a detailed checklist for negotiating a leave of absence. If you won't enjoy your time away without knowing you have a job to come back to, this is the book for you.

That's about it. Without a doubt, the most powerful aspect of the trip for all of us was the service component. Beyond sightseeing, volunteering allowed us to learn from and connect with so many amazing people we would never have met otherwise. Yes, there are amazing people at Club Med, but you know what I mean. There's a world of difference between comforting a crying orphan and tipping your favorite bartender. Martin Luther King Jr. said, "Everybody can be great because anyone can serve," and I believe the same can be said for every vacation. If you feel inspired to reach out, whether as a family or an individual, I wholeheartedly encourage you to do so. If not for the lives you will touch and the connections you will make, do it for yourself, because it feels really good. This much I know.

Beyond this, be smart, travel light, meet the locals, take risks with the languages and the food, face the endless human variations on the concept of "toilet" with good humor, hire a real estate agent to rent your house (especially to screen applicants), make a photocopy of your passport and keep it somewhere safe, WWOOF hard, follow all the *maaawn-kay* rules, notice the beggars, allow your heart to open, be patient, be flexible, have faith even when things are very bad, even if you receive your own black shell, and accept it all with as much grace as possible. Finally—and this is your last travel lesson—know this:

You will not change the world.

But the world will definitely change you.

ACKNOWLEDGMENTS

WHEN AN ASPIRING YOUNG WRITER RECENTLY HEARD I'D SOLD A BOOK, she approached me for advice. "How'd you do it?" she asked, as if I had some secret formula to hand over.

"It's easy," I said. "First: Write for twenty-six years. Then: Sell a book."

She laughed, and then I gave her some actual advice—but I've thought about her question since then. *How did I manage to sell this thing?*

The real answer is actually much more involved and goes back much further.

First: I was lucky enough to be born into a supportive home that encouraged creativity. When I was growing up, my parents made sure I had all the pens, paper, paints, brushes, lessons, instruments . . . whatever I needed for whatever creative task I was into. When I went through a piano-playing phase, my dad came home from work one day with a beat-up baby grand that he'd bought in a bar for fifty bucks. He put it in our basement and it was all mine. I pounded on that thing for years. As they say in Ladakh, my parents are like the precious jewels I have been given but do not deserve. They certainly are my biggest fans. If you see a woman walking around southern Florida wearing a placard that advertises this book, that's my proud mother.

Second: I had the good fortune of attending Manchester Central High School in Manchester, New Hampshire, and having Mrs. Singer as my freshman English teacher. Before I showed up in her class, I had never read a book for fun. I played sports and watched TV. Books, in my mind, were for nerds. But when Mrs. Singer handed me a copy of *The World According to Garp* by John Irving and challenged me to read it, a whole new world opened up for me. She pushed me hard in that class, never letting me settle for the first easy quips I'd dash off on my assignments. And somewhere during that year, without my even knowing it, she planted the seeds that would one day grow into the writer's life I now live.

Third: I had the benefit of many skilled and generous readers who helped shape the early drafts of this book. To Brent Askari, Sarah Skillin Woodard, Molly Friedrich, Meredith Jordan, and Rebecca Gwyn: Thank you for your time, your feedback, and your friendship. Special thanks go to Rebecca's friend Adrienne Blair, a woman I have never met, who gave this story its first professional edit. The fact that such a skilled woman would spend countless hours offering thousands of insightful suggestions to a complete stranger . . . *for free!* . . . makes me believe I must have done something wonderful in a previous life.

Fourth: I am friends with the brilliant writer Colin Woodard, who was generous enough to refer me to his equally brilliant agent, Jill Grinberg. Jill does not need new writers. She has a robust stable of successful authors who keep her more than busy. But Jill also has a passion for talent and an eagerness to discover something fresh. In an industry that is famous for saying no to unproven newcomers, Jill said yes to me, and for that I will be forever grateful. Plus, marching this book around Manhattan with her was a thrill I will never forget. Big thanks also to Jill's team, Katelyn Detweiler and Cheryl Pientka, for making me feel so at home.

Fifth: I hit the mother-flipping jackpot when Susanna Porter became my champion at Random House. A publishing professional told me: "If there was an All-Star team of editors in New York City, Susanna would be one of the captains." Every time she put a smiley face at the end of one of my sentences, my heart sang. Every time I was smart enough to take one of her editorial suggestions, my manuscript got better. To Priyanka Krishnan, Jennifer Tung, Richard Callison, Robbin Schiff, Diane Hobbing, Crystal Velasquez, David Moench, Quinne Rogers, Allison Schuster, Toby Ernst, Donna Sinisgalli, and the entire Ballantine team: Thanks for surrounding me with so much experience and support.

Sixth: I was encouraged to keep writing and dreaming while I raised my family. To my children, Logan and Jackson: Thank you for being not only a part of my life but a part of this story. I know you didn't ask to be treated as characters in anyone's memoir. I just hope it comes across on every page how much I love and appreciate you. And finally, to Traca: I cannot thank you enough. For twenty-six years of encouragement, for helping raise our beautiful kids, for putting up with all the crap that comes with marrying a writer, this book is dedicated to you.

ABOUT THE AUTHOR

JOHN MARSHALL loves to make things. He's worked as a screenwriter, a carpenter, and a cartoonist. He's also a nine-time Emmy Award–winning television producer, earning the industry's top honor in such diverse categories as set design, musical composition, art direction, and writing. He was named Maine's Broadcaster of the Year in 2008. *Wide-Open World* is his first book. After selling his home in Gorham, Marshall embarked on an extended tour of India. He ended up back at the Good Shepherd Agricultural Mission, making videos with the kids, and writing about orphanage life on his website.

johnmarshall.com
Facebook.com/JohnMarshall
@cowlimp

neworphanage

After his daughter Jackson headed off to college, John Marshall sold his house, left his job, and spent most of the next year back at the Good Shepherd Agricultural Mission in India, the orphanage from *Wide-Open World*.

During that time, he helped launch several successful fundraising campaigns for the orphanage, producing videos that inspired people worldwide to get involved.

His new initiative, **NewOrphanage,** will seek to continue this vital work, showcasing the best, most trustworthy orphan projects, telling their stories, and pairing them with interested donors.

Learn more at:
new**orphan**age.org

ABOUT THE TYPE

This book was set in Fairfield, the first typeface from the hand of the distinguished American artist and engraver Rudolph Ruzicka (1883–1978). Ruzicka was born in Bohemia (in the present-day Czech Republic) and came to America in 1894. He set up his own shop, devoted to wood engraving and printing, in New York in 1913 after a varied career working as a wood engraver, in photoengraving and banknote printing plants, and as an art director and freelance artist. He designed and illustrated many books, and was the creator of a considerable list of individual prints— wood engravings, line engravings on copper, and aquatints.